Minecraft® For Dummies®

A Wiley Brand

by Jesse Stay
Thomas Stay
Jacob Cordeiro

Minecraft® For Dummies®

Published by: **John Wiley & Sons, Inc.,** 111 River Street, Hoboken, NJ 07030-5774, www.wiley.com

For general information on our other products and services, please contact our Customer Care Department within the U.S. at 877-762-2974, outside the U.S. at 317-572-3993, or fax 317-572-4002. For technical support, please visit www.wiley.com/techsupport.

Wiley publishes in a variety of print and electronic formats and by print-on-demand. Some material included with standard print versions of this book may not be included in e-books or in print-on-demand. If this book refers to media such as a CD or DVD that is not included in the version you purchased, you may download this material at http://booksupport.wiley.com. For more information about Wiley products, visit www.wiley.com.

Library of Congress Control Number: 2014940495

ISBN 978-1-118-96823-9 (pbk); ISBN 978-1-118-96824-6 (ebk); ISBN 978-1-118-96825-3 (ebk)

Printed by Bell and Bain Ltd, Glasgow

10 9 8 7 6 5 4 3 2 1

Table of Contents

Part III: Mastering Techniques 83

Introduction

The virtual world of Minecraft is everywhere. With more than 17 million purchases total and purchases raking in more than $300,000 a day, Minecraft has become the number-two game in the world, lagging only behind Nintendo Wii's Wii Sports title, which comes bundled with every Wii system. Shortly before this book went to print, Mojang, the company that created Minecraft, was acquired by Microsoft. The Pocket Edition, which appears in iOS and Android app stores, consistently ranks among the top-grossing apps in each mobile app store.

As a parent of seven kids, I quickly became aware of the power Minecraft has on families. When my kids would invite their friends over, and after all of them were engrossed in using a tablet or Kindle device, they would explore and play and sometimes even nag each other in the game. "Dad, JJ just blew up my house!" is a common phrase in our household, and "Dad, can you give me ops?"

Perhaps, as a parent, you've seen a similar situation, wondering what in the world your kids are talking about and whether you should be concerned. Or perhaps you're one of the children who's playing and you want to better understand how to build the largest village or automate your entire world by using farms, iron golems, or even redstone contraptions and circuitry.

Although Minecraft is an amazing game, it isn't really even a game: It's a "world" that encourages exploration. To expand and increase your world, you need to do things to enhance the mind and grow your skills. In Minecraft, you learn about topics such as architecture, geology, farming, and nutrition, and about advanced logic, circuitry, programming, and even server administration and API development (the topics I'm teaching to Thomas, my 12-year old son and co-author).

No one ever officially wins a game of Minecraft. It's a game that encourages collaboration and cooperation, so it doesn't work well when players fight against each other. As a parent, you can feel comfortable knowing that your kids are playing a game that teaches teamwork. As a child or regular player, you can anticipate playing a game that's fun and enjoyable, where other players will, for the most part, help you along the way.

We hope as you read this book that you can see how to enjoy the game as much as we (my sons and I) enjoy it. As a parent, I've been able to bond with my children by engaging in a shared experience. My kids have had some fun in an environment that's familiar to them from sharing it with their dad. Minecraft is an incredibly fun game that enriches your mind and expands your knowledge, and it lets you do both in an environment in which you can learn and grow with your closest friends and family — or meet new people along the way.

About This Book

We wrote this book as a family. Jesse is the dad, and Thomas is Jesse's 12-year-old son. The icons labeled Joseph's Corner throughout this book hold input from Jesse's 10-year-old son, Joseph. Even Jesse's 6-year-old son, JJ, contributed some of the images in the book. It was a family project, and our hope is that other families can benefit from this book, just as we have.

Parents, you might want to start in Chapter 17. Jesse wrote that chapter as a guide to show parents how to get started, to address their concerns, and to help them protect their children along the way. Chapter 17 can help you get ready to let your children advance through the game in confidence — or even embark on an adventure yourself, with your kids.

For everyone else, this book is written in a format that lets you pick up the book and start reading anywhere. Pick your favorite topic, read about it, and then take your game to the next level. Or you may want to start from the beginning (it's a good place to start) and advance to the end.

In a sense, this book operates much like Minecraft does: After you have the basic ingredients, you can take your game wherever you want. Skip to the End. Advance to the Nether. Just pick a chapter and start reading.

Take this book and share it with a close friend. Let your parents read it. Let your children read it. Let your siblings read it. Minecraft, whether it's played with friends or the mobs in your own single-player virtual world, really is a social experience and best played with people you know. We hope that you can share the knowledge in this book with the same people you play with in the game.

Conventions Used in This Book

If you already own a *For Dummies* book, you're likely familiar with the conventions we use in this book. It's simple: URLs use a monospaced font, like this:

`stay.am/minecraftfordummies`

Foolish Assumptions

Minecraft is a constantly changing game, and it's updated regularly, so it may not necessarily look the same now as when we wrote this book. For that reason, we recommend always referring to our Facebook Page at `facebook.com/minecraftfd` or on YouTube at `youtube.com/minecraftdummiesbook`. In addition, be sure to check out the official Minecraft Wiki at `minecraft.gamepedia.com`.

We assume that you have either a Windows PC, a Mac, or an iOS or Android device. You can also play Minecraft on the Xbox 360 and Xbox One, as well as on certain other consoles, though our focus in this book is on the Minecraft PC edition for the Windows and Mac desktops. At the end of each chapter, we briefly describe the differences between Minecraft for the desktop and Minecraft for your mobile device.

Beyond that, Minecraft is a cinch to play. If a 6-year old can play it (Jesse has even caught his 2-year-old trying to figure out how to play), you *know* that it doesn't take much to get started.

How This Book Is Organized

We've organized this book in a way that lets you get started by hitting the ground running. You can find out all about the elements of survival, and how to get everything you need to make the most of the game. You can truly start anywhere in the book though, so pick a chapter and start reading.

Part I: Getting Started with Minecraft

Part I is a great place to start if you have little to no knowledge of Minecraft and you want to survive your first "day" in the game. We show you how to survive your first night, how to construct a crafting table, and how to engage in various methods of staying alive so that you can continue on and expand what you can do in the game.

Part II: Learning Basic Survival Skills

Are you tired of losing hunger points or your characters dying from malnutrition? This chapter shows you ways to stay hydrated in the game and protect yourself from evil at the same time. We show you how to build farms for a supply of food that can be replenished, and we spell out better ways to mine for more minerals so that you can build better tools and weapons.

Part III: Developing Advanced Skills

In Part III, Minecraft gets fun! This part shows you how to build, and take advantage of, villages in the game to earn new supplies and food, and how to protect those villages. It describes how to work with redstone circuitry and how to build items such as chicken farms, which automatically harvest, cook, and store chicken for you to eat. This part talks about enchantments and other ways to make armor stronger, or even perform magic in various ways.

Part IV: Customizing Minecraft

In Part IV, you can read about ways to integrate the game with various Minecraft servers. This part describes how to send commands to Minecraft to make it perform tasks such as switch between Survival mode and Creative mode. We point you toward our favorite YouTube channels and places where you can find out more about Minecraft.

Part V: Making Minecraft a Family Affair

We wrote this book for anyone to read, but we focus particularly on families. In Part V, we show you the various platforms of Minecraft, from PC edition to PE edition, and then we list the game's various difficulty levels. And, we've written a chapter, entirely for parents, on the things they need to know as their kids play the game.

Part VI: The Part of Tens

Each chapter in this part of the book holds ten (or so) items, usually tips, that can help you expand your game. Use our tips and tricks, our redstone contraptions, and our best advice on better ways to build, for example. If you think that you already know everything there is to know about Minecraft, read this part of the book to discover new topics.

Icons Used in This Book

Throughout this book, you see little icons next to extra tidbits of information about Minecraft:

Wherever you see this cute little icon, we leave a tip to make you one step more knowledgeable about Minecraft. These are the places where you're likely to hear yourself say, "Hmm, I didn't realize that."

We created this special icon just for this book. These tips, written by Jesse's 10-year-old son, Thomas (and Thomas's younger brother Joseph), reflect the mindset of the younger generation of Minecraft players (10 years and younger).

We promise not to bore you by becoming too repetitive, but if we ever have to remind you of something, we stick this icon on it. We want this information ingrained in your mind so that you can recite it from memory when the book isn't at hand.

WARNING!

Whenever you see the Warning icon, pay attention. It marks information that you should be aware of — and we don't want you to learn the lesson the hard way (like we probably did).

TECHNICAL STUFF

If you're less technically inclined, you can usually skip the information in this icon — though if you want to see the nuts and bolts of how things work, it's the one for you. This icon tells you that we're briefly getting into the meat of the topic.

Beyond the Book

Understanding your Minecraft goes beyond these pages and onto the Internet, where you can access additional information. There's a handy-dandy cheat sheet that reiterates the basics and web extras.

- **Cheat Sheet:** You can find this book's online Cheat Sheet at `www.dummies.com/cheatsheet/minecraft`. See the Cheat Sheet for Minecraft PE survival tips and quick ways to earn experience points.
- **Web Extras:** Companion articles to this book's content are available at `www.dummies.com/extras/minecraft`. The topics range from trading with villagers, building a dog army, and ten useful crafting recipes.
- **Updates:** If this book has any updates, they'll be posted at `www.dummies.com/extras/minecraft`.

You also can follow this book's Facebook Page as well as Jesse's personal Facebook account and this book's YouTube channel, and we've set up a Facebook Group for you to collaborate with, and learn from, each another. Here's how to find them all:

- *Minecraft For Dummies* Facebook Page: `http://facebook.com/minecraftfd`
- Jesse's personal Facebook profile (follow at your own risk, although all are welcome): `http://facebook.com/stay`
- *Minecraft For Dummies* YouTube channel: `http://youtube.com/minecraftdummiesbook`
- *Minecraft For Dummies* Facebook Group: `http://facebook.com/groups/minecraftfordummies`

We are also working on a *Minecraft For Dummies* Minecraft server, to be hosted by the Stay family, which we'll announce on these channels and pages whenever it becomes available. (We also hope that you'll come by and say hi.) More than anything, get out there and play Minecraft. We hope to see you sometime — look under the username `jessestay` for Jesse, `TheRealStayman` for Thomas, and `expelymarndo` for Joseph. See you in the Nether!

Part I

Getting Started with Minecraft

Visit www.dummies.com for more great *For Dummies* content online.

In this part . . .

- Understand the world of Minecraft
- Start your first game
- Survive your first night

1

Entering Minecraft

In This Chapter

- Understanding Minecraft
- Registering your account
- Buying and downloading Minecraft
- Starting your first game
- Recognizing the basic controls

You're ready to build, fight, create, craft, and brew. But how do you begin? This chapter tells you how to register and begin your first game.

If you're a PE player (PE stands for Pocket Edition, the version of Minecraft for mobile devices), skip to the end of each chapter in this book to find a special section written just for you. In this chapter, PE players can find out how to download the game and understand its unique basic controls.

Getting to Know Minecraft

Minecraft is taking the world by storm! These days it's hard to be a gamer without hearing or coming across the Minecraft brand — in fact, as of this writing Minecraft is the second most-played game right behind Wii Play, which just so happens to ship with the consoles it ships with. Parents and kids alike can't avoid the game.

Minecraft is a massive adventure you can play on your own, or with your friends. The adventure encourages exploration and "mining" of the resources you need to build your world. As you play, there are monsters, zombies, and even dangerous animals that can hurt you along the way. You have to keep yourself fed and nourished in order to stay strong. In so many ways, it mimics real life.

There is so much to learn in this game — from geology to architecture, to farming, nutrition, and even electronics, engineering, and logic, you'll find yourself learning throughout your adventures. Keep exploring, and the more you learn, the more cool things you'll be able to build.

The game is playable on both mobile and desktop. You'll probably find yourself, as a true player, exploring both of them at some point. The desktop version allows you to explore and do the most, but mobile is the cheapest and most widely available version to play. Spend time in each to learn new and different things you can do in them.

Registering a Minecraft Account

To jump into the action, you first have to register a Minecraft account. Then you can play in Demo mode or upgrade to a Premium account, which you need for the full version. Follow these steps to register an account:

1. **Go to** `http://minecraft.net`**.**

   The Minecraft home page opens.

2. **Click the Register link in the upper right corner of the page.**

   The Register New Mojang Account page appears.

3. **Fill out all information requested in the text boxes, specify your date of birth, and answer the security questions (see Figure 1-1).**

4. **Click the Register button to finish.**

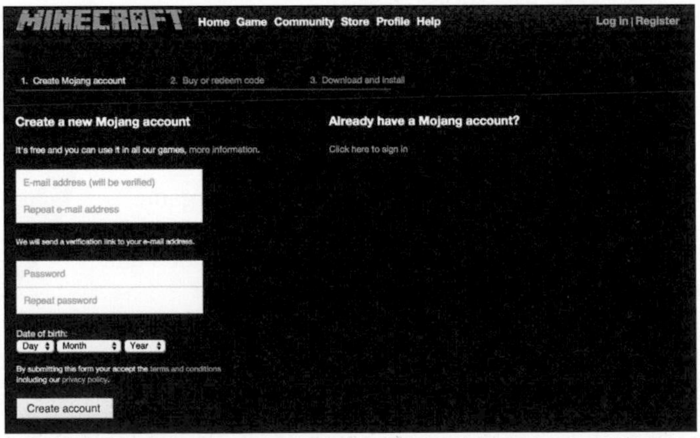

Figure 1-1: The registration page.

5. **Check the email account you entered for a verification message from Minecraft.**
6. **Click the link provided in the email to complete the registration.**

   Check out the next section to find out how to purchase the game.

Purchasing and Installing Minecraft

To buy and install the game, log in to your account at `http://minecraft.net`. (See the preceding section for details on registering.) Then follow these steps:

1. **Click the large Buy Now or Get Minecraft button on the home page.**

   The Minecraft Store page opens. This interface changes often, so the exact wording can also change as you read this.
2. **Select the option to login or register for Minecraft (it might also say "Get Minecraft," but the interface changes often), as shown in Figure 1-2.**

   At the time of this writing, the game cost $26.95.

   If you can't click the button, you may not be logged in (or you may have already bought the game).

Figure 1-2: Buying the game.

3. **Fill out the payment information, and then click the Proceed to Checkout button.**
4. **Follow the necessary steps to complete the purchase.**
5. **Return to the Minecraft home page. On the right side of the screen, the large Buy Now button should now be labeled Download Now. Click this button to open the Download page.**

Redeeming a gift card or code

When you purchase a copy of Minecraft, you can pay using a gift card that you received on your birthday or on Christmas, Hanukkah, Kwanza, Easter, or another "just because" occasion. Here are the steps to redeem your copy of Minecraft (or at least get a discount!):

1. Click the Register button in the upper right corner.
2. Create a Mojang account.

   You can see the instructions for this step in the earlier section "Registering for a Minecraft Account."

3. Create a Minecraft username.
4. Click the Redeem a Code button on the right side of the Payment Details section.
5. Enter the code number and click Redeem.

That's it — now you've got a bona fide, cheap or free copy of Minecraft!

6. **If you're using Windows, click the downloaded file and save it anywhere on your computer.**

   To view instructions for other operating systems, click the Show All Platforms button.

7. **Double-click the file to install the game.**

The payment is immediately attributed to your account, so, if necessary, you can download the file again for free. The Minecraft home page also gives you the option to play from your browser — click the link under the Download Now button.

Playing the Game

After you install Minecraft, you're ready to start playing the game. To start, run the launcher you downloaded in the previous section of this chapter, "Purchasing and Installing Minecraft."

Logging in and operating the main menu

The launcher opens the News screen, which displays game updates and links. Enter your username and password in the lower right corner and click Log In to continue to the main menu, shown in Figure 1-3.

Figure 1-3: The main menu.

This list describes what you can do after you click the buttons on the main menu:

- **SinglePlayer:** Start or continue a basic game. This chapter covers the options for starting a game in SinglePlayer mode.
- **MultiPlayer:** Join other players online. You can find more information about MultiPlayer mode in Chapter 9.

- **Languages:** Change the language of the text in Minecraft. This tiny button, next to Options, is a speech bubble containing a globe.
- **Options:** Manage game options such as sound, graphics, mouse controls, difficulty levels, and general settings.
- **Quit Game:** Close the window, unless you're in In-Browser mode.

Starting your first game in SinglePlayer mode

To start your first game in SinglePlayer mode, follow these steps:

1. **Click the SinglePlayer button to view a list of all worlds.**

   If you're just starting out in Minecraft, this list should be empty.

2. **Click the Create New World button to start a new game.**

   The Create New World page appears, as shown in Figure 1-4.

Figure 1-4: Creating a new world.

3. **In the World Name text box, type whatever name you want and click the Create New World button at the bottom of the screen.**

   I cover more world options in Chapter 13.

To turn on cheats, click the More World Options button, and then click the Allow Cheats button to turn cheats on or off.

Turning on game cheats increases or decreases the level of difficulty as you play and switches between Creative mode and Adventure mode. Cheats give you more control over the world when you're just getting started.

Chapter 2 explains how to use a basic cheat for surviving your first game.

When you finish creating your world, the game automatically starts by generating the world and placing your *avatar* (character) in it.

Understanding basic controls

The world of Minecraft (you can see an example in Figure 1-5) is made of cubic *blocks,* materials such as dirt or stone, that you can break down and rebuild into houses or craft into useful items. A block made of a material such as sand is referred to as a *sand block*. Because the side length of every block measures 1 meter, most distances are measured in blocks as well: If you read about an object that's located "3 blocks up," for example, it's the distance from the ground to the top of a stack of 3 blocks.

In addition to building and crafting, you have to defend against monsters and eventually face them head-on. As the game progresses, your goal becomes less about surviving and more about building structures, gathering resources, and facing challenges to gain access to more blocks and items.

To survive, you have to know how to move around, attack enemies, and manipulate the blocks that comprise the world. Table 1-1 lists the default key assignments for each control.

Figure 1-5: The look and feel of Minecraft.

If you reassign any major keys, you may cause confusion later in the game.

Table 1-1 Default Controls in Minecraft

Action	*Control*	*What Happens When You Use It*
Pause	Esc	The game pauses (only in SinglePlayer mode), and the Game menu opens. Choose Options⇨Controls to change the controls for certain actions. You can also close menus and other in-game screens.
Forward	W	Your avatar moves forward when you hold down this key. Double-tapping the W key makes the character sprint — and makes the avatar hungry, as explained in Chapter 3.
Back	S	Your avatar backs up.
Left	A	Your avatar moves to the left.
Right	D	Your avatar moves to the right.
Look	Mouse movement	Your avatar looks around. The Forward control always makes the avatar move in the direction you're looking.

(cotinued)

Table 1-1 ***(continued)***

Action	*Control*	*What Happens When You Use It*
Jump	Space	Your avatar jumps over 1 block at a time. Use this control while moving to make your way around rough terrain or jump over gaps. Jump while sprinting to leap over a great distance! Hold down this button while swimming to swim upward or keep your avatar's head above water.
Attack	Left mouse button	Your character attacks in the direction of the crosshair in the middle of the screen. Tap the button to punch nearby entities, or hold down the button to break nearby blocks.
Use Item	Right mouse button	Your character uses the selected item, as described in Chapter 2.
Drop	Q	Your character drops the selected item, as explained in Chapter 2.
Sneak	Left Shift	Your character moves more slowly, but cannot walk off edges. In MultiPlayer mode (described in Chapter 9), other players can't see your avatar's name tag if a block is in the way.
Inventory	E	Your avatar's inventory is shown (described in Chapter 2), and any open menus except the Pause menu are closed.
Chat	T	The Chat menu opens. Type a message, and then press Enter to talk to friends in multiplayer worlds or implement cheat commands.
List Players	Tab key	A list of all players in the world is shown (and is disabled in single-player worlds).
Pick Block	Middle mouse button	Click nearby blocks or entities with the middle mouse button to put them into the bottom row of the inventory, possibly replacing the selected item. It works only in Creative mode (see Chapter 6). If the mouse has no middle button, reassign this key on the Pause menu.
Command	/	The Chat menu opens and shows a slash mark (/), used for cheat commands.
Hide GUI	F1	All visual images are turned off, except for the player's view of the world (used for capturing imagery).
Screenshot	F2	A screen shot of the current view is taken (see Chapter 10).
View Performance	Shift+F3	You can view the game performance, and everything on the F3 menu. (This option is rarely used.)

Action	Control	What Happens When You Use It
View Statistics	F3	Your character's coordinates, current biome, and other information are shown. The y-axis points upward.
Change View	F5	The camera view changes between first-person view (recommended), third-person view, and in front of the avatar, looking back at the avatar.
Smooth Movement	F8	This one makes the mouse cursor move more smoothly (used for recording).

Walk around and explore the world. After you get the hang of using the controls and you're prepared to immerse yourself in the fun and challenge of the real game, it's time to figure out how to survive. Chapter 2 gives you the lowdown on surviving the first night.

Watching the Heads-Up Display (HUD)

The little arrangement at the bottom of the screen is known as the Heads-Up Display, or HUD. To show the important details of your character, the HUD features the five sections described in the following list, as shown in Figure 1-6.

- **Health bar:** These ten hearts monitor the health of your avatar. As your avatar incurs damage, the hearts disappear. After all ten are depleted, your avatar dies and reappears at its *spawn point,* a position that can be changed by sleeping in a bed.

  Your avatar can take damage by falling from ledges 4 blocks tall, colliding with harmful blocks or entities, or succumbing to other dangers, such as drowning. When you equip yourself with armor (see Chapter 4), the Armor bar appears over the Health bar, indicating the protective value of your armor.

- **Hunger bar:** This bar represents the food supply. The emptier the bar, the hungrier you are. Hunger is an important concept to understand, so it's covered in Chapter 3.

- **Experience:** The green Experience bar fills up when you collect *experience orbs.* These orbs appear naturally whenever you defeat monsters, smelt items in a furnace, breed animals, or mine any ore except iron or gold. When the bar is full, a number appears or increases over it, indicating your experience level. You can spend levels with Anvils (detailed in the bonus chapter, available for download at `www.dummies.com/go/minecraftfd`) or enchantment tables (detailed in Chapter 6), but you will lose them if you die.

- **Inventory:** These nine squares, at the base of the HUD, contain items you've collected, and they're the only squares in the inventory that you can access without pressing E. You can use the 1–9 keys or the scroll wheel to select items, and right-click to use them. If you're using a sword or a tool for breaking blocks faster (such as an axe), the item automatically functions when you left-click. (I discuss the inventory in more detail in Chapter 2.)
- **Breath:** When your avatar's head goes underwater, ten bubbles appear just above the Hunger bar and begin to pop, one by one. They signify how long you can hold your breath; if all the bubbles are gone and you're still underwater, the Health bar begins to deplete.

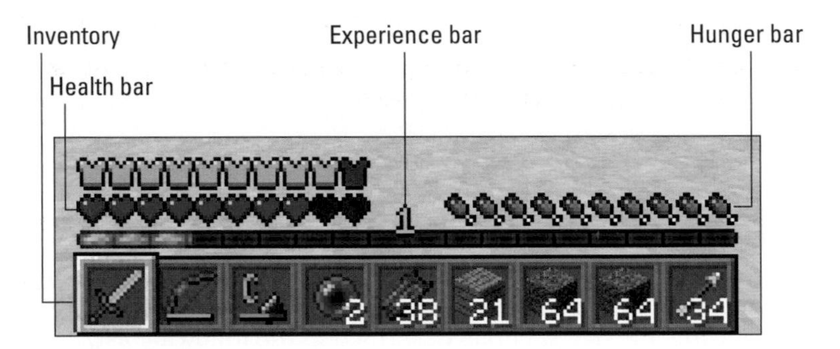

Figure 1-6: The Heads-Up Display.

Carefully monitor the Health and Hunger bars, and organize the inventory slots for easy access.

Minecraft PE

Minecraft PE, or Pocket Edition, is the most widely used version of Minecraft in the world. There's probably a good chance, even if you use the desktop version that you also play with your friends on an iPad, iPhone, iPod touch, Android phone or tablet, or Kindle (and many other devices!). If you couldn't tell already, Minecraft PE is the version built just for mobile and smart devices.

As you'll quickly discover, and as we explain throughout this book, Minecraft PE has a few, slightly more simple features that you need to understand, separate from the desktop version. If you play only PE, most of this book still applies to you —— you'll just want to be sure to skip to the end of each chapter to catch what, of the desktop-focused items, has been changed within Minecraft PE.

For this chapter, we start by showing you how to get started with Minecraft PE.

Purchasing PE

Purchasing Minecraft PE is easy! In just a few steps, you'll be off and running. Much unlike the desktop edition, which requires a much more expensive app download, the PE edition is usually only a few dollars, and you can get started almost immediately. Here's how to get it:

1. **Go to the App Store (if you have an iOS device, such as an iPad or iPhone or iPod touch) or the Google Play store (if you're on an Android device or Kindle).**
2. **Minecraft PE is usually one of the top ten paid games in the app store, or you can search for it by typing** Minecraft**.**

   You may also see the demo, which is free but has fewer features.
3. **Download the game (with a parent's permission, of course, if you're under 18) and you're set to start!**

   See Figure 1-7 for an example of what the game looks like in iOS.

Starting PE

Playing your first game in Minecraft PE is straightforward. Just follow these steps:

1. **Tap the newly installed Minecraft app.**

   You should see the word `Mojang` and the company's red-and-white logo at the beginning (indicating that it's booting up).

   When you see the text `Minecraft Pocket Edition` and a phrase imprinted in yellow (one phrase is randomly chosen at startup) at the top, you're at the title screen.

   In the lower left corner, you see the version information (such as *v0.9.5 alpha*). In the lower right corner, you see the Options button.
2. **In the center, click the Play button.**

   This step opens the Worlds screen. On the Worlds screen, you can click to choose from these three options (shown in Figure 1-8):

   - **New:** Create a new world.
   - **Edit:** Edit worlds. This option is rarely used.
   - **Back:** Open the title screen.

Now you're ready to start a game. Follow these steps:

1. **Tap the New button.**
2. **Tap the Name box, and name the world.**

Figure 1-7: The download page for Minecraft PE in iOS.

Figure 1-8: The Worlds menu.

3. **Tap Done.**
4. **Tap the Survival button.**

   Leave the Seed box blank for the first game. (You can find tips to customize the game with seeds in Chapter 13.)
5. **Tap Create World, and you're set!**

On the Create New World screen, tap the Advanced setting (in the upper right corner of the screen) to open the Advanced Settings screen. The difference between the two screens is that the Advanced screen has three new buttons and omits the mode description. You can use the three new World Type buttons to select the old, limited world; the new, infinite world; or the Creative mode only, flat world. If the Infinite option is grayed out, you cannot play in that mode because your device is too slow to keep up. To exit the Advanced Settings screen, simply tap the Advanced button again.

Understanding the Heads-Up Display (HUD) for PE

You see the Heads Up Display at the bottom of the screen as you play the game (see Figure 1-9). This series of monitors and controls can help monitor your health, energy, and inventory status throughout the game.

Figure 1-9: The Heads Up Display looks like this as you play the game.

Here is a description of the monitors and controls of the Heads Up Display, which is shown in Figure 1-9:

- **Health bar:** The Health bar is displayed in the upper left corner of the screen. You can regenerate your health by eating food.
- **Controls:** The controls are at the left: Press up to move forward, down to move backward, left to strafe (move to the side without turning your head) to the left, or right to strafe to the right; press the middle button to jump. (While you're holding the Up button, two buttons should show up; use them to move diagonally.)

- **The Screen:** The screen isn't technically a control, though moving a finger on top of your device changes the way you're facing. If you want to look to your right and move forward, for example, you swipe your finger across the screen and hold up. Tapping on the screen places a block. Holding the tap breaks whatever block you're holding the tap on.
- **Inventory:** At the bottom of the screen, you see six squares — five empty squares and one square with three dots in it. Tap an empty square to select an item in the slots. Tap the square with three dots to bring up the full inventory. Tap the X at the top left to get out. Tap a square in the inventory to bring it up to the selected square at the bottom. For example, tap the button with the iron chestplate to put on armor in the inventory. Tap the bookshelf to craft whatever you can craft in the 2 x 2 inventory crafting that is in Minecraft PC Edition.
- **Pause and Chat:** In the upper right corner of the screen (for iOS users) are the Pause and Chat buttons. For any other device, you have to swipe the screen to the left as though you were going home, and you press the back arrow.

  Be warned that tapping Pause opens the Pause menu, though it does *not* pause the game. On the right side of the Pause menu is a list of players who are in your world; to the left are three buttons.

  - **Top:** Returns you to the game
  - **Middle:** Opens the Options menu
  - **Bottom:** Returns you to the title screen
- **Chat button:** Clicking the Chat button opens the Chat menu.
- **Back button:** Pressing Back returns you to the game.
- **Keyboard button:** Tapping the text box or pressing the Keyboard button brings up the texting buttons. Typing a sentence and then tapping the arrow pointing to the right "speaks" your message to the other players in the game. Pressing the upside-down triangle closes the texting buttons.
- **Armor bar:** The Armor bar is in the upper left corner of the Inventory screen. It tells you how much armor you're wearing.

2

Surviving the First Night

In This Chapter

- Understanding the basic game plan
- Acquiring resources
- Building a base of operations
- Surviving a day and a night
- Switching modes
- Choosing a strategy

After you create a new world in Minecraft, as outlined in Chapter 1, the first order of business is to survive the first night. A Minecraft day lasts for 20 minutes; it has 10-minute daytimes and 3 minutes of sunrise and sunset, during which the player can prepare for the 7-minute nights, when dangerous monsters spawn in the darkness. This chapter helps you survive your first experience; know what to expect on your first night — and how to spend your remaining minutes of daylight preparing.

Preparing for Your First Night

While the first night can be scary and frustrating for a first time player, a little preparation will make it a breeze. In Table 2-1, we've constructed a basic schedule of what you'll need to do to prepare for the night in the 13 minutes you have available. Then, we've broken down further in the following sections how to prepare.

Table 2-1 Schedule for Surviving Your First Night

Time	*Task*
Minutes 1-5	Find trees and start harvesting.
Minutes 6-8	Build a crafting table.
Minutes 9-11	Build a shelter.
Minutes 12-13	Finalize any last minute preparations, build weapons, and catch animals.

Devising a game plan

After you start the game and your avatar appears, you need to start planning out your day, so you can survive the night. The first thing you will need to do is find a living space with some trees and a suitable area for building (usually flat). Always locate trees when starting a game, because you use wooden materials to craft most of the initial items. To survive the first night, on your first day you need to craft these elements:

- Crafting table (or workbench, used for building)
- Wooden tools
- Shelter with a door

You can also craft useful, non-essential items as daylight allows, often during the first day:

- Stone tools
- Torches
- Furnace
- Bed
- Chest

The rest of this chapter explains how to craft these items.

When you start creating your own world, you may discover that the sun is setting too quickly. If that's the case, you can press Esc to open the Pause menu and choose Options⇨Difficulty repeatedly until the screen reads `Difficulty: Peaceful`. This option makes the world much safer and causes your health to regenerate. Alternatively, if you enable cheats for your world (read more about cheats in Chapter 1), press T, type **/time set 0**, and press Enter to cause an early sunrise.

Using the inventory

Before you start gathering materials and crafting items, you should know how to manage the Inventory screen. The nine squares at the bottom of the game screen display items you've obtained. For example, if you break a block such as wood or dirt (see Chapter 1 for the basic controls), an item pops out that is automatically picked up, causing it to appear in one of the inventory squares. The row of squares at the bottom of the game screen represents a quarter of the inventory.

To see the entire inventory, as shown in Figure 2-1, press E (or the corresponding key binding, as described in Chapter 1).

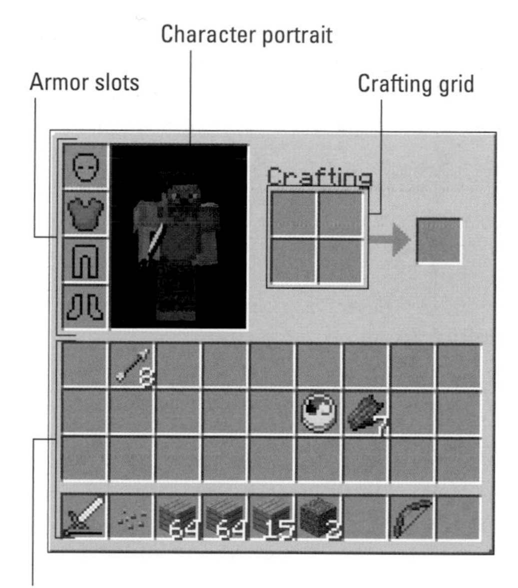

Figure 2-1: Inventory screen.

You should be familiar with these four components of the inventory:

- **Inventory slots:** The four rows of squares at the bottom of the screen, where you see your items. You select the items in the bottom row outside the Inventory screen with the 1–9 keys on the keyboard or the scroll wheel.
- **Crafting grid:** A 2-by-2 square, followed by an arrow pointing toward another square to the right. When you want to craft basic items, such as torches or mushroom stew, place the ingredients on the grid to make the result appear on the other side of the arrow.

- **Character portrait:** A small screen showing what your character looks like now. This portrait can change when your character sits or sleeps, wears armor, gets hit by arrows, drinks invisibility potions, catches fire, and more.
- **Armor slots:** The four squares in the upper left corner, representing a helmet, a suit, leggings, and boots. When you obtain armor later in the game, you can place it in these slots; shift-clicking a piece of armor automatically equips it in the corresponding slot. See Chapter 3 for more information about armor.

Because most items are *stackable,* several similar items such as wooden planks or steak can share the same inventory slot; an item may have a white number next to it in the inventory, indicating how many you have. Most stackable items cannot exceed a 64-stack — you can fit as many as 64 items into one space. Tools, weapons, and armor do not stack, and some items, such as ender pearls or snowballs, cannot exceed a 16-stack.

Manipulating the inventory

While viewing the full inventory, you can use these basic commands for manipulating items in the inventory:

- **Pick up the items in an inventory square:** Click a square in the inventory to pick up the items there.
- **Pick up half of the items in an inventory square:** Right-click a square in the inventory to pick up half (rounded up) of the items there.
- **Place all items you're holding:** While holding an item or a stack of items, click an empty square to place the item(s) there.
- **Place a single item that you're holding:** While holding a stack of items, right-click an empty square to place *one* item there. The rest remain on the cursor. Right-click several times to place several items.

In addition, while holding an item, you can click outside the Inventory screen to drop the item on the ground. While outside the Inventory screen, you can press the 1–9 keys to select an item from the bottom row of the inventory and then press Q to drop the item. If you do this with a stack of items, only one item is thrown.

If you're just starting out in Minecraft, break nearby blocks (as described in the section "Harvesting trees," later in this chapter) and move them around in the inventory to become familiar with it.

Setting Up for Your First Night

Your first night can often be one of the most frustrating parts of Minecraft. Nighttime is when zombies and creepers and other evil and violent mobs ("mobs" are the name for other characters in the game) come out, wanting to hurt or kill your character. In order to survive this first night you need to be prepared. With a few simple measures such as having a shelter, building tools to protect yourself, and improving the tools you have available to mine faster, you will be safe and sound and should be able to continue past your first night in the game.

You should complete a few tasks before nightfall. Start with the essentials, which we discuss in detail in this section:

- **Harvest trees.** Then you can gather wooden planks.
- **Build a crafting table.** It starts off your production.
- **Construct a shelter.** It keeps *you* safe from being attacked.

Harvesting trees

Punching wood, the Minecraft term for harvesting trees, is the only way to begin and advance in any game, and it's the first step regardless of level of difficulty or strategy. Start the crafting process by chopping down nearby trees. Everything you need to build a shelter requires some form of wood, and the most efficient way to get it is to harvest trees. Look for a place with a good number of trees. (If you're too far away from any plants, you may want to create a new world.)

To start, chop down a couple of trees, which are made of wood blocks and leaf blocks. To break a block from the tree, follow these steps:

1. **Walk up to a tree.**

   See Chapter 1 for a rundown of the basic controls for moving in Minecraft.

2. **Using the mouse, position the crosshair over a block in the tree.**
3. **Click and hold the left mouse button to start punching the block until it breaks.**
4. **Collect the item that appears.**

   The item should come directly to you, but if you're too far away, just walk up to the item to collect it. The resource is added to the inventory at the bottom of the screen.

Ignore the leaves on the tree for now because they decay naturally with nothing supporting them. Destroyed leaf blocks sometimes give sapling items, which you don't need for crafting the essential items covered in this chapter.

Building a crafting table and shelter

The crafting table and storage chest require wooden planks to build. Follow these steps to use the wood blocks you've gathered (as described in the previous section) to produce wooden planks:

1. **Press E to display the Inventory screen.**
2. **Click a square containing wood blocks to pick them up, and then click an empty square in the crafting grid to place them there.**

   Four wooden planks appear next to the grid, as shown in Figure 2-2.

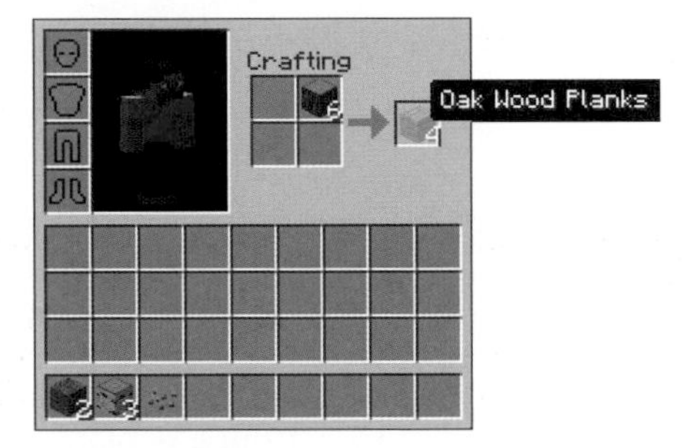

Figure 2-2: Crafting planks.

3. **Click the square that contains the planks.**

   One wood block disappears, but four wooden planks appear on the mouse cursor!
4. **Click the square that contains the planks a few more times to pick up all the planks you can, or Shift-click to send all planks directly to the inventory.**

You can use these planks as building blocks or to build a crafting table and chest.

Crafting the crafting table

Your avatar's crafting grid is a 2-by-2 square (refer to Figure 2-2); however, many items you need in order to survive require a 3-by-3 grid to craft. To unlock this larger grid, you build a crafting table. Follow these steps to build a crafting table, or *workbench:*

1. **Press E to open the Inventory screen.**
2. **Click a square containing your planks, and then right-click each square in the crafting grid to distribute four planks into the squares.**

   A crafting table appears on the right, as shown in Figure 2-3.

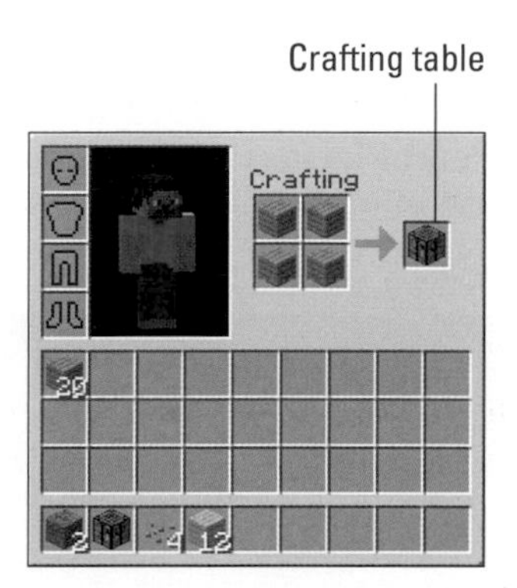

Figure 2-3: Crafting table.

3. **Click the crafting table to pick it up, and then click a square in the bottom row of the inventory to place the table there.**

   You can access items outside the Inventory screen only if they're on the bottom row. This row is always displayed at the bottom of the game screen.

4. **Press E or Esc to close the inventory.**
5. **Use the 1–9 keys or the scroll wheel to select the crafting table.**

   A thick, white outline appears around the crafting table.

   TIP

   You can use either the number keys or the scroll wheel to select items from the bottom row of the inventory. Place the most useful items in the slots you can quickly access.

6. **Right-click a nearby surface to place the crafting table there.**

Right-click the crafting table to view a screen similar to the inventory, with an expanded crafting grid. You use this grid for all crafting recipes in the game, including the chest, described later in this chapter.

Building a shelter and door

Wandering around in the open usually isn't a problem during the day, but the environment becomes much more dangerous at night. If daytime minutes are waning and you don't feel ready to fight back (which is probably true on your first day), you need shelter. By placing many of the blocks you've gathered, you can build shelters, houses, and other structures.

As you gain experience, you can invent your own architectural strategies. To build a basic shelter for now, follow these steps:

1. **Find a good building spot.**

   Flat spots are the easiest to build on, but you can find any spot that you think is feasible for a house to fit. Remember that you can break and replace dirt, sand, and other blocks to flatten a rough area.

2. **Select a block in the inventory with the 1–9 keys, and then right-click a nearby surface to place it there. Place several blocks in a comfortably sized outline for your base of operations, as shown in Figure 2-4.**

Figure 2-4: Starting your base.

   Usually, the frame is a rectangle made of wooden planks, but you can collect blocks such as dirt and use them for building in a pinch. You also need a door, so you can leave 1 block out of the rectangle to make room for it. You can also build the rectangle around the crafting table and chest so that you can work from inside your home.

3. **Place a second layer of blocks on top of the first layer.**

   A structure that's 2 blocks tall is sufficient to keep most monsters at bay.

Next, craft a door so that you have a simple way to enter and exit your shelter. To build a door, use the crafting table and follow these steps:

1. **Right-click the crafting table to open the crafting grid.**
2. **Arrange six wooden planks in two adjacent columns of the crafting grid.**

   This arrangement is the recipe for a door.

3. **Move the door to the bottom row of the inventory.**
4. **Place the door in the wall of your shelter by right-clicking the ground where you want it.**

   You may have to break open part of the shelter wall to fit the door.
5. **Right-click the door to open (and close) it.**

When you place a door in front of you, the door is positioned to open away from you when you right-click it. Usually, a door is placed from the outside of a building so that it opens toward the inside.

Figure 2-5 shows a finished shelter with a door.

Figure 2-5: Crafting a door and finishing your shelter.

To place a block beneath you, jump into the air while right-clicking and looking straight down. This popular method for building and scaffolding is referred to as *pillar jumping*. If you repeat this strategy, you can effectively rise upward on a pillar of blocks, which is useful for building taller structures.

That's it — generally, a basic shelter can ensure your safety for the night.

Making sticks and wooden tools

Sticks and wooden tools set you on your way to obtaining many useful items. To create sticks, open the inventory or right-click the crafting table, and put two vertically adjacent planks into the crafting grid. Four sticks are created for every two planks.

Sticks have no use on their own, but you can use them to craft a variety of other items. By arranging sticks and planks on a crafting table, you can create wooden tools. Tools are used for breaking blocks and fighting quickly and effectively, and although wooden tools break easily and work slowly, they provide a good start.

Here's a rundown of wooden tools to create (see Chapter 4 or the online appendix at www.dummies.com/go/minecraftfd for the recipes):

- **Wooden pickaxe:** You use this item to mine stone-based blocks. (If you try to break stone by hand, it takes a long time and doesn't even drop an item.) Often, a pickaxe is the only wooden tool you need. Any stone-based blocks you break while the pickaxe is selected break faster, so keep it in the bottom row of the inventory for quick access. Breaking stone blocks with a pickaxe provides cobblestone, which is used for stone-based products. (See Chapter 4 for information about the Stone Age.)
- **Wooden axe:** Break wood-based blocks faster.
- **Wooden shovel:** Break granulated blocks faster, such as dirt, sand, and gravel.
- **Wooden hoe:** Till dirt or grass for farming wheat, carrots, potatoes, melons, and pumpkins. (See Chapter 5 for more on farming.)
- **Wooden sword:** Deal extra damage to enemies while this item is selected.

When you use a tool, a green bar representing *durability* appears under the tool (see Figure 2-6); the durability slowly depletes as you continue to use the tool. When the meter runs out, the tool breaks, and you have to craft a new one.

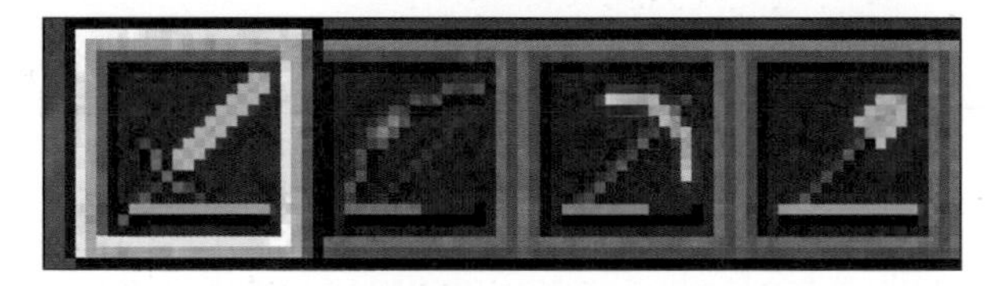

Figure 2-6: When you use a tool, a green bar representing durability appears underneath it.

Only a pickaxe and sword are necessary for the first day. Other tools can be crafted after you discover stone.

Completing Optional Day One Activities

After you've taken care of the basic tasks of creating a crafting table and house, you can move on to the truly fun activities in Minecraft: explore, build, gather, fight, and engage in other outlets of invention. This section details some useful ways you can spend the rest of your daylight minutes.

Use Chapter 4 and Chapter 9 and the appendix (available as free downloads at `www.dummies.com/go/minecraftfd`) for additional information on blocks and crafting recipes.

Constructing a chest

You can place the chest, which is a storage unit, in your world and fill it with items. The benefit is that you drop all items when your avatar dies, but *not* the items in the storage chests.

You can craft a chest by following these steps:

1. **Right-click the crafting table to view the expanded crafting grid.**
2. **Confirm that you have at least eight wooden planks.**

   If you don't, chop down more trees, and then right-click the crafting table.
3. **Click the wooden planks to pick them up and right-click every square, except the center one, in the crafting grid.**

   This arrangement is for crafting a chest. The chest appears to the right of the arrow.
4. **Click the chest to pick it up, and then click a square in the bottom row of the inventory to place the chest there.**
5. **Press E or Esc to close the crafting screen as you would close the Inventory screen.**
6. **Right-click a surface to place the chest there.**

If you right-click the storage chest, you can view an extra grid of squares that's almost as large as the inventory. Placing items into these slots stores them for safekeeping. You can also Shift-click items to sort them from the inventory into the chest, and vice versa. Always keep most of your valuables in storage when you're first starting out. As you become more comfortable playing the game, you can carry more items with you, just in case.

Do not place a block directly above a chest, or else it won't open.

Placing a second chest next to the first one creates an elongated chest, which stores twice as many stacks in the same place for more efficiency.

Mining cobblestone and coal

Cobblestone is a useful building and crafting material. Obtain this item by mining stone (a common, gray block, also known as *smooth stone*) with a pickaxe. You can dig to find stone or look for a cave, mountain, or crag with a visible amount of stone.

This section also covers coal, the most common ore of the game, and how to obtain and use it. Figure 2-7 shows several basic stone- and coal-based items, such as stone, cobblestone, and coal, and also stone tools, a torch, and a furnace.

Figure 2-7: Basic stone- and coal-based items.

Table 2-2 explains how to obtain these items.

Table 2-2 Basic Stone and Coal-based Items

Tool	*Name*	*How to Get It*
	Stone	Crafted in the same way as wooden tools, except with cobblestone rather than wooden planks. Stone tools are faster and have twice the durability of wooden tools. Also, the stone pickaxe can mine lapis lazuli and iron ore (described in Chapter 4 and Chapter 9).

Tool	Name	How to Get It
	Furnace	Crafted with eight cobblestone blocks. After you right-click the furnace, a new screen appears with two input slots and an output slot; place fuel in the bottom slot and an item in the top slot to cook the item. See Chapter 4 for more details about using the furnace.
	Coal	Used to craft torches and fuel furnaces. Coal can be found by mining coal ore, commonly found underground but occasionally aboveground. You can also cook wood blocks in a furnace to get charcoal, which has the same properties.
	Torch	Can be placed on a floor or a wall as a light source. These lights are always important because darkness provides a place for monsters to spawn — and you don't want them to appear in places where you need to go. Use a stick and a lump of coal to craft four torches.

Building a bed

The incredibly useful bed lets you sleep through the night — bypassing all its dangers — as long as you aren't being pursued by monsters. To craft a bed, you need wool blocks, obtained by shearing or killing sheep that roam around grassy areas. Craft three of these blocks with three wooden planks to make a bed (see Figure 2-8). Place the bed in the shelter and right-click it at night to sleep!

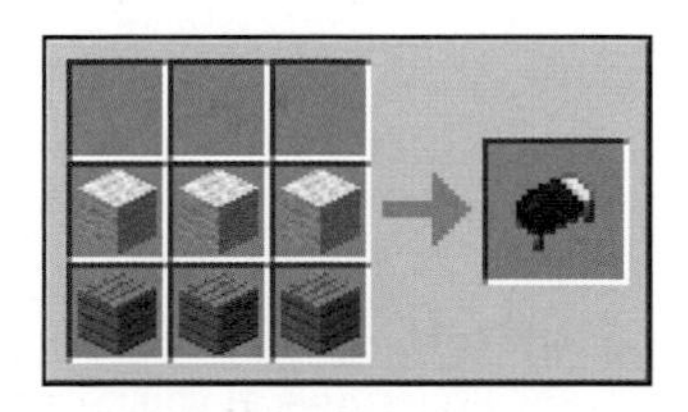

Figure 2-8: Crafting a bed on the crafting table.

Note that these two messages may appear onscreen and prevent you from sleeping:

- `You can only sleep at night.` Wait until the sun sets a little more before trying again.
- `You may not rest now; there are monsters nearby.` You have to look for whatever creature is trying to kill you and destroy it before sleeping.

Continue working on the items in the previous sections of this chapter until nighttime. That's when the fun begins.

Surviving the Night

Unless you set the difficulty level to Peaceful, you *will* face danger during the night. Table 2-3 describes the five types of enemies appear during the night (look over the basic controls in Chapter 1, if you haven't already):

Table 2-3 Enemies and How to Defeat Them

Enemy	*Name*	*How to Defeat It*
	Creepers	Creepers are the most well-known enemies — these cute green shrub-monsters walk toward you, hiss, and explode, harming you and destroying nearby blocks. Attack while sprinting (double-tap the W key) to knock back creepers before they explode. When you play in a higher difficulty mode, creepers can kill your avatar *in one shot.*
	Endermen	Endermen might not appear on the first night, but sooner or later you'll see one. Don't antagonize these monsters — they can be challenging even for experienced players. Endermen normally don't attack you, but if you place the crosshair over one, it turns and glares at you, ready to attack you the moment you remove the crosshair. If you're unfortunate enough to anger these creatures, watch out for their powerful attacks and teleportation. Their weaknesses are water and sunlight.
	Skeletons	Skeletons are downright tricky — they approach you tactically and fire arrows at you. Skeletons are impeccable archers, so hide behind blocks to avoid them. They shoot faster as you get closer, so sneaking up on them is your best bet.

Enemy	*Name*	*How to Defeat It*
	Spiders	Spiders have a relatively small amount of health, but they're fast, small, and jumpy, making them difficult to hit. They can also climb walls, so be prepared to defend your shelter.
	Zombies	Zombies are fairly easy to vanquish if you see them coming. They have more health than other enemies, but they move slowly. Don't let them stall you long enough for other monsters to notice you.

Attacks inflict more damage when you're jumping. You can tell when you score a *jump attack* (jumping and hitting the enemy on your way down) by the sparks that appear on the enemy. Watch out, though: Jumping makes you hungry. (Read more about hunger in Chapter 3.)

Switching from Peaceful mode to Easy mode to Normal mode

If you're playing in Peaceful mode, no mobs can spawn — much less attack, and surviving the first night is not the goal. Instead, your focus should be on advancing through other challenges. You can continue navigating the other challenges of Minecraft in the following chapters. However, if you're ready for a fight, you can switch the difficulty setting to Easy at any time by using the Pause menu tip at the beginning of this chapter (see Figure 2-9).

If you select the default difficulty, Normal mode, you find that the game balances the elements of Minecraft — surviving, building, crafting, gathering resources, and farming, for example. The mobs are challenging, and it can be difficult to combat hunger (see Chapter 3). This chapter tells you how to survive the first night and continue through the game. However, younger players or those who don't want the distractions of mobs and hunger as they explore Minecraft can switch from a difficult mode to an easier one.

Normal mode is a good choice for players who like a significant challenge from the mobs while playing the other parts of Minecraft — such as building, farming, mining, excavating, and inventing.

In Easy mode, you have to protect yourself at night from mobs and worry about hunger (see Chapter 3). Easy mode provides a bit more of a challenge with only a small risk of losing early in the game. This chapter gives you the necessary information to survive your first night in Easy mode.

I like playing in Easy mode because I can deal with the challenges of food and mobs without losing.

Figure 2-9: Using the Pause menu bar to switch between difficulty modes.

Surviving the first night: Three strategies to light the way

The first night can be a doozy if you're not prepared! Knowing a few simple strategies can help you make it out alive, and set the pace to stay alive (you hope) throughout the game.

Strategy 1: Implement the basic strategy

The first approach we suggest that you take to survive the night is basic, and it's one used quite frequently by players of Minecraft. Here's a summary of the basic strategy, outlined earlier in this chapter:

1. Harvest trees by punching wood, as shown in Figure 2-10.
2. Build a crafting table.
3. Construct a shelter.
4. Craft wooden tools and a sword.

If you're playing in Peaceful mode, it isn't necessary to build a shelter or sword. You can choose any optional activities or try your hand at building an effective house.

Figure 2-10: To punch wood, hold down the mouse button while pointing at any wooden structure.

Strategy 2: Use the safe strategy with popular optional activities

Though the first strategy we discuss prepares you for the night, it leaves a bit of risk and little protection. Our second strategy for surviving the night ensures that you've covered all the bases to make yourself completely safe. These steps, though perhaps requiring a little more work to achieve, ensure a peaceful night of sleep with little interruption from mobs on your first night:

Begin by harvesting trees, creating a crafting table and chest. Then obtain tools as described in the optional activities in this chapter. Next, look for sheep and craft a bed. Then look for a place to build a shelter and create your house. Using the remaining daylight, look for animals and trap them by digging a hole, trying to get at least two of each animal except for chickens, which requires only one (see Chapter 5 for more information on animals). Finally, start looking for caves or dig a staircase mine. (This last step is necessary to build a furnace, as discussed earlier in this chapter, in the section "Completing Optional Day One Activities.")

Here are the steps:

1. **Harvest trees.** You can do so by punching wood (refer to Figure 2-10).
2. **Create a crafting table and chest.** See the section "Building a crafting table and shelter," earlier in this chapter.
3. **Craft tools and weapons.** See "Completing Optional Day One Activities," earlier in this chapter.

4. **Find and kill sheep and craft a bed.** Just like real life, in Minecraft sheep are one of the animals you can kill to get meat to feed yourself and wool to build beds and other things. Fortunately, the sheep in Minecraft are 8-bit pixel animals and the killing is hardly violent. See Chapter 5 to find out more about how to kill sheep. After you've killed some sheep, you'll want to craft a bed. See the section "Building a bed," earlier in this chapter, to see how, with the wool you've collected from the sheep.
5. **Create a simple shelter.** See the section "Building a crafting table and shelter," earlier in this chapter, to find out how.
6. **Trap animals other than sheep.** Using the remaining daylight, look for animals and trap them by digging a hole, trying to get at least two of each animal (see Chapter 5 for more information on animals). See Figure 2-11 for an example. Trapping animals allows you to have food and energy when you need it, and by having more than one animal they will spawn and produce even more animals in your hole!
7. **Look for caves or dig a staircase mine.** You can do this by looking for caves or digging a staircase mine. (This step is necessary to build a furnace, as discussed in "Completing Optional Day One Activities" earlier in this chapter.)

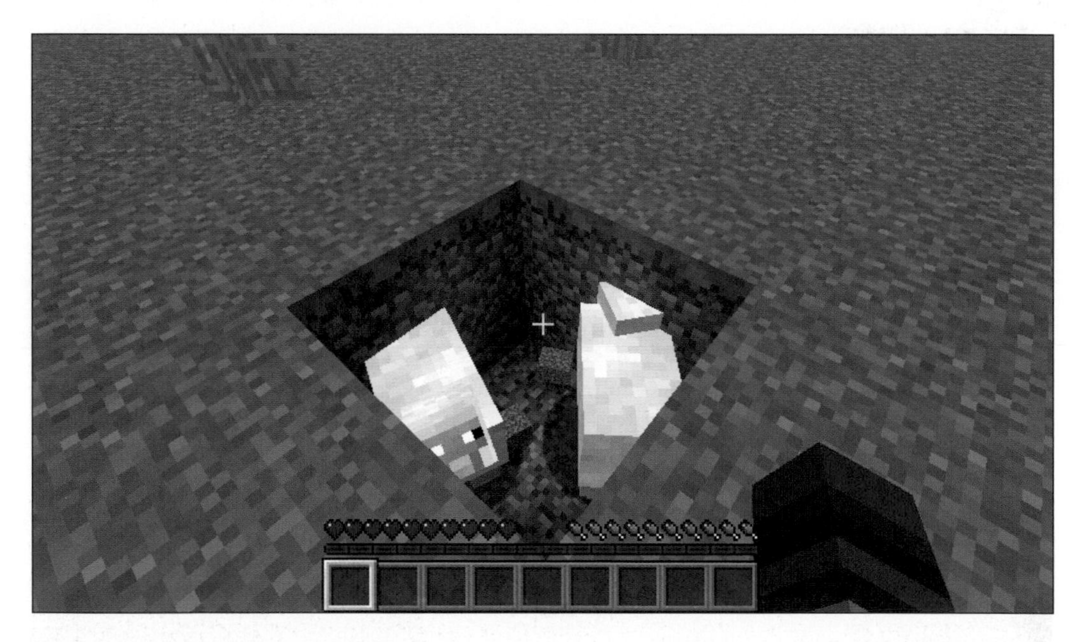

Figure 2-11: Digging a hole to trap animals.

Rather than trap animals and find sheep, we build a wheat farm on the first day (see Chapter 5). We also like digging a staircase during the first night inside the shelter because we get bored simply waiting for daylight.

Strategy 3: Plan an adventure strategy

The strategy we describe in this section is for more adventurous players, who are comfortable fighting a mob or two and who want to take much more risk on their first night. As in all other strategies we describe for surviving the first night, we start by punching wood (harvesting trees). Next, you should craft a sword because you will be fighting. The bed you sleep in won't work if mobs are nearby.

After all the tools you want have been crafted, break the crafting table and take it with you. Look for sheep so that you can craft that all-important bed. Now it's time to travel on your adventure. Start moving and look for anything — a cave, a village, or even a pyramid! Villages work well for starter homes, but you'll have to fight off the zombies (see Chapter 7). This strategy is targeted at exploring the Minecraft world nomad-style rather than create a large house (or base) with connecting farms and mines. There's no single correct way to play Minecraft!

If you have crafted a bed and sword, you do not need a shelter, because you can either fight off mobs or sleep the night away (see Figure 2-12).

Figure 2-12: Fighting off a mob at night with the sword you crafted.

You can choose from plenty of other successful strategies using a combination of required and optional Day One activities. Many players like to experiment with different ideas and strategies every time they play, whereas others stick to a single method that proves effective.

When it's daytime again, the world becomes safer. The undead catch fire in sunlight, spiders no longer attack you, and endermen disappear as they teleport away from the harmful light; creepers are still harmful, but they eventually leave as well. If you're in any mode other than Peaceful mode, congratulations on surviving your first night! Now you can turn your attention to mastering the basic skills needed to survive hunger.

Surviving the Night

If you're playing Minecraft on a mobile device, your experience may be a little bit different! This section details the basic information you need to know to survive your first night in Minecraft PE.

Using the inventoryTo pull up the inventory in PE, you tap the square with three white dots. The inventory in PE (see Figure 2-13) is composed of three main parts: armor, crafting, and inventory. Pressing the three white dots automatically opens the inventory.

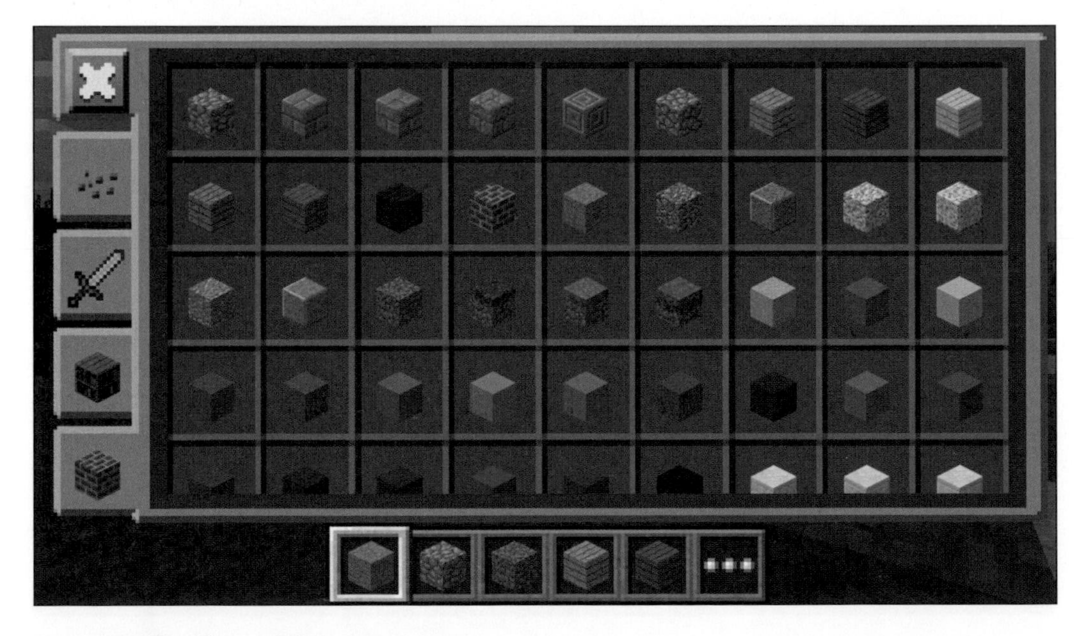

Figure 2-13: The Minecraft PE Inventory screen.

Tap the iron chestplate to open the Armor screen. Tap the bookshelf block to go to the crafting table. To return to the inventory, tap the brick block button. (Say that five times fast.)

To move items in the inventory, tap the square where you want to place an item. Tapping an item already in one of the main slots moves the selected square to the square that holds whatever item you tapped. To throw items out of the main slots, exit the inventory and press on the item you want to throw. It should move the selector over and turn it green while filling up the background of that item with a green bar. When the green bar fills up, you hear a popping sound, and it's automatically thrown out of the inventory. Just walk over to the item, and it automatically returns to the inventory, along with a higher-pitched pop.

Implementing a Minecraft PE strategy for surviving the night

Surviving the first night in Minecraft PE is simple. Your number-one priority is to either find or create a shelter during what little daylight remains. Harvest trees and make tools as soon as possible. We usually make a wooden pick just to mine some stone to get stone tools.

For a shelter, simply dig in the side of the wall or dig into the floor. All the houses we remember building were underground or in the side of a mountain (see Figure 2-14). Just stay inside your little hut all night, or you can fight mobs.

We find that we usually don't die in PE because most mobs are easy to defeat. We find that you can punch the members of most mobs to death without them hurting you. You should trap animals or make a bed if it's an option on your first day.

In PE, if the difficulty is lower than the normal difficulty (about the center of the sidebar), you can recover all health by sleeping in a bed.

For the sake of simplicity, build a shelter underground or in a mountain. Minecraft Pocket Edition is the first Minecraft version Thomas had, and the first time he played, he literally had no idea what he was doing. When darkness started to fall, Thomas dug into the side of a sand dune (this was before sand had gravity in PE) and dug a little tunnel to survive the first night. He had two thoughts: "Why hadn't the sandstone, along with the stone, dropped anything?" and "Why is it taking so long for this stone to break?" Back then, Thomas didn't know how to make pickaxes, so he punched the sandstone and stone with his bare hands!

Figure 2-14: Constructing a shelter in Minecraft PE inside a cave is often the easiest way to survive the first night.

Part II
Learning the Basic Skills

Visit `www.dummies.com` for more great *For Dummies* content online.

In this part . . .

- Get started with farming
- Understand the basics of mining
- Discover how to use blocks

3

Surviving Hunger

In This Chapter

- Preventing and combatting hunger
- Understanding Minecraft PE and food
- Knowing how to attack and defend
- Crafting weapons
- Choosing armor

After surviving the first night, you need to find and eat food while you accomplish the next challenge in the game — implementing blocks, farming, or mining, for example. This chapter can help you understand how food works in Minecraft so that you can keep yourself well fed as you continue in the game.

Understanding and Avoiding Hunger

Hunger is a dangerous, long-term obstacle — try to overcome it as efficiently as possible, which ultimately means gathering as many animals together in an area you control through farming. But you have to eat while you create farms and overcome the obstacles presented in Chapter 4, not to mention nightly mob attacks. As depicted by the Hunger bar at the bottom of the screen, you get hungry over time, and you require food in order to resolve it. (Refer to Chapter 1 for more on the Hunger bar.)

In Peaceful mode (see Chapter 16 to learn more about Peaceful mode), the Health bar doesn't deplete from your hunger, so you can continue to the next challenge without acquiring or eating food. However, you cannot move quickly (by sprinting).

Eating food restores your character's health (as depicted by the hearts on the Health bar) indirectly over time, so keep at least nine out of ten units on the Hunger bar. Though your character never dies from hunger except in Hard mode, it makes you vulnerable to damage that can kill you, including relatively small damage such as touching a cactus, falling from a four-block height, or even facing attacks from neutral mobs (see Chapter 5).

If hunger is significantly limiting gameplay, you can switch to Peaceful mode or Easy mode while you start a farm (see Chapter 5).

Your symptoms of hunger depend on the difficulty level. Except in Peaceful mode, your character grows hungrier by taking action: Sprinting (by double-tapping W) is the easiest way to deplete hunger units, but jumping or absorbing damage also taxes your character.

You cannot sprint if the Hunger bar has three units or fewer.

The consequence of famine (as depicted by an empty Hunger bar) depends on the current difficulty level, as outlined in Table 3-1.

Table 3-1 Effects of Famine on Your Character

Difficulty Level	*What Happens to the Health Bar*
Peaceful	Doesn't deplete
Easy	Assuming that it's more than half full, slowly depletes until it's half full
Normal	Slowly depletes, but not to the point of death
Hardcore	Depletes until it's empty; find some food — quick!

To refill the Hunger bar, you need to acquire and eat food as described in the later section "Finding food."

If you're playing in Minecraft PE, you do not have the Hunger bar. Instead, to restore health, you can eat food or sleep in a bed. Also, the game has no poisonous foods.

Finding food

If you're starting a new game, strive for the foods near the top of Table 3-2, because they are easiest to find and make. Table 3-2 explains how to obtain several useful foods. (Chapter 4 has more information about the items themselves.)

On the Hunger bar, each drumstick represents 2 food units.

Table 3-2 Useful Foodstuffs

Icon	*Food*	*Description*
	Raw porkchop or beef	Killing a pig or cow grants you from 1 to 3 units of this food. However, the food is more effective when cooked in a furnace.
	Cooked porkchop or steak	Cook raw meat in a furnace to obtain an item worth 4 units of food.
	Raw chicken	Avoid eating raw chicken unless you have to. Every item you eat gives you a 30 percent chance of getting food poisoning, draining the Hunger bar.
	Cooked chicken	It has the same effect as cooked pork or beef, but, at 3 units of food, is less powerful.
	Mushroom stew	This item restores 3 units of food, and each inventory space holds only one bowl of stew.
	Bread	Bread isn't quite as satiating as meat, but after you obtain a wheat farm (as described in Chapter 5), you can craft a reliable food source, 2½ units in strength.
	Cookie	Cookies are crafted from wheat, but you also need cocoa beans. Cookies restore only 1 unit of food apiece, so they aren't quite restorative, though you can mass-produce them.

(continued)

Table 3-2 *(continued)*

Icon	*Food*	*Description*
	Carrot	Carrots are found incidentally when you kill zombies or explore villages (as described in Chapter 8). A carrot provides 2 units of food.
	Potato	Potatoes are also found incidentally. Raw potatoes aren't useful, though they can be cooked into baked potatoes.
	Baked potato	Cook potatoes in a furnace to get this item, worth 3 units of food.
	Melon slice	Despite the meager effect of a single slice, or 1 unit, this item can be mass-produced effectively.
	Red apple	This fruit falls from destroyed trees and provides 2 units of food.
	Golden apple	Both types of golden apple yield 2 units of food. The first, crafted with gold nuggets, boosts health and reduces hunger. The second, crafted with gold blocks, gives you 30 seconds of rapid regeneration and 5 minutes of resistance and fire resistance.
	Raw fish	Fishing is mentioned in Chapter 4.
	Cooked fish	Cook fish in a furnace to get this item, worth 2½ units of food; it makes a good food source if you have time on your hands.

Icon	*Food*	*Description*
	Pumpkin pie	Collect eggs (littered by chickens), sugar (from lakeside reeds), and pumpkins to make a pie worth 4 units of food.
	Cake	Making a cake requires 3 buckets of milk, 2 lumps of sugar, 3 units of wheat, and 1 egg. Cake has to be placed on the ground before you can eat it; right-click it to restore 1 unit of food. Cake disappears after six uses.
	Rotten flesh	Eating rotten flesh — obtained from zombies — gives you an 80 percent chance of food poisoning.
	Spider eye	Eating a spider eye — obtained from spiders — has the side effect of poisoning you. The eye is used primarily for brewing potions.
	Salmon	Obtain this item from fishing; it's good for eating and for taming ocelots.
	Cooked Salmon	Simply cook salmon in a furnace to triple your hunger points.
	Poison potato	Restores 2 hunger points but has a 60 percent chance of poisoning a character for 4 seconds; unlike a regular potato, it cannot be planted or baked.
	Mutton	Killing sheep drops 1 or 2 units of mutton, providing 2 hunger units when eaten raw.

(continued)

Table 3-2 *(continued)*

Icon	*Food*	*Description*
	Cooked mutton	Mutton cooked in a furnace offers 6 hunger points — more than chicken but less than pig or beef.
	Rabbit	When a rabbit (or bunny) is killed, it drops 0-1 units of raw food, which can be eaten for 3 hunger points (more than most other types of raw meat); when cooked, it increases the hunger points to 5, just slightly less than cooked mutton.
	Rabbit stew	This complicated recipe involves a bowl, a carrot, a baked potato, a mushroom, and a cooked rabbit; but when crafted and then eaten, it restores an incredible 10 hunger points.

Note that cooked meat provides 2 to 3 times more food points than raw but requires a furnace (see Chapter 2) or killing the animal via fire such as lava.

Eating a poisonous food can significantly impact the Health bar and Hunger bar. Except in Hard mode, you won't die directly from poison, though you're extremely vulnerable to any type of damage and your ability to complete activities decreases. Drinking milk negates the effects of poisonous food. However, obtaining milk isn't possible until you're further into the game, when you have the resources to craft a bucket.

Eating food

You can eat foodstuffs by selecting food and holding down the right mouse button for a second. Your character then finishes eating, and part of the Hunger bar is refilled. Minecraft PE players eat by simply selecting the food and then touching and holding the screen.

If you eat a poisonous food, the poison lasts for only a short time, as shown on the display. During those seconds, a lot of hunger and health points are lost. However, many players survive after eating poisonous food from time to time. Some enjoy experimenting with poisonous foods, especially pufferfish (see Figure 3-1), which makes the screen turn wavy and green.

Figure 3-1: Pufferfish may not kill you, but they surely make gameplay fun by making the screen look wavy and green.

Saturation: Making the most of your food

In addition to restoring the Hunger bar, eating food prevents the Hunger bar from depleting for a while. When the Hunger bar starts jittering, you're becoming hungry again, and the meter continues to deplete.

Different types of food increase or decrease how long you can play before the Hunger bar begins to deplete again. (See Table 3-3 for saturation comparisons.) In this process of *saturation,* the higher the saturation number, the longer the Hunger bar remains before your character needs to eat again.

Table 3-3 Food Saturation Comparison

Food Item	*Saturation Number*
Apple	2.4
Baked potato	7.2
Bread	6
Cake slice	.2
Cake whole	2.4
Carrot	4.8
Clownfish	.2
Cooked chicken	7.2
Cooked fish	6
Cooked porkchop	12.8
Cooked salmon	9.6
Cookie	.4
Golden apple/enchanted apple	9.6
Golden carrot	14.5
Melon slice	1.2
Mushroom stew	7.2
Poison potato	1.2
Potato	.6
Pufferfish	.2
Pumpkin pie	4.8
Raw beef	1.8
Raw chicken	1.2
Raw fish	.4
Raw porkchop	1.8
Raw salmon	.4
Rotten flesh	.8
Spider eye	3.2
Steak	12.8
Cooked mutton	9.6
Cooked rabbit	6
Rabbit stew	12
Raw mutton	1.2
Raw rabbit	1.8

Unfortunately, foods with the highest level of saturation, such as golden apples and carrots, are uncommon and require crafting. As with eating sushi in real life, eating raw meat (avoid raw chicken!) offers a high level of saturation and food points, and you can easily find it in most biomes. (That's why we recommend, in Chapter 2, trapping animals as an optional Day One activity.)

Because cooked meat is the best food option early in the game, build a furnace (see Chapter 2) before starting a farm (see Chapter 5).

Porkchops, even when eaten raw, are our favorite food source when starting a new game because pigs can easily be found, and are a lot of fun to catch!

If you're in one of the few biomes that's short on food, such as a desert or mesa, you need to excavate, find a village, start a farm, or switch to Peaceful mode as soon as possible, or you'll run out of food very quick!

Limiting exhaustion

Another way to make food points last as long as possible is to limit strenuous activity — no sprinting or jumping, and avoid taking damage.

However, don't worry too much about exhaustion and saturation points. Most players simply continue working through the challenges presented in the next few chapters and eat regularly whatever food items are handy.

Table 3-4 shows how different activities in the game can affect your exhaustion levels.

Table 3-4 Exhaustion Levels

Action	*Increase in Exhaustion Level*
Walk and sneak (per meter)	0.01
Swim (per meter)	0.015
Break a block	0.025
Sprint (per meter)	0.1
Jump	0.2
Attack an enemy	0.3
Receive any damage	0.3
Suffer the effects of food poisoning	0.5 per second (15 total) for raw chicken or rotten flesh; 1.5 per second (22.5 total) for pufferfish
Sprint jump	0.8
Regenerate 1 health point by accumulating18 hunger points	3.0

If you don't want to repeatedly run back to your home to eat, you should carry road rations with you, such as steak or bread.

Understanding Minecraft PE and Food

In the PE version of Minecraft, you see only the Health bar and not the Hunger bar. Eating food restores the Health bar directly. The only food items now in Minecraft PE are raw and cooked meats, apples, mushroom stew, beetroot stew, beetroot, potato, and cake. Refer to Table 3-2 for information on most of these food items; see Table 3-5 for food items unique to Minecraft PE.

Table 3-5 Food Items That Are Unique to Minecraft PE

Food	*Name*	*Description*
	Beetroot	Found only in Minecraft PE; can be eaten to restore 1 health point.
	Beetroot soup	Found only in Minecraft PE and crafted from a bowl and 6 beetroots. When eaten, restores 4 health points (not hunger points) directly.

At this point, the Hunger bar and Health bar should be full and the inventory stocked with food. You're now in a position to defend yourself from mobs using basic weapons and armor.

Attacking and Defending

As we mention in Chapter 2, unless the game is in Peaceful mode, you need to fight the common hostile mobs in the first few days of gameplay. Even if you craft a bed, you will likely experience at least one night in which mobs are too close for you to use a bed. That is why we strongly recommend using a wooden sword the first day and then upgrading that weapon as materials become available.

The rest of this chapter discusses making weapons and armor for protection. Many players must wait to make more advanced weapons or armor until after farming and mining, as discussed in Chapters 5 and 6. As you discover more resources, we recommend that you upgrade or add to your weapons and armor list, including enchanting items, as explained in Chapter 10.

Making Weapons

As you start the game, be sure that you have weapons ready, in the event of a mob attack. Knowing the right weapons to build can also help speed up your mining.

Wielding swords

The sword in Minecraft is a weapon that does the most damage and therefore is the most valuable. In addition to helping you fight mobs, the sword can be used as a tool to break blocks quickly. Like a pickaxe (as discussed in Chapter 2), the sword has 5 tiers, listed here in order of strength from least to greatest:

- Wood
- Gold
- Stone
- Iron
- Diamond

When you use a sword, whether in breaking blocks or fighting, you decrease its durability. Over time, swords need to be repaired using the correct ingredients on a crafting grid or an anvil. (For information on anvils, see Chapter 10.) However, a sword should not need to be repaired as often as a tool such as a pickaxe or shovel. Also, the diamond sword has such a high durability that almost always it lasts throughout the game without needing repairs.

As the preceding list indicates, gold is less durable than stone or iron. Because gold is usually scarce and needed in other recipes, primarily in brewing and potions, it isn't a good idea to make a gold sword. The exception to this statement occurs when enchanting a sword as gold is the best medium for enchanting, as we explain in Chapter 10.

Stringing the bow

The bow in Minecraft is a weapon that inflicts different amounts of damage depending on how much the bow is charged. It cannot be fired without arrows. The more charged up the bow is, the farther the arrow goes, the stronger the arrow gets, the slower the player moves, and the more the screen zooms in on the target. Charging also increases the accuracy of the arrow.

A fully charged bow inflicts 4½ hearts of damage with a rare chance of 5. When a bow isn't charged, it deals only half a heart. The bow is a particularly good weapon against skeletons and creepers (and later against mobs). Just remember, the bow cannot be used without arrows.

The bow-and-arrow can be used as an ingredient in redstone, such as in a dispenser (see Chapter 8). Then you can fight mobs using elaborate traps or farm mobs.

An arrow fired from a bow causes significant damage to a mob from a distance (whereas a sword must be used at close range). When the bow is at the perfect angle and is fully charged, it is possible to get the arrow a total of 120 blocks away — that's a lot of blocks! The arrow travels in an arc, and you can pick up the arrows that you have fired. However, skeletons' arrows cannot be picked up, nor can arrows that are fired off from an infinity bow. (Enchantments are detailed in Chapter 10.)

Protecting Yourself with Armor

In the top left corner of the inventory display screen are armor slots (see Figure 3-2) in the following four categories:

- Helmet
- Chestplate
- Leggings
- Boots

Like the quality rating in swords, armor comes in different tiers, from least effective to most effective:

- Leather
- Gold
- Chain
- Iron
- Diamond

Chain armor is not craftable, but can be obtained by trading with villagers or killing a mob that's wearing the armor. It can be repaired via crafting, like other armor that has lost its durability.

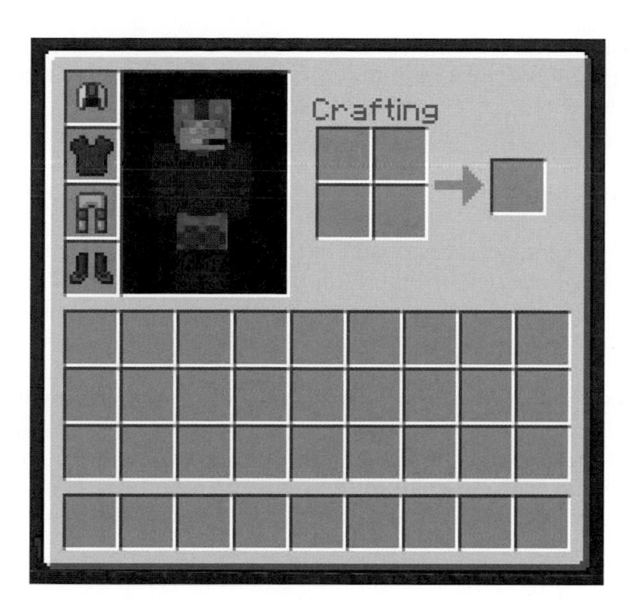

Figure 3-2: The inventory display has armor slots in the top left corner.

Armor protects against not only hostile mobs (and other players) but also other items in the game such as chicken eggs, falling anvils, lightning strikes, injuries from touching a cactus, and explosions. However, armor doesn't protect against all situations such as falling into the void, suffocating, or drowning.

Though leather and golden armor are the least desirable materials for protection, they're the easiest to enchant.

Similar to the pickaxe or sword, armor loses durability over time and needs to be repaired in a crafting grid or on an anvil.

When you repair an item, the newly crafted item will have slightly more durability than the original items combined but will lose any enchantments. The exception occurs when you repair an item using an anvil.

Start crafting armor as materials become available, and then upgrade to more sturdy materials later.

Not all pieces of armor need to consist of the same material. As rare ingredients become available, such as diamond, improving a single piece of armor has tremendous benefit. For example, you can wear a leather helmet with a diamond chestplate and iron leggings.

Armor provides defense points, shown as half a shirt of mail ("mail" is short for chain mail, the type of armor knights wear) on the Armor bar above the Health bar (see Figure 3-3). The higher the number of defense points, the lower the amount of damage dealt to the player in an attack. Many players craft or obtain a full set of armor early in the game to maximize their defense points.

Figure 3-3: Defense points display above the Health bar as half a shirt of mail.

Wearing leather

Leather is the least durable but most common armor material for beginning players. Normally acquired by killing cows, it can also be crafted from rabbit hide.

Leather armor can be dyed, as explained in Chapter 11. This is mostly for decorative purposes to make your character stand out from others.

Donning the helmet

A helmet (also called *cap* when it's made of leather) protects your character's head in an attack. In general, the helmet provides better protection than boots. Leather provides only 1 defense point (represented by half a shirt), whereas diamond provides 3. When enchanted, a helmet can extend underwater breathing time and increase the underwater mining rate.

Pounding the chestplate

Chestplates, also called *tunics* in leather form, are stored in the second inventory slot and provide protection for the upper body. This piece of armor provides significantly more protection than a helmet and should therefore be crafted first if you have enough ingredients and upgrade to a stronger material as soon as possible.

Putting on leggings

Leggings (or pants) provide the second-highest level of protection and are stored in the third inventory slot. This piece of armor should also be crafted early on and upgraded when materials become available.

Walking in your boots

The least effective piece of armor, and the one stored at the bottom of the inventory screen, is a pair of boots. But don't be fooled into thinking that boots are not a vital part of armor. They require only 4 items to craft and offer defense points, and they can be enchanted for additional properties. When enchanted with the depth strider, boots increase underwater speed; when enchanted with feather falling, they reduce fall damage (see Chapter 10).

Though all items can be enchanted with various abilities, helmets and boots have unique enchantments that make them particularly important pieces of armor despite the low number of defense points they provide.

Storing armor

In addition to wearing armor, you can store armor on an armor stand. In Survival mode, you can now only place armor and mob heads on armor stands. Just right-click the armor stand to put on and take off armor.

Another cool feature of the armor stand is that it is an *entity:* It has gravity, it can be picked up with minecarts, and it can even move the armor stand with pistons.

4

Discovering Blocks and Items

In This Chapter

- Exploring the Wooden Age, Looting Age, and Stone Age
- Finding detailed information about blocks and items
- Using the furnace
- Building an effective house

This chapter serves as a guide to the basic components of Survival mode, which you need to know when you're just starting out. This chapter includes information on the Wooden, Looting, and Stone ages (or phases of the game), as well as details on how to use the furnace and where to store all your items. In Peaceful mode, you can skip the Looting Age, but you'll still want to take advantage of discovering all the items and blocks available in the other ages to further their game.

If you're interested in finding out more detailed information about other blocks and items, see Chapter 9; more recipes are in the appendix, and images and detailed crafting recipes are in the bonus appendix. (Both the bonus appendix and appendix are available for download at www.dummies.com/go/minecraftfd.)

Starting In the Wooden Age

When you first start playing Minecraft, most of the items you need are wooden, made from wood blocks (see Figure 4-1). Table 4-1 explains how to find or craft these items and describes what they do. You can break most of these blocks faster with an axe.

Table 4-1 Wooden Items

Item	*How to Obtain It*	*Description*
Boat	Crafted from 5 planks	Right-click some water in which to put your boat, and then right-click the boat to hop in! Press the W,A,S,D keys to drive, and inflict damage on the boat to break it and use it again later.
Bowl	Crafted from 3 planks (makes 4)	The bowl holds mushroom stew.
Chest	Crafted from 8 planks	The storage unit can hold 27 stacks of items. Place two chests next to each other to form a double chest, which can store 54 stacks.
Crafting table	Crafted from 4 planks	Right-click this item to open the expanded crafting grid (see Chapter 2).
Fence	Crafted from 6 sticks (makes 2)	Its posts are decorative blocks that automatically connect to adjacent blocks or fences. Though you can still place blocks on top of fences, you cannot jump over them.
Fence gate	Crafted from 2 planks, 4 sticks	Click to open and close its sideways latch. It connects to, and acts like, the fence.
Ladder	Crafted from 7 sticks (makes 3)	Ladders can be placed on walls, and you can climb ladders by simply moving toward them. Hold the Shift key to hang on a ladder.
Log	Found on trees	Wooden logs come in six textures, used for crafting. You can place logs on walls to make them appear sideways.
Sign	Crafted from 6 planks, 1 stick (makes 3)	When you place this item on a wall, or at any angle on the ground, a screen appears on which you can write.
Stick	Crafted from 2 planks (makes 4)	Make it with wooden planks for more crafting recipes.
Trap door	Crafted from 6 planks (makes 2)	Place this hatch on the side of a block. Click the hatch to open or close it.

Item	How to Obtain It	Description
Wooden axe	Crafted from 2 sticks, 3 planks	A weak axe, it makes lumberjacking somewhat quicker.
Wooden button	Crafted from 1 plank	This simple item provides power when you click it or hit it with an arrow (see Chapter 6).
Wooden door	Crafted from 6 planks (makes 3)	This tall block can be opened and closed when you click it. It has six different variants, all crafted from their respective wood types. Zombies can destroy it (see Chapter 8).
Wooden hoe	Crafted from 2 sticks, 2 planks	The easily broken garden tool is helpful for starting a small farm at a low cost.
Wooden pickaxe	Crafted from 2 sticks, 3 planks	This weak pickaxe is the most basic tool for breaking stone blocks. It's your ticket to the next age.
Wooden plank	Crafted from 1 log (makes 4)	This basis for wooden items is a useful building material. Its texture depends on which logs were used to make it.
Wooden pressure plate	Crafted from 2 planks	It provides power when anything lands on it (see Chapter 6).
Wooden shovel	Crafted from 2 sticks, 1 plank	The weakest shovel in the game is a cheap one.
Wooden slab	Crafted from 3 planks (makes 6)	Walk up and down this decorative block without jumping. Stack the slabs on top of each other, and place them as either ceilings or floors.
Wooden stair	Crafted from 6 planks (makes 4)	The wooden stair allows for denser stairwells and can be placed upside-down on ceilings, like the slab. ***Note:*** Stairs are always placed facing you.
Wooden sword	Crafted from 1 stick, 2 planks	A brittle, basic sword that increases the damage you inflict; it's a good go-to weapon for new players.

Of course, you may come across many other natural blocks during the Wooden Age. Table 4-2 lists the common aboveground blocks and describes the items you can make with them.

Table 4-2 Basic Naturals from the Wooden Age

Item	*How to Obtain It*	*Description*
Apple	Occasionally, from oak leaves	A food item that can be used to make golden apples
Cacti	Found in deserts	A farmable plant (see Chapter 5) that damages anything that touches it; can be made into green dye
Clay ball	By breaking clay blocks (4 per block)	Used to make bricks and clay blocks
Clay block	Found near water	A softly colored building block; drops 4 clay balls when broken
Cocoa bean	Occasionally, from natural cocoa pods in the jungle	Used as brown dye or to make cookies; can also be farmed (see Chapter 5)
Dead shrub	Found in deserts	Used as decoration
Dirt	Found in most biomes, usually with grass on top	Can be used as farmland; nearby grass eventually spreads onto dirt
Flint	Found while mining gravel	Used for crafting flint and steel, or arrows
Flower	Found in grassy biomes	Can be picked up and replanted or crafted into dyes
Grass, dead bush, fern	Found in grassy biomes	A grass that can be grown manually using bone meal; sometimes drops seeds when broken without shears
Gravel	Found randomly aboveground and below it	Falls if no block is under it; sometimes drops flint
Ice	Found on the surface of frozen lakes and rivers	A slippery block that commonly appears in bodies of water that have frozen over
Leaf	Found on trees	Unless you break it with shears, drops only saplings or apples
Lily pad	Found in swamp biomes	Can be placed on water, allowing you to walk across it with ease
Mushroom	Found in dark places or swamps or near trees	Can be used to make stew, but cannot be placed in bright areas

Item	*How to Obtain It*	*Description*
Mushroom stew	Crafted from 1 brown mushroom, 1 red mushroom, 1 bowl	A useful food item, though only one bowl fits in an inventory slot
Packed ice	Found in the Ice Spike biome	A slippery block that doesn't melt and isn't transparent
Paper	Crafted from 3 sugar canes (makes 3)	Used to make maps and books; purchased by librarians for emeralds (see Chapter 8)
Pumpkin	Appears occasionally in patches	A fruit that can be farmed (see Chapter 5), converted to a jack-o'-lantern, used to build golems, crafted into seeds, or made into pie
Pumpkin seed	Crafted from 1 pumpkin (makes 4)	Used to farm pumpkins; see Chapter 5
Red sand	Found in the mesa biome (see Chapter 5)	Falls if no block is under it; can be used to make red sandstone or glass
Sand	Found in deserts and around bodies of water	Falls if no block is under it; can be used to make sandstone or glass
Sapling	Found from leaf blocks	Planted when you right-click grass or dirt; grows into a tree (see Chapter 5)
Snow	Appears in snowy biomes	A thin layer of snow over cold biomes that can be scooped up into snowballs
Snow block	Crafted from 4 snowballs	A decoration block that can be used to build snow golems
Snowball	Appears when shoveling snow	Can be thrown to knock back mobs and deal damage to Blaze and the ender dragon; can be crafted into snow blocks
Sugar	Crafted from 1 sugar cane	Used to brew potions and to make fermented spider eyes, pumpkin pie, and cake
Sugar cane	Appears in patches near water	A reed that can be farmed (see Chapter 5) and crafted into paper or sugar
Vine	Appears on trees in swamps and in jungles	Can be climbed; grows if left untended; if hanging, disappears if its roots are destroyed

Figure 4-1: Most items in the Wooden Age are made from wooden blocks, like this house.

Making It Through the Looting Age

You reach the Looting Age early in the game — sometimes, even parallel to reaching the Wooden Age. You begin by slaying enemies for loot, and by using the loot to improve your crafting repertoire. Many more items then become available to you, as listed in Table 4-3. I don't mention some rare loot, like iron, in this section; these items are described in their respective tables.

All tools increase the amount of damage you inflict. The sword and bow are the most powerful, but an axe still fares well in combat. Shovels are the weakest.

Table 4-3 Items in the Looting Age

Item	*How to Obtain It*	*Description*
Arrow	By killing skeletons; crafted from 1 flint, 1 stick, 1 feather (makes 4)	A type of ammunition used with bows and dispensers

Item	*How to Obtain It*	*Description*
Bed	Crafted from 3 wool, 3 planks	Can be right-clicked during nighttime to sleep, skipping the night and allowing you to reappear by the bed if you die (You cannot sleep while monsters are pursuing you.)
Bone	By killing skeletons	A useful item for taming wolves; can be crafted into bone meal or white dye
Bone meal	Crafted from 1 bone (makes 3)	Can right-click grass while holding this strong fertilizer to grow a patch of tall grass and flowers (Right-click any immature crop to grow it.)
Book	Crafted from 1 leather, 3 paper	Can be used to make a book and quill, a bookcase, or an enchantment table
Book and quill	Crafted from 1 feather, 1 ink sac, 1 book	Lets you write in the book or read a signed book by right-clicking while holding it
Bookshelf	Crafted from 3 books, 6 planks	An expensive decorative item that serves as a buffer for the enchantment table (see Chapter 6); returns 3 books when broken
Bow	Crafted from 3 string, 3 sticks	A powerful weapon that's useful throughout the game (As long as you have arrows in the inventory, you can hold the right mouse button to charge the bow, and release it to fire.)
Carrot	Rarely, by killing zombies	Can be eaten or farmed (see Chapter 5); also used to make golden carrots
Egg	Occasionally laid by chickens	Thrown when you right-click while holding it, occasionally spawning a baby chicken where it lands; also used to craft cake and pumpkin pie
Ender pearl	Sometimes, by killing endermen	An ingredient for an eye of ender, which helps you find the Stronghold (see Chapter 3); if you throw the pearl by right-clicking, teleports to where the pearl lands but incurs damage
Feather	By killing chickens	A useful ingredient for arrows; also used to make the book and quill
Fermented spider eye	Crafted from 1 spider eye, 1 sugar, 1 brown mushroom	The key ingredient in negative potions (see Chapter 6)

(continued)

Table 4-3 *(continued)*

Item	*How to Obtain It*	*Description*
Fishing rod	Crafted from 2 string, 3 sticks	Lets you cast its bobber by right-clicking while holding it; can be right-clicked again — if the bobber floats in the water for a little while and then suddenly dips — to pull out a fish
Gunpowder	By killing creepers (without exploding them)	An explosive material used to craft TNT, fire charges, and splash potions
Ink sac	By killing squids	Used as black dye or as an ingredient for the book and quill
Item frame	Crafted from 8 sticks, 1 leather	Can display an item (when mounted on the wall) when you right-click it while holding the item; rotates when you right-click it again
Leather	By killing cows	Useful for making books and leather armor
Leather cap, tunic, trousers, boots	Crafted from 5, 8, 7, or 4 leather, respectively	The weakest armor that negates a good amount of damage
Painting	Crafted from 8 sticks, 1 wool	Can be placed by right-clicking a wall; measures up to 4 blocks wide by 4 blocks tall
Poisonous potato	Obtained (rarely) instead of a normal potato	Can be eaten but causes poison damage; no real use for it
Potato	Rarely, by killing zombies	Can be eaten or farmed (see Chapter 5); a low-profit food item unless cooked into a baked potato
Pumpkin pie	Crafted from 1 pumpkin, 1 sugar, 1 egg	An effective food item — reliable if you have several pumpkins and eggs
Raw beef	By killing cows	Essentially the same as raw porkchop
Raw chicken	By killing chickens	A weaker food source that can sometimes poison you when eaten raw, draining the food meter; should be cooked before eating!
Raw fish	Obtained by fishing	Restores a tiny segment of the Hunger bar and can be used to tame ocelots in the jungle
Raw porkchop	By killing pigs	A basic food item that isn't effective unless you cook it

Item	*How to Obtain It*	*Description*
Rotten flesh (see Figure 4-2)	By killing zombies	A fairly useless item and volatile food source; however, heals wolves when fed to them; sometimes, village priests exchange an emerald for it (see Chapter 8)
Slime block	Crafted from four slimeballs	A bouncy block that sticks to other blocks when pushed with a piston. Additionally, sends anything that is on it flying if pushed by a piston
Slimeball	Dropped by slimes in the swamp	A gooey item, used to make sticky pistons and magma cream
Spider eye	By killing spiders	A potion ingredient, a poisonous food, and an ingredient of a fermented spider eye
String	By killing spiders or breaking cobwebs	A useful ingredient in making bows, fishing rods, and tripwire lines
TNT	Crafted from 5 gun-powder, 4 sand	When set off by redstone or fire, sizzles and then causes a large block-destroying explosion; affected by gravity when activated
Wool	By killing or shear-ing sheep; crafted from 4 string	A decorative block used for beds and paintings; can be colored with dye

Figure 4-2: Rotten flesh and gold-colored experience points, dropped by a defeated zombie. (Puffs of smoke show a zombie despawning.)

Surviving the Stone Age

A significant milestone in Minecraft Survival mode, and one achieved by some players on the first day, is reaching the Stone Age. After you craft a wooden pickaxe and you either find a cave or dig a hole, the items in Table 4-4 become available to you.

Most stone-based materials are more solid than other blocks, and you have to break them with a pickaxe to obtain loot.

Table 4-4 Items in the Stone Age

Item	*How to Obtain It*	*Description*
Andesite	Found naturally underground; crafted from diorite and cobblestone (makes 2)	A variant of stone that can be crafted into its smooth variant
Coal	Found when mining coal ore; dropped by wither skeletons	A handy material that's used as furnace fuel; can be used to make torches and fire charges
Coal ore	Found commonly underground	A plentiful source of coal that you can find in veins while mining
Cobblestone	Found by mining stone or cobblestone	An excellent building block and the basis for stone-based crafting
Cobblestone slab	Crafted from 3 cobblestone (makes 6)	The cobblestone equivalent of the wooden slab
Cobblestone stairs (see Figure 4-3)	Crafted from 6 cobblestone (makes 4)	The cobblestone equivalent of wooden stairs
Cobblestone wall	Crafted from 6 cobblestone (makes 6)	The cobblestone equivalent of wooden fences; connects to fence gates
Diorite	Found naturally underground; crafted from 2 nether quartz and 2 cobblestone (makes 2)	A variant of stone that can be crafted into its smooth variant
Furnace	Crafted from 8 cobblestone	A useful block that's used to smelt items into other items

Item	*How to Obtain It*	*Description*
Granite	Found naturally underground; crafted from diorite and nether quartz	A variant of stone that can be crafted into its smooth variant
Jack-o'-lantern	Crafted from 1 pumpkin, 1 torch	A spooky, brightly glowing pumpkin
Lever	Crafted from 1 cobblestone, 1 stick	A power source that can be turned on and off by right-clicking; see Chapter 6
Red sandstone	Appears in the mesa; crafted from 4 red sand	The "stone" version of red sand; can occur naturally or artificially
Red sandstone slab	Crafted from 3 red sandstone (makes 6)	The red sandstone equivalent of the wooden slab
Red sandstone stairs	Crafted from 6 red sandstone (makes 4)	The red sandstone equivalent of the wooden stairs
Red smooth, chiseled sandstone	Crafted from 2 red sandstone slabs for chiseled, or 4 red sandstone (makes 4) for smooth	A decoration block
Smooth, chiseled sandstone	Crafted from 2 sandstone slabs for chiseled, or 4 sandstone (makes 4) for smooth	A decoration block
Stone axe	Crafted from 3 cobblestone, 2 sticks	A tool that chops wooden blocks much faster than normal
Stone hoe	Crafted from 2 cobblestone, 2 sticks	As efficient as a wooden hoe, but with more durability
Stone pickaxe	Crafted from 3 cobblestone, 2 sticks	A more durable pickaxe, capable of mining more blocks
Stone shovel	Crafted from 1 cobblestone, 2 sticks	A tool for digging quickly; can be used to level out dirt, gravel, sand, and other types of soft blocks
Stone sword	Crafted from 2 cobblestone, 1 stick	A strong, reliable blade that deals a moderate amount of damage
Torch	Crafted from 1 coal, 1 stick (makes 4)	A common, helpful, and cheap way to light up areas

Figure 4-3: Mining a staircase downward.

Using the Furnace

You use the furnace, an important part of the Stone Age, to craft many more items. Many players mine for cobblestone and make a furnace on their first or second day because of its importance. Placing a furnace on a surface and right-clicking it opens a menu with three slots: fuel, input, and output, as shown in Figure 4-4.

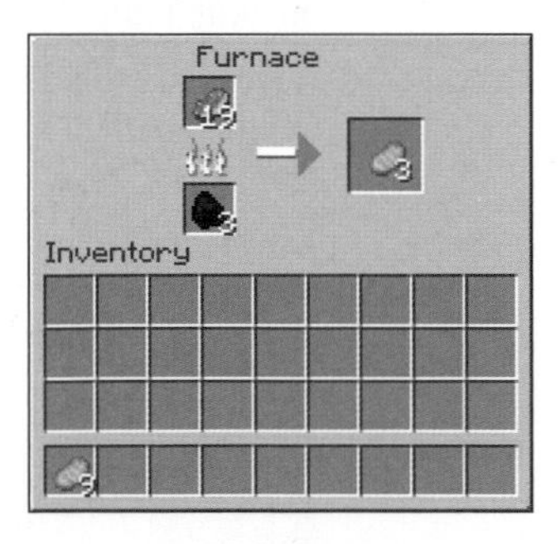

Figure 4-4: Using a furnace in Minecraft PC.

The fuel slot can take coal (eight uses per lump), wooden objects (three uses per 2 planks), and items such as blaze rods or lava buckets. It also takes a variety of other flammable items.

A more effective way to use wood as fuel is to place a wood log in the top and place wooden planks in the bottom of the furnace, creating charcoal. Charcoal then burns in the bottom of the furnace longer than the wood used to make the charcoal.

Using a furnace grants experience orbs, and the items described in Table 4-5 become available.

Table 4-5 Furnace Items

Item	*How to Obtain It*	*Description*
Baked potato	By cooking a potato in a furnace	A moderately effective food item
Brick	By cooking clay balls in a furnace	A simple ingredient for clay pots and brick blocks
Brick block	Crafted from 4 bricks	A dusty, red building block
Brick slab	Crafted from 3 bricks (makes 6)	The brick equivalent of the slab
Brick stairs	Crafted from 6 brick blocks (makes 4)	The brick equivalent of the stairs
Cactus green	By cooking cactus in a furnace	Used as green dye
Charcoal	By cooking wood (logs, not planks) in a furnace	Can be used for fuel, torches, and fire charges, just like coal
Cooked chicken	By cooking raw chicken in a furnace	A food item, slightly less effective than pork or steak
Cooked fish or salmon	By cooking raw fish in a furnace	A food item that's easy to obtain but not effective
Cooked porkchop or steak	By cooking raw pork or beef in a furnace	An effective food item
Flower pot	Crafted from 3 bricks	Can be placed on blocks and filled with any plant

(continued)

Table 4-5 *(continued)*

Item	*How to Obtain It*	*Description*
Glass	By cooking sand in a furnace	Lets sunlight shine through windows
Glass bottle	Crafted from 3 glass (makes 3)	Fill with water to start brewing potions
Glass pane	Crafted from 6 glass (makes 16)	A thin window material that connects to adjacent blocks
Hardened clay	Found in desert temples and in mesa biomes; you can cook clay in a furnace to obtain	Has a terracotta look; can be dyed in the same way glass or wool can be dyed
Stone	By cooking cobblestone in a furnace	A smooth, gray block commonly located underground; restored to its smooth (from cobblestone) state by using a furnace
Stone brick	Found in the Stronghold; crafted from 4 stone (makes 4)	A refined, popular decoration block
Stone brick slab	Crafted from 3 stone bricks (makes 6)	The stone brick version of the slab
Stone brick stairs	Crafted from 6 stone bricks (makes 4)	The stone brick version of the stairs
Stone button	Crafted from 1 stone	A power source that activates for a few seconds when pressed (see Chapter 6)
Stone pressure plate	Crafted from 2 stone	A power source that activates when a heavy mob steps on it (see Chapter 6)
Stone slab	Crafted from 3 stone (makes 6)	A smoother version of the cobblestone slab
Water bottle	By right-clicking a water source or full cauldron while holding a water bottle	The base ingredient for brewing potions (see Chapter 6)

Using the Stonecutter with Minecraft PE

The PE version introduces the stonecutter, which is a crafting block that allows the crafting of stone and stone-related items. It was created to decrease the number of items found on the crafting table menu, which would be overwhelming in the PE format. Any item made out of cobblestone (except for a furnace, tools, and the stonecutter itself) is made using the stonecutter.

Building an Effective House

Once you've built a basic shelter in the game, you'll want to move on to a more effective dwelling place. The first of these, leading up to a much more elaborate and complex home base, is a house. Houses are little fragments of a base.

A house is usually built as your first base and then you either find a new base or expand on your starter home. Houses can also be for decoration, just because you want to make your environment a little nicer. In addition, if you are building a homemade village (see Chapter 6), the villagers in your village will need an effective house to protect them from zombies.

One creative goal in Minecraft is building things. Although a wooden rectangle with a door is likely to satisfy most of your needs, having a giant house full of storage chests, crafting tables, beds, farms, and other tidbits is always satisfying — and a welcome sight after completing a long adventure. The type of house reflects the personality and skill of the builder and can even be a status symbol in multiplayer games.

Though building is primarily left to your creativity, a few tips can help you build quickly and easily:

- **To build upward,** jump and quickly place a block underneath yourself. Repeat this action to make a pillar.
- **To build off a ledge,** hold the Shift key (so that you don't fall) and walk up to the rim of the ledge. Then you can place blocks on the side of the ledge (see Figure 4-5).
- **To build a floor,** move backward while placing blocks in front of you to make a line. To fill a space, repeat in any pattern you choose.

Figure 4-5: House on a ledge.

Moving from Effective Houses to Bases

After you've built a basic house, it's time to start creating a much bigger, more stable and protected base (see Figure 4-6 for one of Thomas's bases). The base should be the main attraction in your survival world. It should be strong, big, easy to repair, mob resistant, useful, and, most importantly, good looking. If the base just got exploded by a creeper, you fix the base with the blocks you have, hurry to collect the blocks you need in order to repair it, and repair it quickly before mobs come in.

Now that you know of an example of how a base works, it is time to get you to Thomas's real estate and car dealership (patent pending). Let's see what is the right house for you. Here we have an ordinary base — a simple house on a flattened-out area, easy to build, but you will have a hard time defending your base. The basement acts like a warehouse, whereas the roof acts as your garden.

Or maybe you decide that's not the best house for you. Perhaps you should try a fancy air base. It can be expanded almost infinitely. Sadly, it has no basement, but you can definitely enjoy the view from the balcony! Because of how high up it is, you will have no trouble from mobs as long as you keep the base well lit. Good luck getting up to that base, though.

Hmm, maybe that's not the best base for you either. How about we show you the exotic underwater base — no mobs, no problem. If you're looking at building a base like this one, we recommend that you not build the base anywhere close to a water monument! This base looks cool with a glass ceiling. It has plenty of room for underground expansion. When the zombie apocalypse attacks, they can only float above the base. Just make sure the base is lit to avoid coming back and finding a creeper inside!

When it comes down to it, there are many more bases out there, like a base in the side of a mountain, or a man-cave base, or just about anything your mind can imagine! As you can see, the whole decision of how you design the base is up to you.

Figure 4-6: All your base belongs to you – this is an underwater base.

Part III
Mastering Techniques

In this part . . .

- Surviving mobs
- Getting advanced with mining
- Getting what you need from villages
- Excavating for resources
- Working with redstone
- Getting through later block ages
- Gaining superpowers
- Advancing to the End and beyond

5

Understanding Biomes and Mastering Farms

In This Chapter

- Exploring biomes
- Creating farms
- Raising animals
- Farming with and protecting against mobs

After you advance through the Stone Age and you develop basic food sources and weapons — in addition to gathering items from looting mobs — it's time to begin farming.

Farming in Minecraft is based largely on the type of biome your avatar spawned into at the beginning of the game. Some biomes lend themselves to mining earlier than farming, so you might want to read Chapter 6 first. Some types of farming and mob interaction are common in all biomes.

All worlds have more than one biome (as in real life), so you can gather resources as you move through the biomes. Because punching wood is important early in the game, many players need to find a wood-based biome as soon as possible. In this chapter, we look at the staggering array of biomes (61 of them) that you can explore. Then we look at farming and, finally, explore the different mob types.

Knowing Your Biomes

When you spawn into a new world, you're greeted by a wide range of landscapes. Whether you have big trees that shield you from the sun or colorful clay and sand scattered everywhere, you're in a biome. Some biome hills reach the building limit! Others have special structures, such as the incredible ocean monument.

Generating worlds

As you start your world, you can spawn using the default settings or specify the type of world you want to create. Minecraft has six different types of world generation, including the default world — normal. We cover the other types of world generation and customization options in Chapter 13.

Growing flowers

Flowers are wonderful additions to Minecraft — they add a little spunk to the place. Many flowers are biome-specific. Most of them are found only in flower forests, but some can be found elsewhere. An example of a biome-specific flower is the sunflower: It's generated in the Sunflower Plains biome.

Playing in snowy biomes

Minecraft has a total of six snowy biomes. Each one features snow and ice as main features, and add an interesting dynamic to the game. This list describes the snowy biomes:

- **Frozen River:** This biome is characterized by its ice river, allowing you to harvest ice.
- **Ice Plains:** This one has vast amounts of snow-covered plain, but few trees. It also has frozen rivers and lakes. And, it never rains — it only snows in the Ice Plains. Sugar cane grows naturally, but little else. Because of its difficulty level, many players leave this biome as soon as possible, in order to survive.
- **Ice Plains Spike:** This beautiful and rare variation of the Ice Plains biome has frozen hoodoos creating a picturesque, though barren, landscape (see Figure 5-1).
- **Cold Beach:** In this interesting biome, ice plains and ocean intersect, creating a snow-covered plain, a sandy beach, and an ocean.
- **Cold Taiga:** This winter wonderland features ferns, spruce trees, flowers, and wolves (and of course, snow).
- **Cold Taiga M:** The M in its name stands for *m*ountains. This biome has cold taiga with a mountainous terrain.

Figure 5-1: Ice Plains Spike is known for its beautiful frozen hoodoos.

Chilling in cold biomes

Though snow may not always be the main feature of cold biomes, the terrain is reminiscent of any colder environment. Cold biomes are known for their evergreens, fewer trees, and lots of gravel, stone, and dirt. Here's a description of the cold biomes:

- **Extreme Hills:** This exciting biome offers natural emerald ores and silverfish exclusively, thanks to its extensive tunnel system. However, your character is likely to die from fall damage from its numerous cliffs and ledges. This biome, shown in Figure 5-2, offers oak and spruce trees, snow, and monster eggs.
- **Extreme Hills M:** With higher peaks that touch the clouds, this variation of Extreme Hills offers fewer trees, more gravel, and snow.
- **Extreme Hills+:** This one truly mixes the two Extreme Hills biomes, providing high peaks and trees with plenty of stone and dirt.
- **Extreme Hills+ M:** Though this variation offers gravel mountains and even a small clearing of grass, it is, again, short on trees.
- **Taiga:** This biome, shown in Figure 5-3, boasts of plenty of spruce trees and ferns with wolves naturally running amok.

Figure 5-2: Extreme Hills.

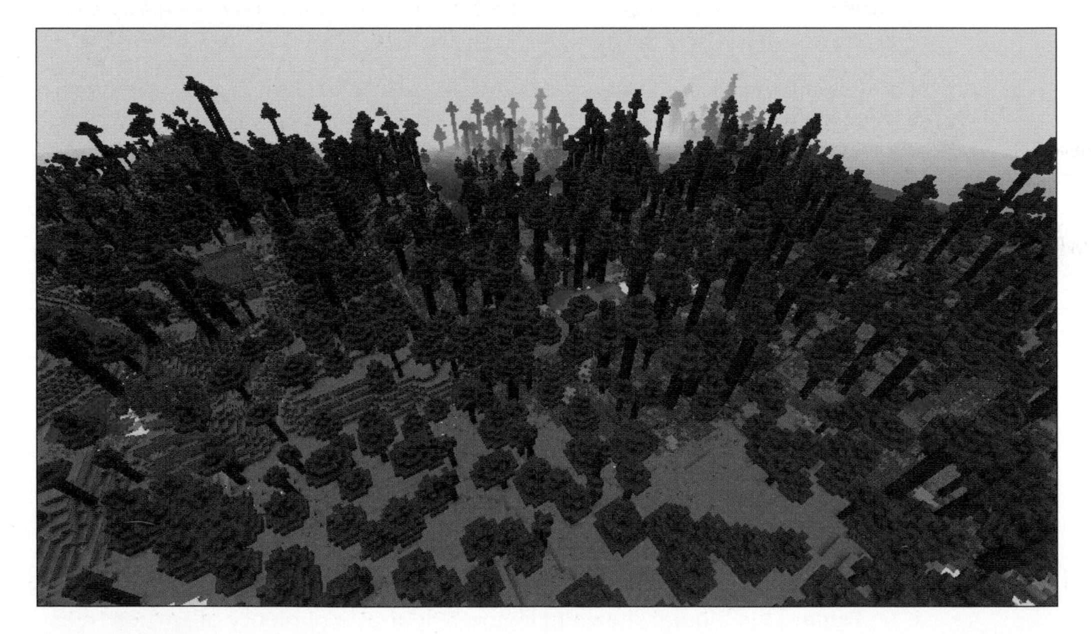

Figure 5-3: Taiga.

- **Taiga M:** This biome adds mountains, but no snow, and an abundance of sheep.
- **Mega Taiga:** This uncommon variation has spruce trees that are so tall and thick they practically become jungle trees. Podzol dirt (which is useful for growing giant mushrooms and other plants), moss stones, and wild brown mushrooms are also common.
- **Mega Spruce Taiga:** This one is similar to Mega Taiga, but with shorter spruce trees.
- **Stone Beach:** Also called Cliff biome, this one occurs whenever mountains meet the ocean, offering a large amount of stone.
- **The End:** Your world doesn't naturally create this biome; instead, you must advance and create this dimension. Also called Sky biome, it's where the ender dragon naturally spawns. (For more information, see Chapter 11.)

Living in medium biomes

The biomes we describe in the preceding section are too cold. The biomes we describe in the following section are too hot. The biomes we describe in this section, however, are just right. As their name implies, medium biomes have a rather average climate, and less extreme geology to accompany that climate. A medium biome tends to be quite comfortable. This list describes medium biomes:

- **Plains:** It's one of the best biomes for resources, because it has villages, cave openings, lava, water sources, and plenty of grass and flowers. Also, horses and other passive mobs regularly spawn there. Wood, however, is limited, and it's virtually flat. Many players love this biome, with its excessive number of passive mobs.
- **Sunflower Plains:** Just add sunflowers, which is handy for making yellow dye (see Figure 5-4).
- **Forest:** This biome is relatively small, so players often collect wood and move in and out of it as necessary. In addition to oak and birch trees, forests provide tall grass, flowers such as poppies, and mushrooms. Forests also offer more hills than the Plains biome. The problem is that mobs can hide around every tree, making this biome a deathtrap at night. Zombies are particularly fond of the Forest biome.

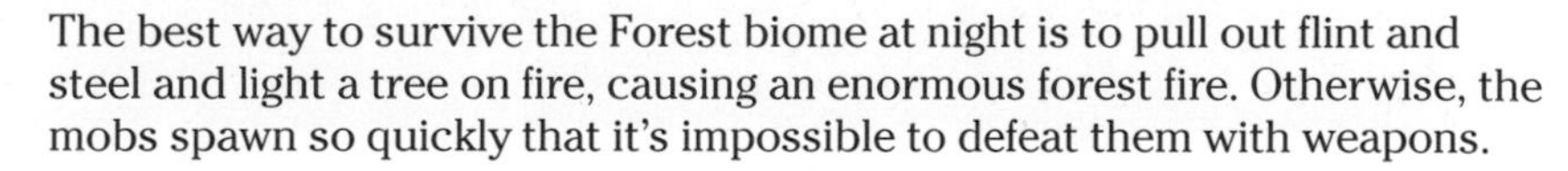

The best way to survive the Forest biome at night is to pull out flint and steel and light a tree on fire, causing an enormous forest fire. Otherwise, the mobs spawn so quickly that it's impossible to defeat them with weapons.

- **Flower Forest:** With fewer trees and a staggering array of flowers in this biome (see Figure 5-5), you can collect unique flowers for dyes and bonemeal used in farming. (For more about farming, see the section "Building the Perfect Farm," later in this chapter.)

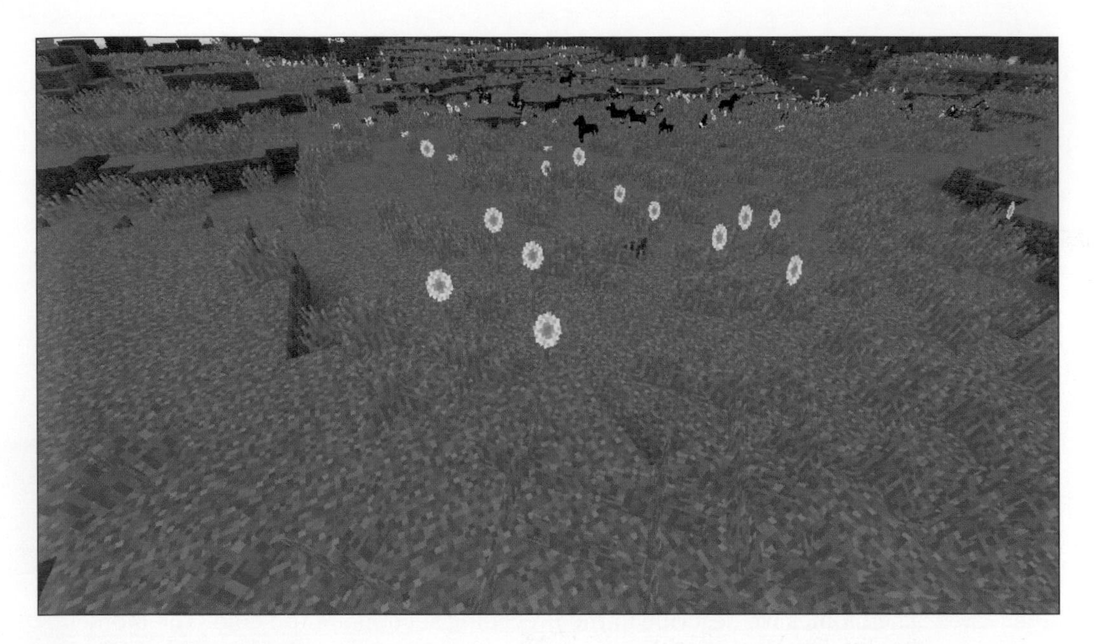

Figure 5-4: Sunflower Plains.

Figure 5-5: Flower Forest.

- **Birch Forest:** This forest contains birch trees exclusively.
- **Birch Forest M:** This one has taller birch trees, but not mountains (despite the letter *M* in its name).
- **Birch Forest Hills M:** This one has taller birch trees and mountains, which spawn cows and are good for mining.
- **Roofed Forest:** Also called the Black Forest (like the one from Germany), this biome features dark oak trees, mushrooms (including giant mushrooms), rose bushes, and a canopy so thick and dark that mobs can spawn during the day.
- **Roofed Forest M:** Add steep cliffs and ledges to the Roofed Forest, which increases the danger and, possibly, the mushrooms.
- **Swampland:** This dangerous biome is flat with shallow pools of dark water. Lily pads, mushrooms, and sugarcane are common. Vines grow on trees and in the swampy water. Witch huts and slimes spawn there (see Figure 5-6), making this place almost not survivable at night. It also features oak trees and clay.
- **Swampland M:** It's simply a hill variation of swampland with slightly lighter green grass.
- **River:** Rivers often separate biomes and are excellent sites for fishing. Some oak trees also grow. Rivers don't have currents but usually lead to an ocean. This biome also offers sand, clay, and a water source.

Figure 5-6: Swamp with witch hut.

- **Beach:** Beaches line the ocean biomes with sand (or, occasionally, gravel) blocks. Fishing is also good in this biome.
- **Jungle:** This rich biome is home to tall jungle trees, melon plants, jungle temples, cocoa beans, flowers, ocelots, ferns, and vines. This landscape includes hills and small pools of water.
- **Jungle M:** The hills in this biome allow the trees to grow above the cloud line and the floor to become invisible in a sea of ferns. It's another rich biome with unique melon plants, cocoa pods, and jungle temples.
- **Jungle Edge:** The edge of the jungle (as its name implies) connects a Jungle biome to another biome. The jungle trees are significantly shorter, but ocelots, vines, and melons still spawn there.
- **Jungle Edge M:** This mountainous version lacks the tall trees connecting a Jungle biome to another.
- **Mushroom Island:** This unusual biome is isolated and filled with mushrooms and giant mushrooms (see Figure 5-7). The only mob that spawns there is mooshrooms, which means that it has no hostile mobs — which is extraordinary for exploring caves and mine shafts. The only challenge is replacing the natural mycelium with farmland, which requires digging up the mycelium, placing dirt, and immediately tilling it. Many players simply harvest the mushrooms rather than create farms in this biome.

Figure 5-7: Mushroom Island.

Mushroom Island is my favorite biome because of its easy food source and lack of hostile mobs.

- **Mushroom Island Shore:** This flat area of the island connects it to the ocean and is dotted with mushrooms.

Roasting in warm biomes

Warm biomes are, well warmer than most biomes. Warm biomes usually have more desert and less water than most biomes. Expect to keep a good storage of water in these biomes to keep you hydrated. Here's a description of the warm biomes:

- **Desert:** This difficult biome is composed of sand dunes, sandstone, and deadly cacti. Occasionally, sugar cane grows on its edges. No passive mobs spawn here. The only benefits of this biome are its desert temples, desert village, and desert wells (all described in Chapter 7).

The Desert biome is my least favorite biome because it's almost impossible to survive if your game starts there.

- **Desert M:** This variation has a small oasis of water, allowing sugar cane to grow.
- **Savanna:** This rainless biome (see Figure 5-8) offers flat, tall grass with arcadia trees, sheep, cows, and villages Like the plains biome, this is the only other place to naturally find horses.
- **Savanna M:** Mountains reach above the clouds to the highest level their world allows in the game (without using an amplified world type, which you can set before starting Minecraft in order to manipulate the size of mountains). Plenty of tall arcadia trees and tall grass and breathtaking peaks adorn its surface.
- **Mesa:** This extremely rare biome offers red sand, hardened clay, red sandstone, occasional cacti, and six colors of stained clay. Small pools of water are found in all Mesa biome variations.
- **Mesa (Bryce):** This desert-like Mesa biome variation offers spire-hardened clay columns, similar to the hoodoos of Bryce Canyon in Utah (from which it draws its name — and where we authors live!). Figure 5-9 shows what Mesa (Bryce) looks like. If you want to see a pretty view of the real-life Bryce Canyon, check out the photo in Figure 5-10 that Jesse shot on a recent family vacation.
- **Mesa Plateau:** This biome is characterized by its flat-topped hills. In this case, the hills are the red hardened clay of the mesa.
- **Mesa Plateau F:** Mesa Plateau F has flat-topped hills but covered layer of dirt and grass with a few short trees growing on it (almost like a savanna).

Figure 5-8: The PE Savanna biome looks like this.

Figure 5-9: Mesa Bryce biome.

Figure 5-10: The real-life Bryce Canyon looks like this.

- **Mesa Plateau M:** This variation offers steeper cliffs and longer flattops.
- **Mesa Plateau F M:** This savanna variation offers tremendously high grassland, flattop mountains, often reaching the world height limit.
- **Hell:** More commonly called the Nether, this biome is created in the game; you don't naturally spawn there. It contains rivers of lava, is surrounded by bedrock, and features large quantities of netherrack and nether quartz, as well as nether wart. This biome is the only home of blazes, wither skeletons, zombie pigmen, ghasts, and magma cubes. Glowstone and soul sand are also found here. Many nether resources are found in nether fortresses.

Exploring in neutral biomes

Neutral biomes tend to connect all the other biomes. From oceans to hills, you can't miss these biomes. This list describes the neutral biomes:

- **Ocean:** Large oceans, often extending over 3,000 blocks, offer water, squid, and gravel. The ocean floor includes small mountains and plains, including the rare cavern entrance. ***Note:*** Console versions have oceans on the edges of world maps.

- **Deep Ocean:** A deep ocean is often twice the depth of a normal ocean and is home to ocean monuments (as shown in Figure 5-11), including the hostile guardians and elder guardians. These monuments also feature prismarine blocks and 8 gold blocks (as a treasure prize).

Figure 5-11: An ocean monument in the deep ocean.

- **Hills:** Hills can be added to jungle, ice, taiga, desert, and forest biomes. Some players find climbing and building minecart tracks discouraging in these biomes, whereas other players enjoy creating bases among the cliffs.

Building the Perfect Farm

Just like natural history in the physical world, people are much more productive at farming than they are at hunting and foraging for food and other supplies. Minecraft lets you farm just like you would in the physical world, and you may be surprised at what you learn as you begin to automate food processes.

Growing crops

Harvestable items such as wheat, melons, and pumpkins fit the raw definition of Minecraft farming by requiring well-irrigated farmland. Follow these general steps to set up a farm:

1. **Find a well-lit area made of grass or dirt.**

   If the area isn't well lit, craft some torches. A flat workspace makes this task easier, though it isn't mandatory.

2. **Craft a gardening hoe (as described in Chapter 4) and use it.**

   You can right-click the ground to use the hoe to till farmland.

3. **Locate a water source nearby, and then right-click it while holding a bucket. Right-click again while holding the full bucket to dump the water near your crops.**

   Dig an irrigated hole or canal in your future farm, allowing any nearby farmland to thrive. Dry farmland grows more slowly and wears out after too much time passes without crops being planted on it.

   (You can find the recipe for a bucket in the appendix, which is available for download at `www.dummies.com/go/minecraftfd`.)

4. **Lock up your farm.**

   Jumping on farmland destroys it. Keep crops safe from animals and mobs by building walls around the crops. Fences and fence gates work well.

Rabbits in particular can eat crops quickly, so build a fence around your crops.

After these steps are finished, you're ready to harvest crops!

Farming wheat, carrots, and potatoes

Wheat, carrots, and potatoes are relatively simple to farm. Simply follow these steps:

1. **Collect seeds and vegetables.**

   Breaking tall grass blocks or tilling grass blocks sometimes provides wheat seeds. You can find carrots and potatoes in villages or by killing zombies.

2. **Right-click the farmland to plant seeds, carrots, or potatoes.**

   Tiny, green stems appear on the block.

3. **Wait until the crops are fully grown. Speed up this process by using bone meal or artificial light.**

   Wheat is mostly yellow and brown when it's fully grown, and carrots and potatoes are ready to harvest when the heads of the vegetables begin to emerge. Work on other tasks while you wait. You can also use bone meal (crafted from skeleton bones) to grow crops instantly.

   Adding bone meal by right-clicking the crop with bone meal makes it grow one stage, significantly decreasing the growing time. Also, crops grow only with light. To supplement natural sunlight, place torches or glowstone around your farms.

4. **Break the crop blocks to obtain your profit.**

   Replant seeds, carrots, and potatoes until your farmland is refilled, and keep the remainder as profit. Figure 5-12 shows a thriving farm.

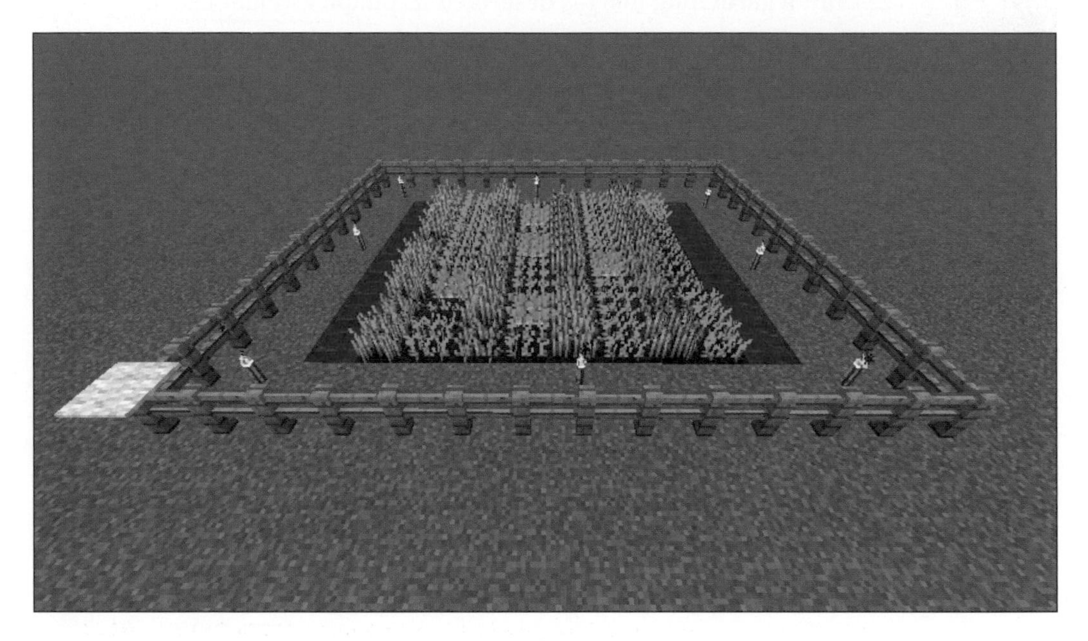

Figure 5-12: Growing crops.

Using this strategy, you can start a farm that obtains items for you while you go out and enjoy the game.

Rather than place fence gates, you can place carpets on top of your fence. Mobs, including animals, don't see the carpet as a block that they can jump on, but you can jump on the carpet to get in and out of your cropland. This strategy is particularly helpful when farming animals, because it prevents animals from leaving through a fence gate.

Harvesting melons and pumpkins

Growing large plants such as melons and pumpkins takes quite a bit of work. Follow these steps to start a farm similar to the one shown in Figure 5-13:

1. **Collect seeds.**

   You can find both melon and pumpkin seeds in treasure chests hidden in abandoned mineshafts. In addition, naturally found pumpkins can be crafted into seeds. Melon seeds can be crafted from melon slices, which you can get by trading with villagers, as described in Chapter 8.

Figure 5-13: Growing melons and pumpkins.

2. **Right-click the farmland to plant seeds.**

   Unlike wheat, this farmland has to be adjacent to grass or dirt. When these seeds grow into stalks, they tip over and grow melons or pumpkins next to them. To grow lots of melons or pumpkins, till a row of farmland next to a row of dirt, with water pools spaced throughout.

3. **Wait.**

   Using bone meal on seeds speeds them into mature stalks, though they don't yet bear fruit. Pumpkins and melons take a while to grow. Ensure that these crops have growing space, and work on other tasks in the meantime.

4. **Harvest the crops.**

   Don't break the stalk blocks — instead, break the pumpkin and melon blocks that appear nearby. If you've grown pumpkins, you can craft them into pumpkin seeds to expand your farm. If you've grown melons, breaking the blocks produces melon slices that can be eaten or crafted into seeds.

Knowing the basic plants

The preceding section deals with the classic crops, which provide a moderate farming experience. The next several sections describe other "growing things" that can be exploited.

Reaping sugar cane

Sugar cane consists of green reeds that grow naturally near bodies of water, and collecting at least one sugar cane block is enough to start a farm, similar to the one shown in Figure 5-14. Sugar cane is useful to mass-produce: Paper and items such as bookcases require a lot of reeds to craft, and you can make sugar for items such as cake and potions of swiftness.

Figure 5-14: Growing sugar cane and cacti.

Fortunately, sugar cane is easy to farm. Simply follow these steps:

1. **Find (or make) a place that holds water.**

   Reeds grow only near lakes or pools. Note that they can grow only on grass, dirt, or sand.

2. **Place canes next to the water in the same way you would place any block.**

   When a patch of reeds is placed where it can grow, it extends vertically until it's three blocks tall.

3. **After the sugar cane is fully grown, harvest all but the bottom block.**

   When you break the stalk blocks in the middle, the top section breaks down into items. The reeds at the bottom begin growing again.

The essential concept is to plant a short patch of reeds, let it grow, and then mow it down so that it can grow again.

When the ground is flat, you're at eye level with the point at which you should break the sugar canes. Walk around with the crosshair at eye level while holding the left mouse button to break all the reeds quickly.

Utilizing cacti

Cacti are sharp desert plants that can be used for creating traps or making green dye. (Refer to the small cactus farm shown on the right of the sugar cane in Figure 5-14.) You can typically find cacti in the desert, and you can grow them similarly to sugar cane (as described in the preceding section). However, growing them is unique because they

- Require no water and must be placed on sand
- Cannot be placed next to other blocks
- Are sharp, and they destroy items

Destroy the entire cactus and replant it to ensure that some of your profits aren't destroyed by other cactus blocks.

Enjoying cocoa beans

Cocoa beans are used to make brown dye and as an ingredient in cookies. The best way to find cocoa beans is to explore a jungle — the beans are found in pods growing on the trees. Though green and yellow pods aren't fully matured, orange ones provide several cocoa beans when you smash them.

Farming cocoa beans is easy. To place a pod, right-click some jungle wood while holding cocoa beans. Then break the pod when it turns orange to harvest lots of cocoa beans. Make a large wall of jungle wood to start your farm.

Finding nether wart

You can find *nether wart* growing in special rooms in the nether fortress (described in Chapter 8). You can pick up nether wart by breaking fully grown crops, as shown in Figure 5-15. Nether wart is useful for brewing potions (described in Chapter 6). You can farm nether wart by planting it in soul sand blocks and waiting for it to grow, similarly to wheat. (You don't need to till soul sand.)

Chopping down trees

Tree farms aren't commonly established. They're usually useful when you live in a place with few trees nearby or when you want a wood source while underground. To grow trees, collect saplings — occasionally dropped when breaking leaf blocks — and then right-click to place them on dirt or grass in a well-lit area. (Remember that trees need lots of space to grow.)

Figure 5-15: Growing nether wart.

Plant a square of four jungle saplings and apply bone meal to one of them to make a giant tree grow.

Farming animals

You can use animal farms to acquire resources such as pork or wool without having to endure a lot of hassle. Animals follow you while you're holding wheat, so lure some into a fenced-in area to start your farm (see Figure 5-16). Chickens are lured by seeds instead. Pigs and rabbits are lured only by carrots.

Right-clicking two animals of the same species while holding wheat (use seeds for chickens, and carrots for pigs) causes them to spawn a baby animal. Thus, you can make use of your animal farm however you want and keep it populated.

A lamb's wool is the same color as its parents' wool. To farm a specific color of wool, right-click some sheep while holding dye to paint them, and then start a farm with them. Sheep regrow shorn wool by eating grass.

Growing mushrooms

Though mushrooms slowly spread if their climate is dark enough, the spacious, dark areas of a farm can attract monsters. If you don't want to have to perfect the lighting, use bone meal on a planted mushroom so that it grows into a giant mushroom (see Figure 5-17). Giant mushrooms provide a huge profit when you break them, and they can be used to quickly get lots of mushrooms. Because of the difficulty in providing enough lighting to prevent mobs, but not too much to prevent mushrooms to grow, many players don't farm mushrooms or use mushrooms to farm mobs.

Figure 5-16: Animals in pens.

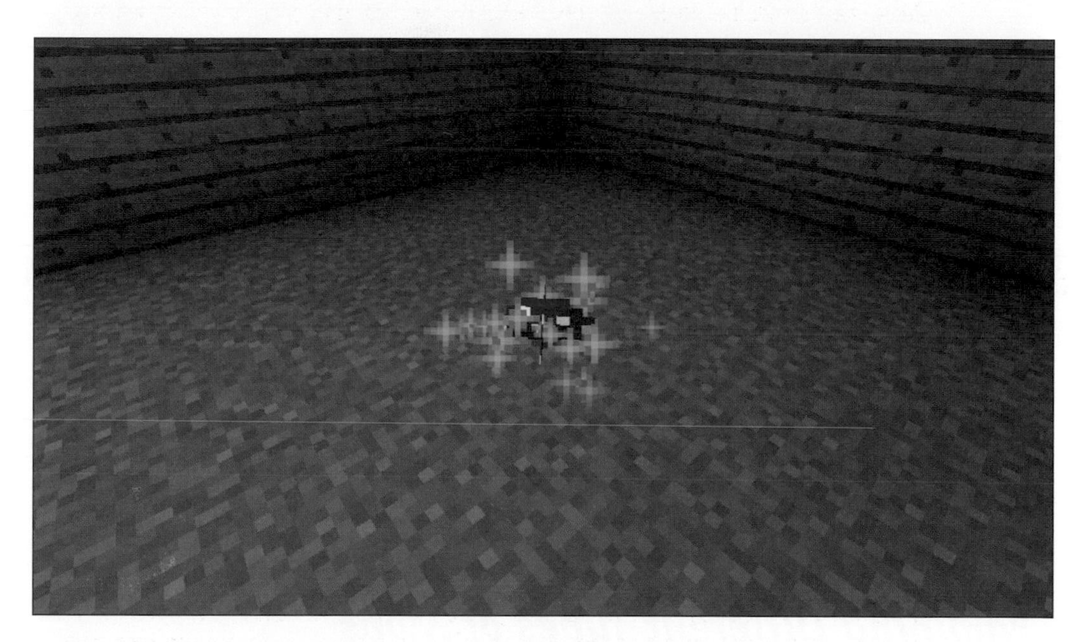

Figure 5-17: Growing a giant mushroom.

Mobs don't spawn in the Mushroom Island biome, allowing a player to farm mushrooms effectively.

Knowing the PE Farming Differences

PE farming is almost exactly the same as PC farming. There is no redstone, so no fancy contraptions.

However, Minecraft does have one crop that's exclusive to the PE edition: beetroot. It is used to make beetroot soup. Just like carrots, potatoes, and wheat, beetroot grows in four stages. When fully grown, it drops seeds and beetroots (of course), which you can farm, as shown in Figure 5-18.

Figure 5-18: Beet root farm.

Examining Different Types of Mobs

A *mob* refers to any creature, monster, or other living entity that you may find in the world. At the time of this writing, Minecraft has 37 different mobs, each with different faculties that drop various loot when slain, including experience orbs.

Living with docile mobs

Some mobs in Minecraft are *docile:* They can't harm you, and they won't try. All land-based docile mobs (such as pigs, cows, sheep, chickens, ocelots, villagers, and mooshrooms — see Figure 5-19) flee when attacked. You can lure cows and sheep anywhere around the game by holding wheat, and you can right-click two animals of the same species while holding wheat to feed them and cause them to spawn a baby animal. Chickens and pigs have this same faculty, but they require seeds for chickens and carrots for pigs instead of wheat.

Table 5-1 describes the types of docile mobs.

Table 5-1 Docile Mobs

Mob	***What It Does***
Bat	A member of a flying mob, the *bat* adds atmospheric visual elements to dark caverns. In addition to flying, it sleeps on the underside of blocks.
Chicken	The *chicken,* which is easier than other creatures to kill, is a good source of feathers. It can be bred (with seeds instead of wheat), and it occasionally lays eggs, which can be picked up. It incurs no damage from falling.
Cow	The common *cow* provides useful loot, and it can be bred. To get a bucket of milk, right-click a cow while holding an empty bucket.
Mooshroom	A *mooshroom* is a red cow that appears on the Mushroom Islands. It can be bred, and you can shear it to get red mushrooms and turn it into a standard cow. Right-click a mooshroom while holding a bowl to create mushroom stew.
Ocelot	The timid jungle cat known as an *ocelot* can be tamed and domesticated. Living only in the jungle, it's frightened by an avatar's movement. If it tentatively approaches you while you're holding raw fish, right-click to feed it. You can feed an ocelot five times or so to tame it.
Pig	A commonly occurring animal and a good food source, the *pig* can be bred, and it turns into a zombie pigman when struck by lightning. It also spawn naturally in the Nether and can move to the overworld through a nether portal you create.

(continued)

Table 5-1 *(continued)*

Mob	***What It Does***
Sheep	The common *sheep* can be used to obtain wool and food. Its wool comes in several different colors. It can be bred: Right-click a sheep while holding shears to obtain 1 to 3 blocks of wool; right-click a sheep while holding dye to recolor the sheep. Baby sheep have the same color as their parents including a mixing of the colors if the parents are of two different colors; sheep eat grass to regrow wool.
Squid	The water-dwelling *squid* is a source of black dye. It can swim, and it dies if it has no water to breathe.
Villager	The *villager* lives in a village and trades items with you, as described in Chapter 7. Villagers remain indoors at night, and they can fall in love and have children. They can also trade with players.
Horse	Your trusty steed, the *horse,* gives you a fast way to get to places. It can travel as fast as 14 blocks per second (BPS) and can jump over blocks such as fences. As in real life, each horse has a unique combination of speed and jumping ability. Offspring average the speed and jumping ability of their parents. Horses can be tamed and healed by using certain foods — sugar, hay, wheat, golden carrots, golden apples, and apples. Horses are naturally afraid of water. Horses have their own inventory, which stores their equipment such as saddles and armor. Using a cheat command, zombie horses and skeleton horses, 2 fun mobs intended mostly for decoration and fun can also be added to the game. Refer to the official Minecraft wiki to learn more about these mobs.
Donkey	A variation of the horse is the *donkey.* It's more rare than the horse. In addition to riding one, you can place a chest on it. Mules don't spawn naturally but are bred from a horse and donkey (as in real life). Mules can also carry a chest. Pigs, horses, donkeys, and mules all can wear saddles. When saddled, these animals can be ridden, which shows the animal's Health bar. If the animal is damaged from a mob or natural event, the Health bar depletes and can be restored with certain foods.

Mob	*What It Does*
Rabbit	Also called bunnies, *rabbits* can be led by carrots. Rabbits are fast and usually jump aimlessly. They eat fully grown crops, so add a fence around your garden. You will want rabbits for the items they leave behind, such as rabbit leather, rabbit meat, and rabbits foot. One in every 1,000 rabbits is a killer bunny, which is a hostile mob. (The killer bunny is based on the movie *Monty Python and the Holy Grail,* which features a killer bunny character.)

Figure 5-19: The docile mobs.

Protecting yourself from hostile mobs

Hostile mobs, as shown in Figure 5-20, cause most of the danger in Minecraft: They attack without provocation. However, hostile mobs tend to provide especially useful loot.

Table 5-2 describes hostile mobs in detail:

Table 5-2	Hostile Mobs
Hostile Mob	***What It Does***
Blaze	A powerful guardian of the nether fortresses, the fiery construct known as the Blaze provides a useful item, the blaze rod. It can fly, it shoots fireballs, and it takes damage from snowballs. To protect yourself, hide behind physical structures that can't get hit by the blaze's fireballs.
Cave spider	The poisonous cave spider lurks around abandoned mine shafts. An *arthropod,* it's fast, and it climbs walls and jumps. It poisons targets in Normal mode or Hardcore mode. To properly defeat the cave spider, use weapons that don't require close proximity, such as a bow and arrow. Ensuring your house has a roof over it will also keep cave spiders can't enter.
Creeper	The plant-like enemy known as the *creeper* walks up to you and explodes. It's destructive, and it deals massive damage by exploding, though it cannot use melee attacks. It becomes incredibly powerful when struck by lightning. To stay safe from creepers, keep your distance, and attack from a distance if you can.
Ender dragon	The *ender dragon* is the giant dragon that constitutes the final battle of the game. It's an enemy that appears in the End, flying around and occasionally charging for massive damage. See Chapter 11 for details and tactics for defeating the ender dragon.
Ghast	The giant, floating beast of the Nether, the *ghast* spits fireballs that can be hit back at it. It can fly, and it's destructive, hard to hit, and not resilient. To protect yourself, stay inside stone bricks of any sort, because ghast fireballs can't blow up stone blocks.
Magma cube	A *magma cube* is the slime of the Nether — it bounces like a spring. It splits into smaller cubes when killed. Larger cubes are more armored. Magma cubes are generally pretty slow, so it's easy to stay away from them or kill them.
Silverfish	A *silverfish* is a nipping bug that burrows into stone. An *arthropod,* it can hide inside stone, cobblestone, and stone bricks. Active silverfish can awaken hidden silverfish to rally a swarm. Silverfish are very easy to defeat, so the easiest way to protect yourself is just to kill them when they are around.

Hostile Mob	*What It Does*
Skeleton	A *skeleton* is a powerful, skilled archer that drives off foes with its arrows. It's an *undead,* and some skeletons can equip armor or weapons. To defend yourself, hide behind tree trunks or other physical objects so they can't shoot you. Then, when the skeleton comes to you, attack — wait for them to come to you!
Slime	A bouncing blob of *slime* appears in various sizes in swamps and, occasionally, in deep caves. It splits into smaller slimes when killed: Tiny slimes are harmless and can be kept as pets. Slime, like the magma cube, is pretty slow so you should either destroy them or stay away from them to protect yourself from dying. Slime is very weak and easy to kill.
Spider	The *spider,* a quick enemy, is difficult to outrun and escape. An *arthropod*, it becomes neutral in daylight and doesn't attack unless provoked. It's fast, wall-climbing, and jumping. To protect yourself from a spider, keep a roof over your head, or keep your distance.
Witch	A *witch* is a master alchemist who lives in a hut in the swamp and attacks with an assortment of potions. She drinks potions of regeneration to heal and uses potions to mitigate fire damage. She throws potions of weakness, poison, slowness, and harming. Witches are rarely encountered, but when you do, hide behind a physical object so the witch can't throw potions at you. Attack the witch the same way you would a creeper, rushing them as fast as you can, attacking, and getting away.
Wither	The *wither,* which is a powerful foe, is a flying undead construct. It's a destructive, unique undead. You can create the wither with 4 blocks of soul sand and 3 wither skeleton skulls. (Refer to the "Constructs" section of the bonus chapter, available for download at `www.dummies.com/go/minecraftfd`.) Stay away from the wither as it comes to life, because it creates a sizable explosion. The wither flies around and throws exploding skulls at everything it sees, and it can smash its way through blocks. It also regenerates over time, and it drains health from its victims to heal itself. After the wither loses half its health, it becomes immune to arrows. It drops a nether star. To defeat the wither, either fight it in a cave, or shoot it with a bow (until half of his health is gone) and finish with the sword (or both).

(continued)

Table 5-2 *(continued)*

Hostile Mob	***What It Does***
Wither skeleton	A *wither skeleton* is a powerful warrior that patrols nether fortresses. It's an undead, it inflicts high damage, and it's immune to fire. (Some wither skeletons can equip weapons and armor.) It inflicts wither damage to the player in either Normal or Hardcore mode, draining the Health bar temporarily and potentially causing death. To stay safe from the wither skeleton, keep 2 blocks above or below you and the wither skeleton. A wither skeleton can't jump higher than 2 blocks, and you can easily fight them from above or below.
Zombie	A *zombie* is a slow, lumbering enemy that inflicts damage on contact, and it appears commonly at night. An *undead* mob, it burns in daylight and slightly resists damage. Some zombies can equip items and wear armor. To beat a zombie, just attack them over and over again to kill them. Zombies are usually pretty slow and easy to hit.
Zombified villager	A *zombified villager* can appear naturally or whenever a villager is killed by a zombie in Normal mode or Hardcore mode. It has the same faculties as a zombie. To beat a zombie villager, fight them the same way as the zombie.
Guardian	*Guardians* are the protectors of their home, the ocean monument, and their elders. Hitting them when they are not swimming also does damage to you. When they are swimming, you can hit them without hitting yourself. They flop around, trying to return to water whenever they are out of the water. There is no avoiding the guardians when you need to get inside ocean monuments and similar structures. The only way to defeat them is to attack them, but you will usually incur damage in the process!
Elder guardian	The *elder guardian,* which is bigger than a guardian, gives you mining fatigue if you get too close. Like the guardian, it flops around to the nearest water source. The elder guardian fights just like the guardian, but is a bit slower and easier to fight. The only way to get around them is to fight them!
Endermite	An *endermite* spawns as long as an enderman teleports away or an enderpearl is thrown. It has the same sounds as silverfish. Just like silverfish, the easiest way to protect yourself from endermite is to just kill them.

Figure 5-20: Various hostile mobs.

Ignoring neutral and allied mobs

Some mobs are *neutral*, leaving you alone until you provoke them. Minecraft has only a few neutral mobs, and some of them can become *allied* and fight alongside you, as described in Table 5-3 and shown in Figure 5-21.

Table 5-3	Neutral and Allied Mobs
Neutral or Allied Mob	***What It Does***
Cat	A *cat,* which is a tamed ocelot, can follow you around. It attacks chickens and scares creepers. Right-click a cat to have it sit or follow you. It can be bred like certain passive mobs. (Use raw fish instead of wheat.)
Enderman	The *enderman* is a mysterious and rare nightfolk that originates from the End. Powerful and tall, it teleports for locomotion and to avoid damage; it dodges projectiles and detests water and sunlight. The enderman is provoked whenever you place the crosshair over it.

(continued)

Table 5-3 *(continued)*

Neutral or Allied Mob	***What It Does***
Iron golem	The *iron golem* is a slow but powerful village guardian that is built by placing a pumpkin on top of a cross of iron blocks. (See the bonus chapter, available for download at `www.dummies.com/go/minecraftfd`.) Giant but slow, it attacks nearby hostile mobs or any player who attacks a villager. It flings targets into the air and inflicts massive damage, and it spawns naturally in some villages (see Chapter 8) or when built by the player.
Snow golem	A *snow golem* can be built by putting a pumpkin on top of 2 snow blocks. This guardian trails snow as it walks, and it lobs snowballs at hostile mobs, knocking them back. Though harmed by water, with enough numbers it can kill Blaze. It explodes into snowballs when killed.
Wolf	The *wolf* is a wild dog that can be tamed. Don't attack it or else its entire group will charge you. While holding bones, right-click an unprovoked wolf a few times to feed it until it's tame; right-click tamed wolves while holding meat to feed and heal them. Right-clicking tamed wolves also tells them to sit or follow. Following wolves appear next to you if they can't reach you; tamed wolves attack your enemies but avoid creepers.
Zombie pigman	The *zombie pigman* is a wanderer from the Nether that attacks you if you attack one of its brethren. Undead, it attacks in a swarm and wields a golden sword. Some zombie pigmen can equip better weapons and armor.

Figure 5-21: The neutral and allied mobs.

Raising pets

A *dog* (which is a tamed wolf) is your noble companion. It fends off zombies from your base. Skeletons run away from dogs because the dogs know that skeletons are made of bones, and every dog loves a good bone! For that reason, it takes longer for a dog to kill a skeleton. Dogs don't go after creepers and if you have a dog with you, the creeper will still blow you up.

A *cat* is a tamed ocelot. It likes the warmest places in your home. It sits on a bed or a lit furnace or on your chest, making only the chest inaccessible. The cat doesn't get up unless pushed off that block. Cats often like exploring around players. After creepers notice a cat, they go running away.

The smallest of slimes even counts as a pet (see Figure 5-22). They are often cute, trying to fight against the big guy. It always follows you and tries to attack you, but because he is the weakest mob in the game (he only has half a heart), he does no damage to you.

Your horses define your place. Minecraft has 35 horse breeds (seven colors, five patterns). A horse has three different abilities which makes them valuable. The three abilities are how high they can jump, how fast can they run, and how much health they have.

Figure 5-22: Pet slime looks like this.

Playing with PE mobs

This list shows the only types of mobs in the PE edition of Minecraft. In the PC edition, there are no guardians or more complicated characters. The PE edition, as we've said before in this book, is pretty simple!:

- **Allied:** Sheep, chicken, cow, pig and mooshroom, villager
- **Neutral:** Wolf and enderman
- **Hostile:** Zombie, skeleton, slime, spider, silverfish, creeper, and zombie pigman

As we've said earlier, after some time playing the more popular PE edition of Minecraft, many players opt to switch to the PC Edition because of the many more mobs, minerals and rocks, and items that can be built. It is also much more challenging!

6

Mastering Mines

In This Chapter

- Beginning a cave mine
- Starting a branch mine
- Mastering a staircase mine
- Creating a quarry mine

Building out your Minecraft empire requires that you explore and find all the necessary ingredients, ores, supplies, and food necessary to be able to do everything you possibly want. One of the basic parts of exploring Minecraft is to build your own mines and extract all the necessary ores you need to build things in the game. The more advanced your mine, the more advanced your game will become. When you want something more strategic than simply crafting blocks and items, look to this chapter to find the basic techniques for mining ores.

Mining Efficiently

Mining is an incredibly useful practice that gives you a fast (though challenging) means of obtaining strong minerals such as iron, redstone, and diamond. You can mine in a number of ways, as described in this section, so use whichever method suits you best.

These mining tips aren't strict guidelines. Try your own methods, too.

Cave mining

Cave mining is challenging yet fruitful. To start, you must find a large cave — perhaps while working on another mine or exploring. If you can find a large cave, you have a useful resource at your disposal.

Caves are generally *very* dark — and in Minecraft, darkness means monsters! Always be on your guard, carry weapons (and perhaps armor), and light up the cave with torches, as shown in Figure 6-1.

Figure 6-1: Lighting the way in a cave adventure.

Cave mining is useful — you can obtain many scattered resources without wearing out your tools trying to plow through stone. However, caves can sometimes be deadly labyrinths, and you may lose your items if your avatar dies. You have to decide whether the payoff in resources is worth the risk of losing them.

Cave mining tips

When mining in a cave, simply light the way and skim the walls for minerals you can use. Iron ore is common, but keep an eye out for it to collect it, anyway.

If you can mine deep enough, you may find useful materials such as redstone, gold, and diamond. However, you may also come across lava — the bane of careless miners. Lava flows slowly and destroys items (and you!), so avoid it and ensure that your precious ores don't fall anywhere near it. To learn more about lava, check out Chapter 9.

Navigating ravines and canyons

Sometimes, while exploring or mining, you come across *ravines*. These narrow, deep gaps can appear underground or on the surface. Although ravines can contain lots of lava and monsters and are cumbersome to navigate, they expose a lot of surface area and are useful for finding minerals.

Ravines are great places to find iron and coal. Ravines are usually on the surface, making them easy to spot. However, because they are not deep, you cannot mine some types of valuable material, including diamonds, gold, and redstone.

A ravine also provides an excellent shelter (see Figure 6-2) because mobs cannot spawn on the walls of the ravine. You need to light the bottom around you using torches.

If you enjoy mining and spend most of your time using a pickaxe, build a little rest area underground. You might want to include a bed, chests, and even a farm to provide you with food. Your house doesn't have to be located on grass.

Figure 6-2: A house inside a mine.

Digging into branch mining

If you're new to Minecraft and you don't yet have the weaponry necessary to brave a cavern, branch mining is an effective way to obtain lots of stone and minerals.

Understanding simple branch mining

Follow these steps to dig a simple branch mine:

1. **Dig your way underground.**

   You can dig any way you want, but do not dig straight down; you might fall into a pit, or into lava. A common technique is to use staircase mining, which is described in the later section, "Staircase mining."

   At the bottom of every world is a layer of unbreakable *bedrock*. Statistics have proven that ores in Minecraft are most commonly located only a few blocks above this layer, so dig until your character's y-coordinate is 11. (Press F3 to see this value.)

2. **Dig a tunnel.**

   The smallest tunnel that your character can fit into is 1 block wide and 2 blocks tall. Use torches to light the area, or else your tunnel will attract unwanted guests.

3. **Build more tunnels that branch off from the first one.**

   By building extra tunnels that split off from the main route, you can look for ores over a large area. Position the tunnels two blocks apart to be able to inspect a large surface area and not miss anything (see Figure 6-3).

Figure 6-3: Checking a large surface area.

Branch mining is effective because you can acquire a lot of ores efficiently. However, this type of mining consumes many tools because of the volume of stone you dig through and produces much more cobblestone than valuables. Branch mining is a helpful method if you have patience and a project in which you can invest your fortune of cobblestone.

Spinning into pinwheel branch mining

A simple way to set up a lot of branch mines is to use a pinwheel mine (see Figure 6-4). Follow these steps:

1. **Make a small 4 x 4 area.**

   Use this space as a staircase to get to the surface along with your chests, bed, and furnaces.

2. **Make 2 x 2 tunnels in all four directions.**

   This step determines how many branch mines you have, so dig a reasonably big tunnel. Make sure the tunnels are centered with your base. Dig one of the tunnels until your inventory is full.

3. **Make tunnels in the "corridors" you created in Step 2.**

   The spacing is up to you, but for maximum efficiency, put them about six spaces apart. If you want to be thorough, put them two spaces apart. It will get all the ores for sure, but you might find that you've already collected all the ores from half of the tunnel. Keep digging until only three spaces remain in the inventory. Then head back.

Emerald ore can be found only in the Extreme Hills biomes (see Chapter 6) and spawn only 1 ore instead of a vein. Only 3 to 5 emerald ores in one chunk. Emerald ore isn't the only ore that is found only in a certain biome. Nether quartz ore is found only in the Nether (the "Hell" biome), but unlike emerald ore, nether quartz spawns in veins.

Figure 6-4: Pinwheel branch mine.

Digging into tiered branch mining

This method of branch mining is to not miss a single ore in your branch mine. Tiered branch mining can be quite efficient. Tiered branch mining is basically a strip mine on separate levels (see Figure 6-5). Follow these steps:

1. **Dig 16 blocks once, down to Level 11.**

   This is the base of your tunnels. Mining at Level 11 gives the most ores.

2. **Dig four tunnels.**

   Make sure that the four tunnels are 3 blocks apart. Dig one tunnel until the inventory is almost full. When coming back, dig out all the ores you missed.

3. **Dig 4 blocks under the main shaft you made in Step 1.**

   This is the second level of your branch mine.

4. **Dig another 16 blocks for the second shaft.**

   The second main shaft is for another layer of the branch mine.

5. **Dig another four tunnels in the second shaft.**

   This should be offset from the first four tunnels: Where the first tunnels are spaced is where the second tunnels should be. On the second space of the first tunnel's spacing is exactly where the new tunnel should be.

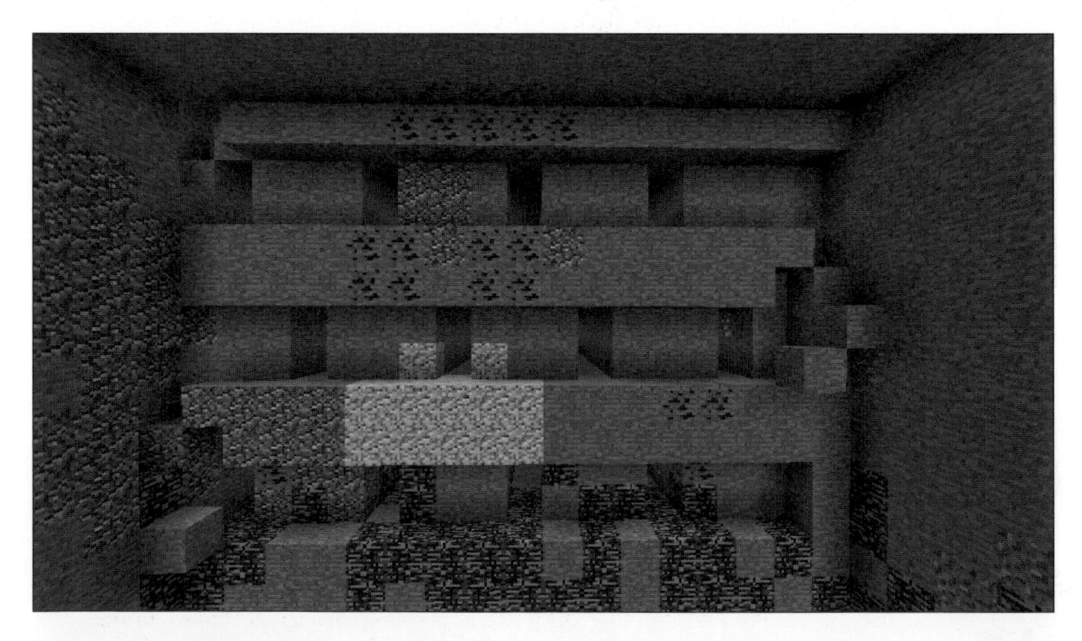

Figure 6-5: Tiered branch mine.

6. **Repeat Steps 1 through 5.**

   Repeat until you get down to bedrock. If this happens, lengthen the shafts to create more tunnels.

Stepping into staircase mining

In the staircase method, you dig deeply and quickly to search for caves, find a suitable spot for a branch mine, search for minerals en route to destinations, or simply build an attractive staircase.

Descend only 1 block at a time, or else you can't get back up. Figure 6-6 shows a staircase, which requires a minimal amount of work.

Figure 6-6: Descending a staircase in a mine.

TIP

Craft stair blocks (wooden stairs, cobblestone stairs, and others are described in Chapter 4) to make the staircase's ascension less taxing. (As Chapter 3 specifies, your character becomes hungry when jumping.) Raise the ceiling of the staircase to make your descent faster and less cramped.

If you build a shelter on your first night, you can simply begin a staircase mine descending below your house (see Figure 6-7). If you build this way, mobs cannot get in easily. However, they can still spawn unless you use torches, so make sure to create enough sticks and charcoal before your first night begins. I mine on the first night so that I don't waste my time waiting for daylight.

Figure 6-7: A house on top of a staircase mine.

Many players build a staircase mine to Level 5 or Level 12 because those are the most diamond-rich levels. At that point, you would build a branch mine. However, you might encounter a cave before you reach those levels. You need to immediately light up the caves and kill the mobs within. Caves are usually the most ore rich, so do not miss the opportunity.

Building a quarry

A *quarry* is the simplest type of mining, and digging one is a useful way to gather lots of cobblestone — and to ensure that you don't miss any materials. Simply dig a rectangle out of the ground, and then another one under it, and so on, until you have a sizeable hole from which you've unearthed every possible resource. Most players build a stairwell or ladder to exit and reenter the quarry. A natural and more efficient method is to use vines, which grow automatically (see Figure 6-8).

Although quarries produce lots of materials and can be mined safely, digging one requires great patience and generally isn't advisable. However, if you take that route, you can easily repurpose quarries into underground buildings.

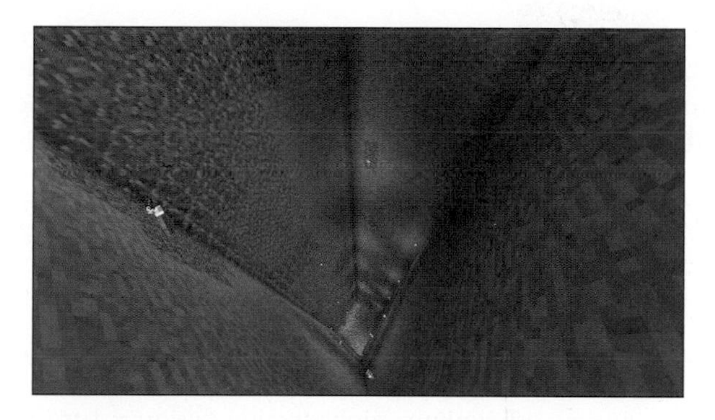

Figure 6-8: A classic quarry, with vines for ascending and descending.

Ripping into strip mining

An alternative version of quarry mining involves the use of TNT (see Figure 6-9). When you flatten out a large area on which to build your house, that's strip mining. In this example, we flatten out a giant mountain. The first five layers consist of dirt and other elements. (We are almost certain that blowing up dirt won't hurt anyone. Just don't get too close to the TNT.) Placing TNT 2 blocks in the ground and 4 blocks apart should destroy the fifth and a little of the sixth layer if all layers were dirt. After that, destroy one layer at a time, 1 block by 1 block.

Figure 6-9: Mining with TNT.

Newer players often waste resources, especially tools, in mining inefficiently. They build elaborate branch mines, placing their tunnels too close together. Or they pick up ores that they already have in large quantities. They also fail to bring enough food, weakening their players against mob attacks. Finally, new players do not usually bring enough weapons or armor to adequately protect themselves.

Rushing into speed mining

An expensive way to mine, but one used by advanced players, is to speed-mine. This is where you take advantage of the Haste Two effect, which you get from a beacon, and an efficiency 5 pickaxe, which you get from enchanting (see Chapter 10) to instantly mine stone. This is not fast enough to mine ores, it's fast enough to mine stone, allowing you to come back with a fortune pick (also from enchanting) and mine the ores that you didn't mine out the first time around. Be sure to not move out of the beacon's effect range.

Within an hour, Etho (a YouTuber, or YouTube account featured in Chapter 14) mined 3 stacks of iron and a stack of gold using this method of mining. He also collected 10 diamonds and 4 stacks of redstone blocks, and many unmined ores. He threw away the diamonds to demonstrate how efficient this mining strategy is.

PE Mining: Random Mining

In random mining, you dig, dig, dig wherever and whenever you want. This type can be most beneficial. You have no idea what you will find: a dungeon, an abandoned mineshaft, or maybe a whole lot of iron ore. Who knows?

It can also be quite "unbeneficial" at times — you might run into lava or have water rush in your face. Or you could miss a 16-block diamond vein that is only 2 blocks away from your mining location. The possibilities are endless.

This is the most-often-used type of mining in Minecraft PE, because it's the easiest and simplest approach to mining in the game. Due to the limitations of a touch-screen interface, it's much easier just to dig wherever, and whenever you are and start exploring that way!

7

Increasing Resources through Villages and Excavation

In This Chapter

- Trading in villages
- Defending and building villages
- Exploring structures
- Raiding structures

Minecraft not only produces natural landscapes that look different every time you play, but it also spawns structures such as bustling villages, treasure-filled pyramids, or dangerous dungeons. This chapter helps you find and benefit from these structures and communities to enhance your experience.

Trading in Villages

A *village* is a group of structures — such as hovels, smithies, churches, and roads — arranged as a community for its residents, as shown in Figure 7-1. A village can appear in a plain, a savanna, or a desert, and its inhabitants are quite helpful to you. Villages spawn naturally in the world, and most people find them throughout the game. By spawning zombie villagers and then curing them through a simple hack (see the section, "Building a village" later in this Chapter), you can actually create your own villages as well!

Villages can be an automated way to farm and increase your resources throughout the game. With many villagers at your disposal, you now have a workforce of villagers to tend to your crops and livestock. In addition, each villager has a profession that, by right-clicking on the villager, you can trade emeralds with them for items in their possession that can help you in the game. Also see Table 7-1 for more benefits you can gain from villages.

Figure 7-1: Village.

Exploring village features

Villages are composed of several different structures, each of which can be useful. Some of the components of a village are described in Table 7-1.

Table 7-1 Village Features

Structure	*Description*	*How to Use It*
Hut, hovel, or house	A place of overnight shelter for villagers	Homes appear naturally, but you can build your own housing for villagers. (See the later section "Building a village.")
Farm	A flat stretch of farmland on which villagers grow crops	Help farm these crops to grow wheat, carrots, and potatoes.
Smithy	A cobblestone building that holds a forge and a storage chest with useful treasure; one or two may appear in a village	Look for these valuable items in the chest in the back room. You can also borrow the lava.

Structure	*Description*	*How to Use It*
Well	A small structure that appears in a village and holds water	Use it as a reliable source of water; it's renewable.
Other buildings	Structures such as butcher shops, libraries, and churches	House villagers with specialized trading options (as explained in the later section "Trading with emeralds").

Villages that appear in deserts provide a source of smooth sandstone blocks. Replace broken blocks so that villagers' homes are safe during the night. Otherwise, zombies will successfully attack the village.

Trading with emeralds

To trade with a villager, right-click him and use emeralds as currency to buy and sell materials.

Though the most common villager is the farmer (wearing a brown robe), you have other trading options, from butchers (white aprons), blacksmiths (black aprons), librarians (white robes), and priests (purple robes).

To trade with villagers, follow these steps:

1. **Right-click a villager to open the Trade menu, as shown in Figure 7-2.**

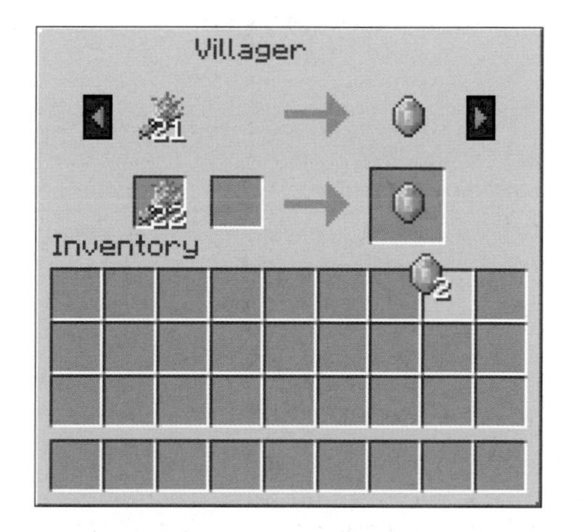

Figure 7-2: Trading inventory.

The top of the Trade menu shows a large, gray arrow with an item to the right and one or two items to the left. The items to the left of the arrow are the ones the villager wants. If the villager wants to buy materials such as raw meat or paper, find some. If he wants to sell you items for emeralds, obtain some by selling to other villagers.

2. **Place the items that the villager wants in the corresponding slots of the Trade menu.**

   The item you want to buy appears on the right side of the menu.

3. **To buy the item that appears, click it.**

   If you invest enough resources into the trade for multiple items, Shift-click to buy as much as you can.

4. **Close the Trade menu and wait for a moment. If green sparks appear around the villager (indicating that the villager has unlocked a new trade option), repeat Steps 1 through 3 to trade new items with the villager.**

   When you trade with the villager again, press the arrow buttons to cycle through available trades. Some trades close if you use them too many times or if you harm the villager who is offering them.

5. **Find other trading opportunities.**

   Villagers have not only professions (easily recognized by their clothes) but also careers. A career is a subset of the profession. The villager changes what is sold depending on the career. When you meet a villager, right-click the person to open a trading inventory menu displaying the career name at the top. Otherwise, you cannot determine the career of a villager and the available trades. Table 7-2 describes the types of villagers and their careers.

Table 7-2 Types of Villagers and Their Careers

Villager	*Profession*	*Career*	*Description*
	Farmer	Fletcher or farmer or fisherman or shepherd	Brown robe; only farmers plant, harvest, and replant crops; the other careers are for trading only.
	Butcher	Butcher or leatherworker	White apron; the butcher sells meat, and the leath-erworker sells leather armor and leather.
	Librarian	Librarian	White robe; has 3 random enchanted books to trade.

Villager	*Profession*	*Career*	*Description*
	Blacksmith	Toolsmith or armorer or weaponsmith	Black apron; sells tools, armor, or weapon, depending on career.
	Priest	Cleric	Purple robe; buys zombie flesh or gold in trade for emerald.
	Zombie	Zombie villager or baby zombie villager	Green; a zombie villager can be cured by throwing a splash potion of weakness and right-clicking it with a golden apple; baby zombie villagers can ride chickens and cannot be cured until grown.
	Baby	All careers, but cannot trade until grown	Follows other baby villages in a game of tag; grows into a villager after 20 minutes.

You can trade with villagers by using emeralds directly or a complex list of other trades to obtain emeralds, which are then used to buy other items you want. Please see the online chapter to discover the various types of trades available with villagers.

I combine mob farming (see Chapter 9) with a cleric villager. That way, I can trade zombie flesh with the cleric for emeralds. This strategy gives me an almost endless supply of emeralds so that I can quickly make other trades.

If you help farm crops in a village, you can trade what you reap with other villagers. Your profits (resulting from farmers buying wheat from you) can fetch you a number of emeralds. Farm fast though, because farmer villagers will harvest and replant the wheat you sow, collecting the wheat and seeds for their own farms.

Surviving zombie sieges

For the seasoned player, zombies may be no problem for you, but they're quite dangerous to villagers. Zombies chase villagers and can easily kill cornered villagers. In Normal mode or Hardcore mode, zombies turn these victims into *more* zombies, causing them to form swarms as they tear through the village.

Occasionally, a nearby village experiences a zombie siege at night, in which a horde of zombies appears and gains the ability to break down wooden doors in Normal mode. (They can already do this in Hardcore mode.) During these sieges, the village may lose many inhabitants unless you do something. Losing your villagers means precious time wasted in accumulating more resources from that village.

Defending a village

Do your best to stop zombie sieges, as they can significantly decrease your village size, meaning you'll have to rebuild your village to receive the multitude of resources it used to provide. You'll also have a village full of "zombie villagers," which are mostly just a nuisance until you can restore them back to their human state. Use torches to build a somewhat safe zone around the village, and kill off zombie infestations before they can reach villagers and expand. Take extra preemptive measures too, such as building iron golems (described in Chapter 9) and adding extra doors to houses.

I like to add fences around the village in addition to torches. This creates a further barrier to prevent zombie invasion. Or, if I can get enough iron, I make iron golems to patrol the villages instead. The iron golems will fight the zombies for you within your village!

Restoring a village

Villagers can repopulate their own cultures, but sometimes a zombie attack leaves an entire population devastated. Just like an episode of "The Walking Dead," your entire village will be replaced by zombie villagers! Have no fear though — you can restore any zombie villager back to their normal state. To restore a villager, follow these steps (see Figure 7-3):

1. **Find a zombie villager.**

   This type of villager burns in the daylight, so make sure that a few are indoors. A zombie villager wearing a helmet is also immune to daylight.

2. **Throw a splash potion of weakness at the zombie villager, and then promptly right-click him with a golden apple.**

   The effect from the potion lasts only briefly, so act swiftly with the golden apple. (Chapter 6 has the lowdown on potions.)

3. **Wait.**

   The zombie villager shakes slightly and emits red swirls, indicating that he's reverting. Wait it out for a minute or so, and you have a villager.

If the new villagers can remain safe until the zombies have been either converted or slain, you will have restored a village to its former glory.

Figure 7-3: Restoring a villager.

Building a village

If you can't find a village, build your own! Zombie villagers have the slight possibility of appearing in the same places as zombies do, so if you follow the steps in the preceding section to turn a zombie into a villager, you can start your colony.

A villager needs a home, of course. A villager lives in any enclosed space that has a wooden door. If you add extra doors, more villagers will decide to live in the same building — essentially, a door defines a living space.

After your colony has at least 10 villagers and 21 houses, iron golems may appear and defend your work. You can build a large colony by organizing a large number of houses or by building large manors or apartments that have numerous doors.

Exploring PE Villages

The PE edition has villages, but you cannot trade within those villages. The blacksmith houses still have chests, which you can and will want to raid. Beginning players may also use a villager's house as a shelter. In the PE edition, villagers do not become zombies and cannot open doors.

In addition, be careful in the Smithy — in PE edition, it can often catch fire, setting your entire village or nearby structures on fire! Unfortunately there is not much you can do about this — it's just a feature (or could some call it a bug) of the game. Because villages are a relatively new feature of Minecraft PE there are bound to be things that come and go between the time we write this, and the time you read it, so explore and see what you can find!

Excavating Structures

The village is by far the most advanced structure in Minecraft, but many other types can appear throughout the world. These structures often provide useful materials and can contain treasure chests for you to find.

Excavating a Desert temple

You occasionally find a sandstone pyramid while exploring the desert. As shown in Figure 7-4, this useful resource is worth excavating.

Figure 7-4: Desert temple.

This pyramid structure is composed of several different types of sandstone, including hieroglyphics that can be collected and used as building blocks. The pyramid, which is a single room with numerous entrances, has a spiral staircase in each of its towers and a secret tunnel leading to 4 treasure chests.

You have to dig in the correct spot to find the treasure of the temple. Watch out, though: A long fall and a trap await you. The trap in particular is quite dangerous, using TNT and a pressure plate, but you can scavenge good resources from it.

Though a desert temple can be partially caved in with sand, you can generally see it easily in the flat parts of the desert. Be sure to look for one when you're in the biome.

Finding jungle temples

The moss-covered jungle temple is much more difficult to find than a desert temple. You can find jungle temples hidden among the trees in the jungle, as shown in Figure 7-5.

Figure 7-5: Jungle temple.

The jungle temple is composed primarily of mossy cobblestone, crafted from vines and cobblestone. The temple has two floors and a basement: The top floor is a balcony, and the bottom floor holds the empty main room. The basement contains tripwire traps and a couple of secrets. Two treasure chests are available in jungle temples — you can find one in the basement and the other beneath a secret passage on the first floor. To open the secret passage, you have to solve the combination lock in the basement.

If you're not in Adventure mode (described in Chapter 13), you can bypass many jungle temple challenges. Use shears to cut tripwire, and use a pickaxe to smash your way through the combination lock. You can also scavenge useful materials such as dispensers, chiseled stone bricks, and pistons.

Breaking into a dungeon

The small, rare dungeon structure, shown in Figure 7-6, appears underground as a cobblestone room. It usually has no entrance, so you can use a pickaxe to break in and find treasure chests, which contain moderately useful items. It's also the only way (other than trading) to get the elusive saddle item, which allows you to ride pigs as a means of transport.

Figure 7-6: Dungeon.

The center of the dungeon contains a fiery grate with a spinning figurine in its center, called a *spawner.* This block sporadically spits out monsters in nearby dark areas. You can break this block quickly with a pickaxe or neutralize it by lighting the area around it. You can also exploit this block's capabilities to obtain loot from the monsters that appear.

Invading the witch hut

The witch hut structure, as shown in Figure 7-7, found exclusively in the swamp biome, is used as living space for evil witches. The witch hut contains a potted mushroom, a crafting table, and a cauldron. Though witches commonly spawn in huts, witches can also spawn elsewhere, like any hostile mob.

This structure is useful because the witch that appears in it drops potion ingredients when it's slain. However, it's also worthwhile to take the cauldron, because it's rather expensive to craft.

Figure 7-7: Witch hut.

Exploring an abandoned mine shaft

Large, abandoned mine shafts can be found underground, as shown in Figure 7-8. You can find several useful treasure chests in these complex webs of broken rails and tunnels, and you can forage lots of minecart rails. However, you can also easily get lost.

Figure 7-8: Abandoned mine shaft.

While exploring an abandoned mine shaft, you may discover a room packed with cobwebs, which can slow you down considerably. At the center of the cobwebs is a grate, similar to the one inside a dungeon. The grate spawns cave spiders (described in Chapter 5), which are smaller, blue bugs that crawl from the cobwebs and attack you. The cave spider's poisonous bite makes it a distinctive threat.

To reach the spawner and shut it off (by breaking it with a pickaxe or lighting possible spawning areas with torches), hack your way through the cobwebs — a sword does this job quickly. Cobwebs also provide lots of string, which you can use to craft items such as wool, bows, and fishing poles.

Finding a Stronghold

The incredibly rare (and giant) Stronghold structure (see Figure 7-9) is home to the End portal. Only three exist in most worlds, and all are generally far away from you at the start of the game. You can find the general direction of one, as detailed in Chapter 11, by right-clicking while holding an eye of ender and watching in which direction it points.

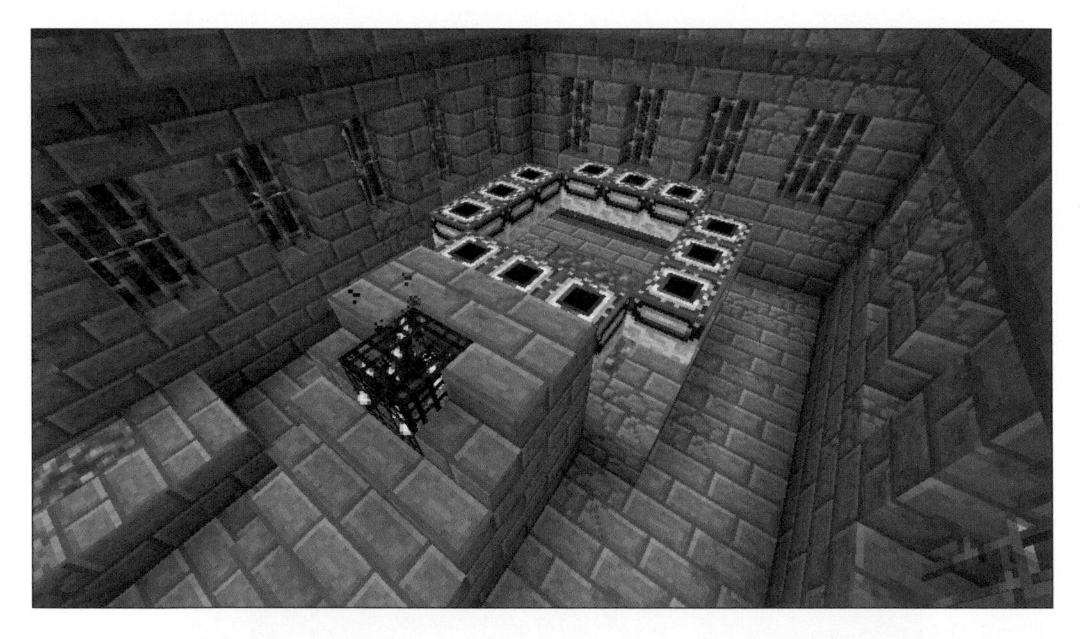

Figure 7-9: Stronghold.

The main feature of the Stronghold is that it contains the portal to the End. However, the Stronghold itself has plenty of features to explore, as described in this list:

- **Rooms:** A Stronghold has many rooms, which can contain fountains, prison cells, and stairwells. Most rooms contain lots of high-end building materials, such as iron bars, iron doors, and stone bricks. You can also get mossy stone bricks and cracked stone bricks.
- **Treasure:** Strongholds generate a huge number of valuable treasure chests. Find as many as you can!
- **Libraries:** Sometimes, you find in a Stronghold an abandoned library that contains many bookshelves and, possibly, a balcony and chandelier. The bookshelves are useful to collect, and treasure is hidden throughout the library.
- **Danger:** Use torches to light up the Stronghold quickly! When you break a wall, be careful — a silverfish might pop out and attack you. If you can break a wall quickly with your hand (hold down the left mouse button to see whether the cracks in the block expand quickly), you know that a silverfish is inside.

Exploring the nether fortress

The *nether fortress*, is a dark, elaborate castle that you can find — where else? — in the Nether. The fortress, shown in Figure 7-10, consists of dark rooms and giant, bridge-mounted hallways. The nether fortress is important throughout the game because it's home to both Blaze and wither skeletons, as detailed in Chapters 5 and 11. In certain rooms, you can also find nether wart growing, which you can collect and farm. Additionally, you can find chests at the corner of hallways, which includes all kinds of goods — even obsidian.

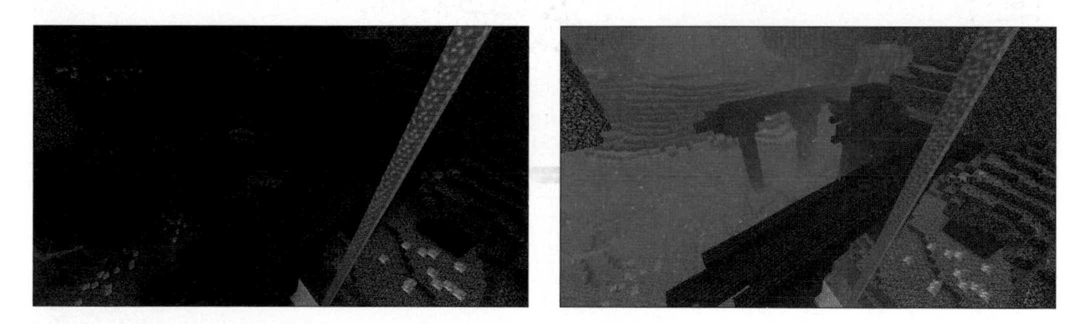

Figure 7-10: Nether fortress.

Discovering ocean monuments

The ocean monument is gigantic — see Figure 7-11. It is so big that it's almost the size of a Stronghold. This area is the only one that spawns guardians. It's also the home of three elder guardians. They cast the mining fatigue 3 effect, making it incredibly slow to mine out blocks.

Figure 7-11: Ocean monuments.

The point of venturing into the ocean monument is to collect its treasure — 8 gold blocks encased in dark prismarine. (This is the only spot where you will find this block in the monument.) If you want to get the treasure, therefore, you have to kill all three elder guardians. (We describe the guardians and elder guardians in more detail in Chapter 5.) You can find the elder guardians in the top, left, and right sections of this monument.

This monument is amazing to excavate but requires you to have advanced skills. Add respiration enchantment and aqua infinity enchantment to your helmet and add depth strider enchantment to your boots (see Chapter 10) so that you can breathe longer underwater, mine quicker, and move faster.

Understanding Minecraft PE Excavation

Players in PE mode can enjoy excavating all structures except for the nether fortress and ocean monuments. The other structures operate similarly in PE mode as they do in PC mode with the exception of witch huts. PE mode has witch huts in the swamp biome, but no witches or potions (commonly raided in the PC version). Players can gather useful items in other structures such as diamonds, gold, iron, and bones (for bone meal), among other rare items such as armor and swords. Many players enjoy this bit of adventure to spice up a game that has become largely building and farming.

8

Developing Redstone

In This Chapter

- Getting to know Creative mode
- Engineering with redstone
- Understanding Minecraft ticks
- Running commands when you can't be there yourself
- Applying redstone to farming

Most of this book focuses on the various faculties of Survival mode. As a player begins to experiment with redstone, Survival mode alone can prove tricky for acquiring enough blocks and ingredients to build redstone contraptions.

You can "playthrough" and skip this chapter entirely, continuing to advance through survival gameplay toward the Nether and End. If you're interested in learning to use redstone, however, you should switch to a notable feature in Minecraft: Creative mode.

Redstone is considered difficult to use in Creative mode — and impossible to use in Survival mode — so don't get frustrated as you attempt your first redstone creations. Figuring out the different redstone items, timing of contraptions, and building designs takes plenty of experimenting. But first, you need to get into Creative mode.

Playing in Creative Mode

You enter Creative mode by creating a new world and clicking the Game Mode button to change the game type. Alternatively, in a world where cheats are available, you can enter Creative mode by using this command:

```
/gamemode 1
```

You can return to Survival mode by using this command:

```
/gamemode 0
```

In Creative mode, you can build whatever you want with no fear of restraint or resource consumption. You can use this mode whenever you're feeling creative rather than adventurous and you want to try new ideas. In Creative mode, you can

- **Place blocks while retaining inventory:** If you use a consumable item in Creative mode, it takes effect, but the item isn't consumed.
- **Break blocks instantly:** Clicking blocks always breaks them immediately, unless you're using a sword, and then you can't break anything.
- **Press the spacebar while airborne to fly:** While flying, press the spacebar to move up and the Shift key to move down. You can stop flying by touching the ground or double-tapping the spacebar.
- **Avoid all damage:** You have no health or hunger points, and nothing can kill you. The only way to die is to dig through the bedrock at the bottom of the world and fall deep into the Void, which is difficult to do accidentally. Another thing that's difficult to do accidentally is to use the command `/kill`.
- **Use items without consuming durability or ammunition:** Tools, weapons, and armor don't lose durability when used, and you can fire a bow without consuming arrows. You can also perform any enchantment without the necessary experience orbs or lapis lazuli.
- **Add any item you want to the inventory:** Rather than see the standard inventory screen, you pick and choose the items you want in the Creative mode inventory. The inventory consists of 12 tabs. The 10 on the left are categories of items; the Compass tab lets you search for items by name; and the Chest tab shows your Survival-style inventory, as shown in Figure 8-1.

In addition to using Creative mode for redstone, this mode is used whenever a player attempts any large projects, such as creating large homes or bases, and creating transportation systems, including railways (see Chapter 9).

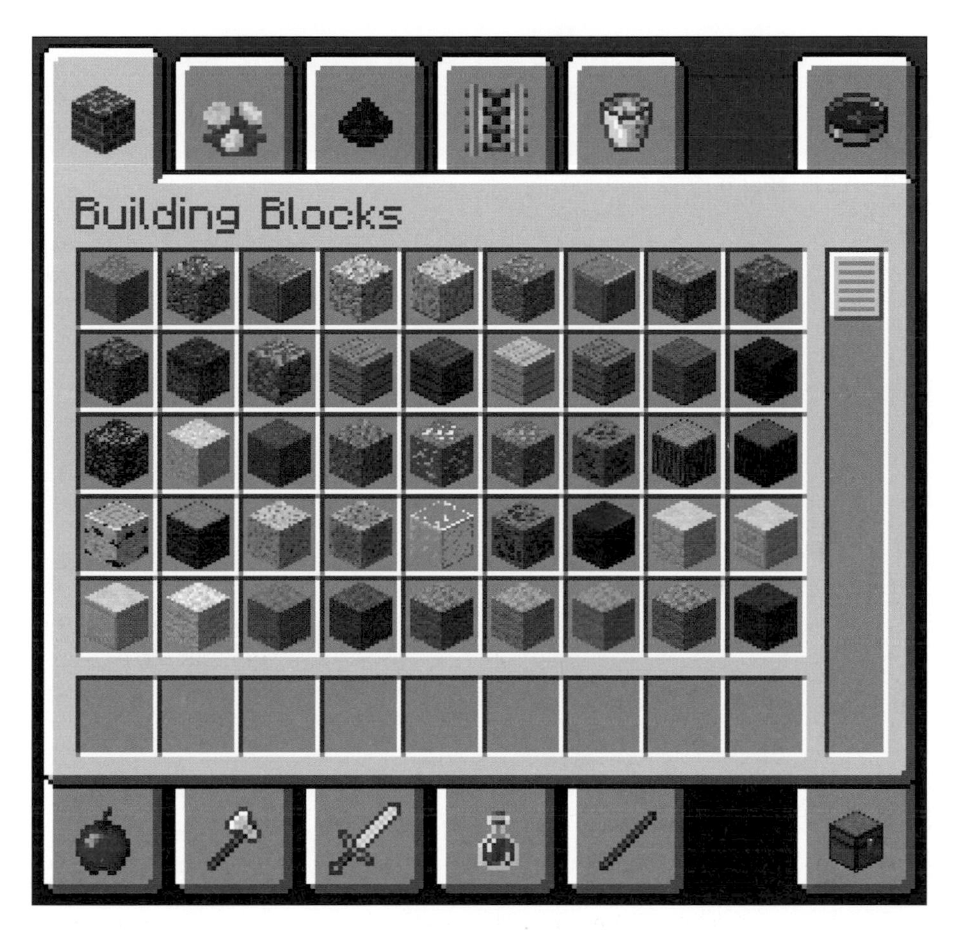

Figure 8-1: Creative mode inventory.

Understanding Redstone Basics

Redstone is one of the more advanced concepts in Minecraft. You can obtain *redstone* dust by mining redstone ore underground. You can spread this dust across the ground as wire, attach it to levers or doors, and craft it into torches and repeaters to build machines. Whether you want a lever that performs two tasks at a time, a combination lock, or a giant virtual computer, you can build it by cleverly arranging redstone dust.

If you read this section from start to finish, start a new game in Creative mode and follow along by building machines yourself. If you're new to Minecraft, this chapter is somewhat advanced. Use the later section "Applying redstone circuits" as a technical reference guide.

Transmitting power with redstone wire

Put simply, redstone dust carries power. While holding a lump of redstone dust, right-click the ground to place it there, at which point it becomes a *redstone wire*. In its default state, the redstone wire is uncharged, which means that it does nothing.

When the redstone is powered by a device such as a lever, tripwire, button, or pressure plate, the wire begins to glow red and transmits power to open doors, ignite explosives, or activate dispensers. Figure 8-2 shows a lever connected to a mechanism that ignites three explosives at one time.

Figure 8-2: Basic mechanism.

Redstone dust can transmit power and perform more tasks than you can normally complete by pulling a lever. You should know these concepts about redstone dust. It can

- **Orient itself automatically:** When you first place some redstone dust, it appears as a small lump of wire that can transmit power in all directions. By placing more dust or certain mechanisms near it, the wire stretches into lines, corners, and bends to meet its task.
- **Extend 15 blocks from the power source:** Charged redstone wire gets dimmer as it moves away from its power source. After the wire travels 15 blocks from any power source, it can no longer transmit energy that far. Use mechanisms or items such as redstone repeaters (described in the next section) to extend it further.
- **Climb blocks:** Your designs don't have to be only two-dimensional. Redstone wire can run up or down the side of a single block so that you can build staircases to carry the circuit vertically. However, the redstone still has to have an unbroken path, as shown in Figure 8-3.

By carrying power in your world, you can achieve great accomplishments by simply pressing a button.

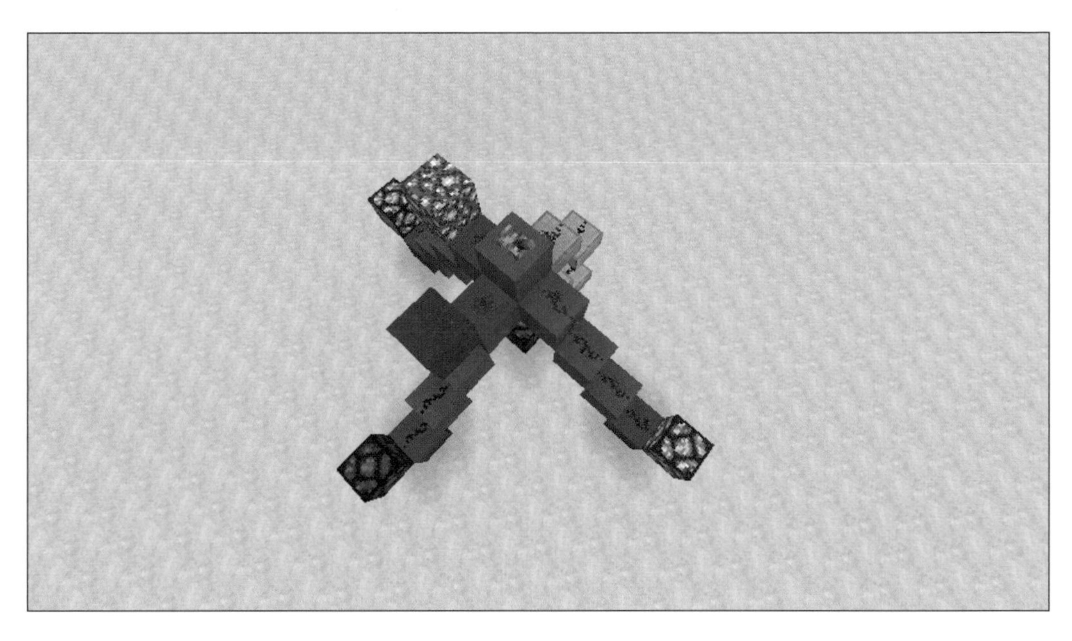

Figure 8-3: Redstone staircase.

Using other redstone mechanisms

Of course, you can craft other items to improve your redstone creations. These allow you to build advanced circuits and accomplish more interesting goals.

Although a block such as grass or iron technically absorbs no current, we sometimes refer to it as *powered*. See the later section "Applying redstone circuits" for rules governing powered blocks.

Lighting a redstone torch

A *redstone torch* is a useful resource that's crafted with redstone dust and a stick. It provides a constant source of power to everything next to it, above it, and below it, and it can be placed on floors or walls. It can even power the block directly above it.

Redstone torches never burn out on their own, but you can turn them off by powering the blocks they're placed on, as shown in Figure 8-4.

Redstone torches are important because they power sources that can be turned off by other parts of the circuit. Thus, the clever arrangement of redstone torches can allow for powerful circuits such as combination locks or programs.

Figure 8-4: Redstone torches.

Using a redstone repeater

Redstone repeaters are interesting little mechanisms that can be placed on the ground like redstone wire, though they have a few extra faculties. They

- **Transmit current in only one direction:** When you place a repeater, the output faces away from you. A repeater also transmits current after a brief delay.
- **Allow you to add a delay to the circuit:** Right-click a repeater to edit the time it takes for the current to pass. Use a delay to make timers and choreograph large circuits.
- **Extend a wire's 15-block range:** Then the circuits can move as far as you want.

Figure 8-5 shows examples of using redstone repeaters.

In addition, if you place a redstone repeater so that it powers a second one from the side, it locks the second repeater's On–Off value. Then the circuit can store binary memory, which is useful in advanced designs.

Run a redstone repeater into a block to easily make a powered block.

Using a redstone comparator

A redstone comparator, as shown in Figure 8-6, looks similar to a repeater but has an additional input from the side and doesn't extend the signal. When the torch is lit (by right-clicking), the comparator goes into Subtraction mode and subtracts the two signals from the back and side input to determine the strength of the output signal. The back input must be larger than the side input or else the comparator doesn't give out an input (similar to a transistor).

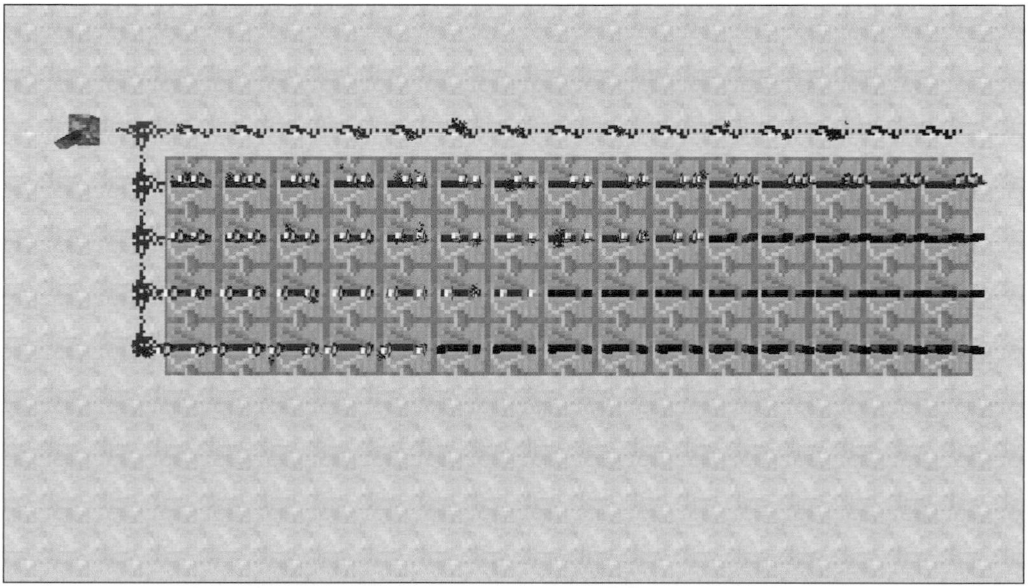

Figure 8-5: Redstone repeaters.

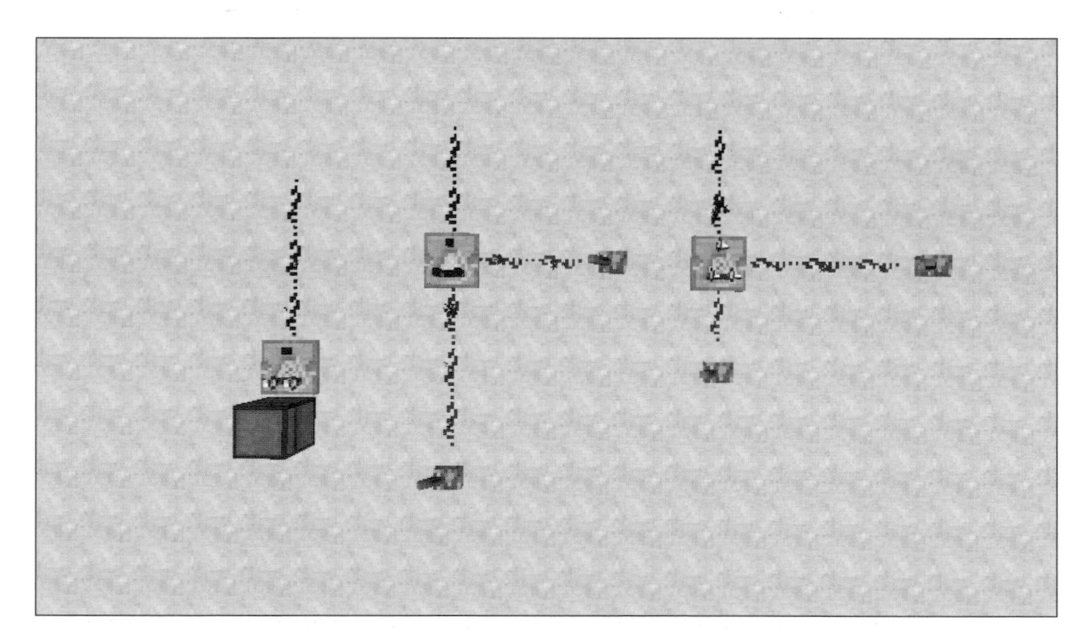

Figure 8-6: Redstone comparator.

After you right-click again, the torch turns off and the output signal is the full strength of the back input if the back signal exceeds the side. When placed by a block with an inventory (such as a chest), the output of the comparator is based on the amount of used inventory space in the block.

Storing things in a hopper

A hopper, as shown in Figure 8-7, picks items up and stores them in its own inventory of 5 slots (see Figure 8-8). It also drops items to a block that has an inventory from its end. A hopper can send items sideways and down but not up. When connected to an item that has an inventory (such as a chest), the hopper places items directly into that inventory.

Figure 8-7: Hopper.

A major capability of a hopper is that it can remove items from storage containers and pick up items off the ground. Its "sucking" feature allows a simple collection system that can be used in farms. This feature is also used in bulk storage — multiple chests connected by hoppers — making it seem that you have 1 chest that has the space of 4 double chests.

Hoppers are often used with storage minecarts to place items into the storage carts, or they can be connected to a storage minecart and pick up items from the storage minecart as it travels over the hopper. A hopper can also be crafted into a *hopper minecart,* which is a moveable hopper (see Figure 8-9).

Hoppers are also used to feed dispensers, droppers, furnaces, and brewing stands. You can then automate some of the work of item collection and make traps. Hoppers are deactivated by using redstone.

Figure 8-8: Hopper inventory.

Figure 8-9: Minecart with hopper.

Pushing things with a piston

A piston (see Figure 8-10) pushes most blocks when activated up to 12 blocks away. Pistons are commonly used to open and close doors, create traps, combine with redstone repeaters to create logic gates (yes, just like a transistor, if you're an electronics geek) without a redstone torch, or to build escalators, for example. A unique feature of the piston is that it extinguishes a block that is on fire.

Figure 8-10: Piston.

Despite their wooden appearance, pistons aren't flammable. Pistons are activated using redstone. It isn't uncommon to activate a piston using a pressure plate or lever wired some distance away. This method is particularly helpful in automating farms or creating mob traps.

Redstone dust and repeaters activate pistons not only directly in front of them but also power pistons below them. Some items aren't moved by pistons including obsidian, bedrock, blocks with extra data such as chests or furnaces, nether portals, and anvils. Items including cactus, pumpkins, jack-o'-lanterns, sugar cane, and dragon eggs are dropped when pushed. Melons and cobwebs return to slices and string, respectively. Water and lava are simply moved in their path.

Pulling things with a sticky piston

A sticky piston operates the same as a piston but also pulls blocks in addition to pushing them. The same rules apply in pulling blocks as in pushing them. A sticky piston cannot pull back a block that is affected by gravity if it pushed the block over a hole. (That is, the block will fall.) Similarly, sticky pistons cannot keep sand and gravel in the air when pushed horizontally.

Dispensing items with a dispenser

A dispenser (see Figure 8-11) is one of the coolest redstone contraptions in Minecraft. When right-clicked, a dispenser has its own inventory, allowing you to place items inside. When activated by a redstone charge, a random item is discharged from the inventory. The selected item is random and based on stacks, not on individual items.

Figure 8-11: Dispenser.

So if a stack of 6 arrows and a stack of 3 snowballs are in the inventory, the chance is equal for arrows and snowballs, even though there are twice as many arrows. Many items are simply dropped 3 x 3 blocks away. However, arrows, snowballs, fireworks, fire charges, chicken eggs, splash potions, and bottles of enchanting are shot out of the dispenser. Bombs away!

Boats and minecarts can be dispensed, but only above water and rails, respectively. Armor can also be dispensed, quickly equipping a player who is only 1 block away. Bone meal can be dispensed automatically on a farm, improving the crops. Mob eggs can also be dispensed and consequently spawned. Also, liquids can be dispensed from buckets. Finally, pumpkins and command blocks can be placed in their block form from dispensers. When the command block is placed by a dispenser, the command in the command block runs (if a command is in the command block).

Dispensers are activated by a redstone pulse running into the block or 1 block adjacent. By placing redstone wiring in a crossing pattern, 5 dispensers can be triggered at one time. A dispenser is also triggered by opening a trapped chest if the two are adjacent, so you can see the fun tricks you can play on your friends!

Dropping things with a dropper

A dropper (see Figure 8-12) works similarly to a dispenser, holding its own inventory and activated by a redstone circuit. It cannot dispense projectiles (it simply drops them). However, droppers can push items upward. This feature is handy in pushing up items from a mine.

Figure 8-12: Dropper.

A dropper also puts items into other blocks that store items. For example, a dropper can place fuel into an adjacent furnace.

Droppers and dispensers are quite similar and look almost identical. A dispenser has a cross mouth, whereas a dropper has a U-shaped mouth.

Applying redstone circuits

Of course, you can accomplish a great deal by using circuits: Open doors, move blocks with pistons, ignite explosives, play music, or complete basic tasks, for example. The following list describes additional redstone-based items and their uses, as well as mechanical items that can be powered by redstone:

- **Redstone wire:** A wire that powers adjacent wires and repeaters, the block it rests on, and any block or mechanism it faces. For more information, see "Transmitting power with redstone wire," earlier in this chapter.
- **Powered blocks:** Technical terminology used in this chapter. These blocks power all adjacent mechanisms. Ice and glass cannot be powered.
- **Redstone torch:** A power source that affects every adjacent mechanism, including ones above and below; it also powers the block just above it. I discuss redstone torches in more detail in the earlier section "Redstone torch."
- **Redstone repeater:** A block that's powered by anything behind it and powers anything in front of it with a slight delay. See the earlier section "Redstone repeater."
- **Redstone block:** A block of redstone that acts like a redstone torch that is always on.
- **Lever:** A type of switch that affects adjacent mechanisms as well as the block it's placed on. You can turn a lever on or off by right-clicking it. You can place a lever on any surface.
- **Button:** A type of switch that sends a temporary current to adjacent mechanisms and to the block it's placed on. In addition to right-clicking it, you can activate a wooden button by shooting it with an arrow. You can place buttons only on walls.
- **Tripwire hook:** A type of switch that affects adjacent mechanisms as well as the block it's placed on. Tripwire hooks can be placed only on walls. Place string in a line between two hooks to make *tripwire* — the hooks are powered when the tripwire is stepped on or when the string is broken without shears.
- **Pressure plate:** A type of switch that transmits power to adjacent mechanisms and to the block it's placed on, when weighted down. Wood pressure plates can be activated by any entity, whereas stone pressure plates can be activated only by an entity that is at least as large as a chicken.
- **Detector rail:** A type of rail that works similarly to a pressure plate. It transmits power when a minecart crosses over it, and it affects adjacent mechanisms and the block it's placed on.
- **Redstone lamp:** A lamp that emits light as long as it's powered. It is also a full block, so it can share the properties of a powered block.

- **Powered rail:** A charged minecart track that powers other powered rails (within a 9-block range). When powered, the powered rail speeds up minecarts; when it isn't powered, it slows them to a halt.
- **Piston:** A device that pushes blocks but destroys redstone devices. Pushing blocks can affect circuits. A piston can be activated by any power source.
- **Doors:** These open automatically when powered by redstone.
- **Fence gates:** Like doors, these open automatically when powered by redstone.
- **Trapdoors:** Special doors that open automatically when powered by redstone.
- **TNT:** Explosive material that ignites when it's powered by redstone (and it's time to think up redstone schemes).
- **Dispensers:** A block that shoots out items and can launch a few projectiles.
- **Note blocks:** Blocks that play sound when powered by redstone. The sounds can be adjusted by right-clicking the note block.
- **Hoppers:** Devices that take inventory, and can spit them out into other blocks that have inventory (such as a chest).
- **Comparators:** Devices that take a signal in the side, and output a varying powered signal out the back. When a signal is applied by way of the attached redstone torch, an output signal is sent at the equivalent strength to the difference of the signal from the back, minus the signal from the side. When a signal is not applied, the full signal sent through the back, if greater than the side, will be sent as output.
- **Dispensers:** Contraptions that allow you to randomly drop one item from the contents when a redstone signal is applied.
- **Droppers:** Devices that work similarly to dispensers, but can place items from their inventory upward into blocks above the dropper.
- **Pistons:** Blocks that, when combined with other contraptions such as redstone repeaters, can push blocks on command.
- **Sticky pistons:** A type of piston that can pull items rather than push them.

Advanced redstone circuitry

You can do lots of fun things with redstone, even such tasks as building computers, calculators, and virtual RAM. First, you need to understand how to build redstone circuitry. If you want a head-start on all this, spend some time researching the topics *binary logic* and *binary calculations* on your favorite search engine. Jesse studied these topics in his childhood math classes, and they can significantly help you understand why these concepts work. A little study of transistor logic can also help. (You didn't realize that this book would help you become an expert at electronics, did you?)

The NOT gate

Suppose that a redstone wire passes through a circuit you've created. If you run the wire through a NOT gate, the wire reverses its value: Off becomes On, and On becomes Off. This is useful for commands such as, "If the pressure plate isn't being triggered, play the All Clear music." The NOT gate, shown in Figure 8-13, is based on torches being naturally active, though they can be turned off by active current.

Figure 8-13: The NOT gate.

The OR gate

Arguably one of the simplest gates, the OR gate (see Figure 8-14) says, "If either of these redstone currents is activated, turn on this third current." To make one of these gates, you simply connect two separate circuits.

The NOR gate

The NOR gate (see Figure 8-15) is the opposite of the OR gate. In Chapter 20, we discuss the RS-NOR latch, a memory unit composed of NOR gates. The NOR gate says, "If either of these redstone currents is activated, turn off this third current." To make one of these gates, place a redstone torch where the two circuits meet.

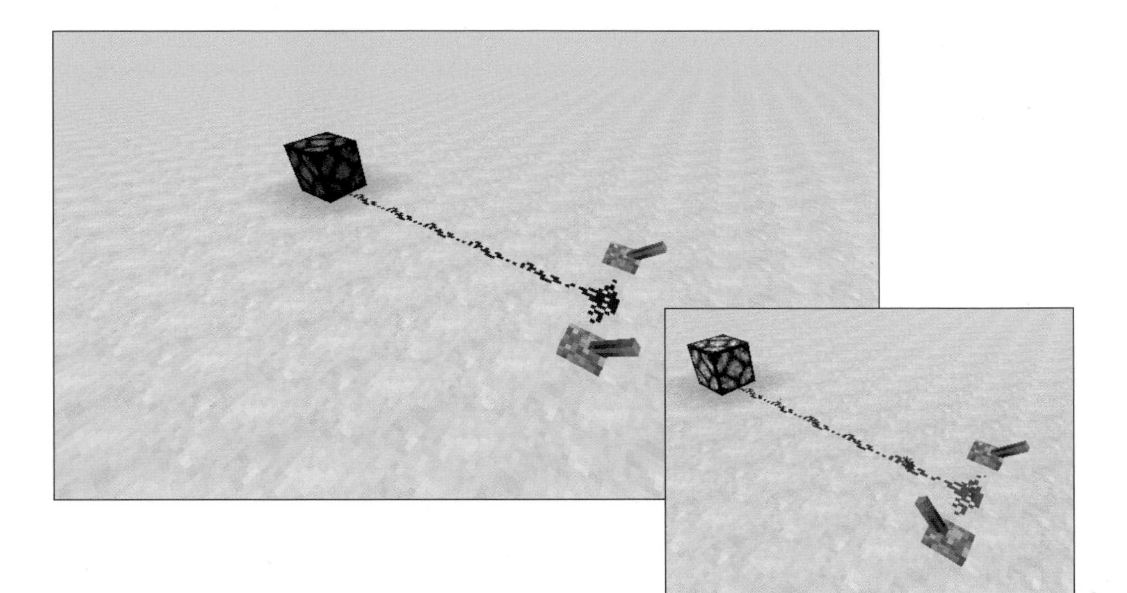

Figure 8-14: The OR gate.

Figure 8-15: The NOR gate.

The AND gate

The AND gate (see Figure 8-16) is tricky to set up. How do you say, "Turn on this circuit only if both of these two other circuits are running?" The setup shown in Figure 8-16 is one of the easiest, though the concepts behind it are useful to understand.

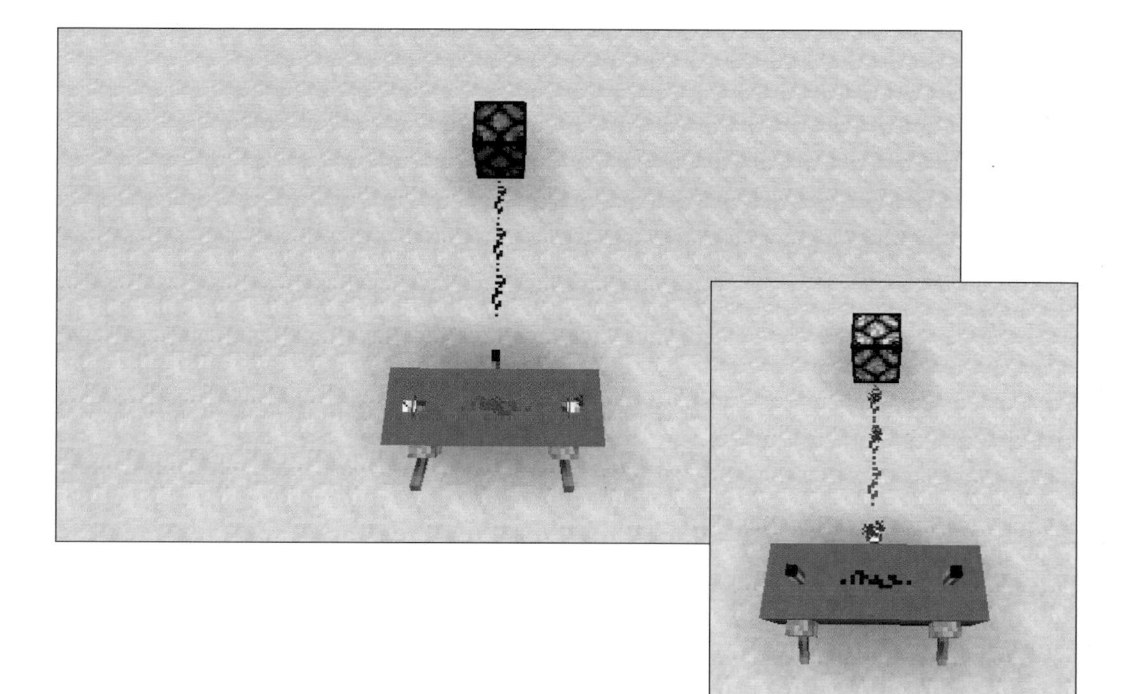

Figure 8-16: The AND gate.

The NAND gate

The NAND gate (see Figure 8-17) is pretty much the opposite of the AND gate. This is how you say, "Turn off this circuit only if both these two other circuits are running." This is simply taking off the third torch in the AND gate.

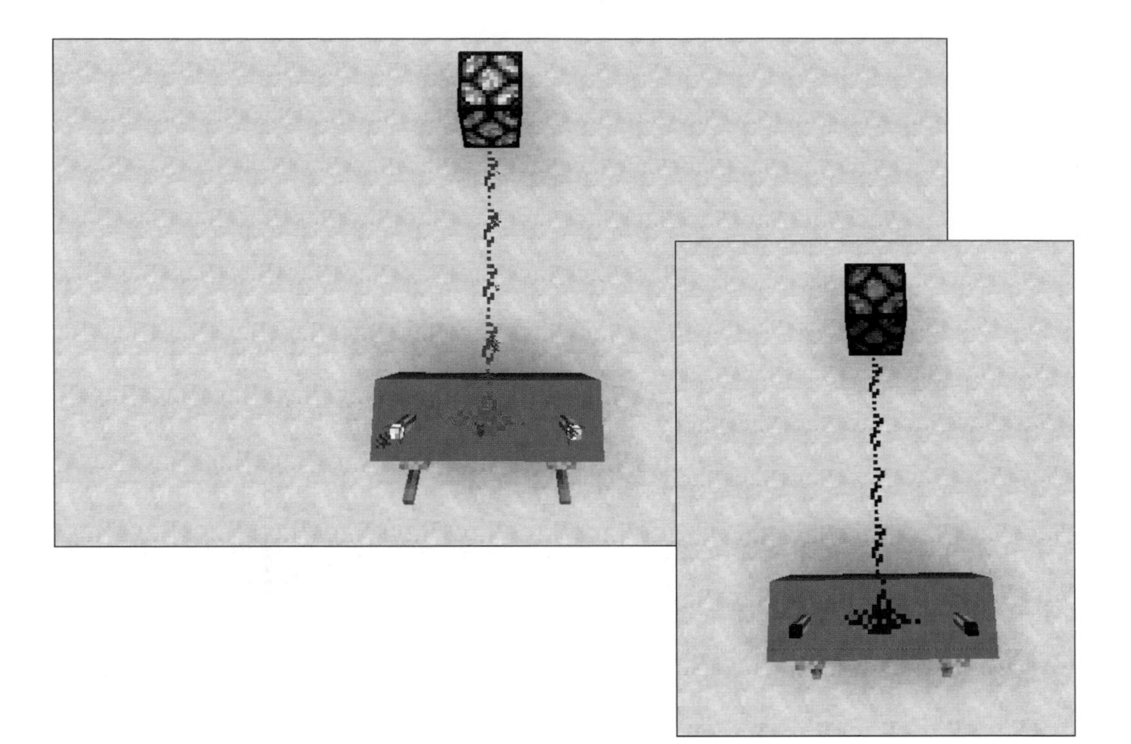

Figure 8-17: The NAND gate.

The XOR gate

The XOR gate means, "Turn on this circuit if only one of these other two circuits is running." The solution shown in Figure 8-18 may be somewhat complicated, but it's simply AND, NOT, and OR rolled into one: The OR gate turns on the output if either lever is activated, and the AND NOT gates turn it off again if both levers are down.

The XNOR gate

The XNOR gate (see Figure 8-19) is the opposite of the XOR gate. It means, "Turn off this circuit if only one of these other two circuits is running." You just have to add an extra NOT gate at the end.

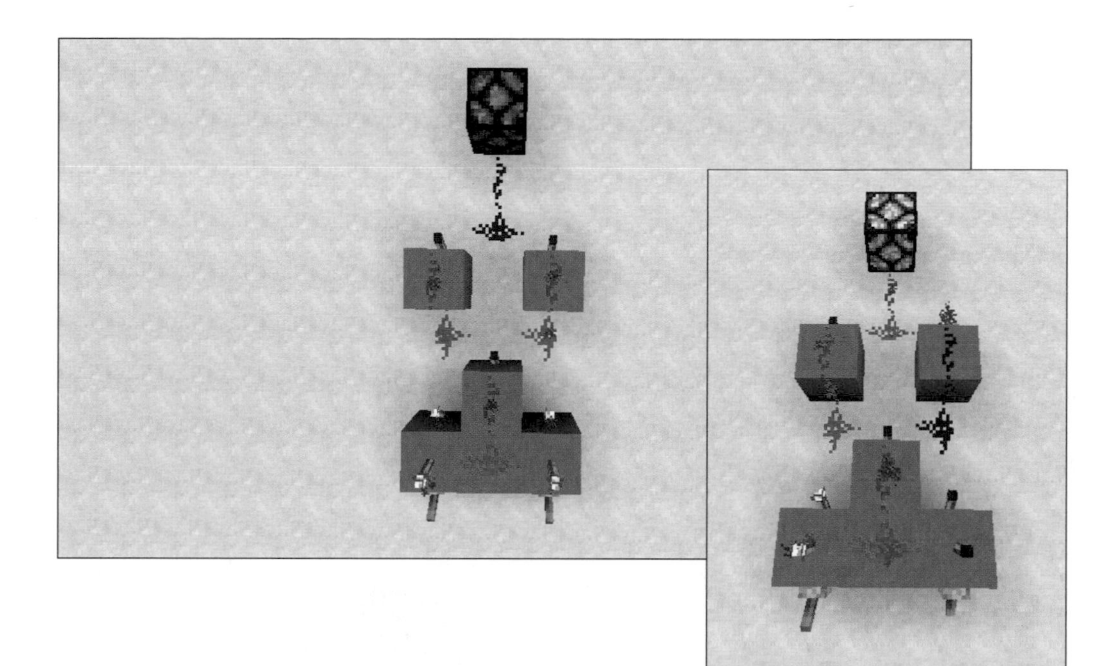

Figure 8-18: The XOR gate.

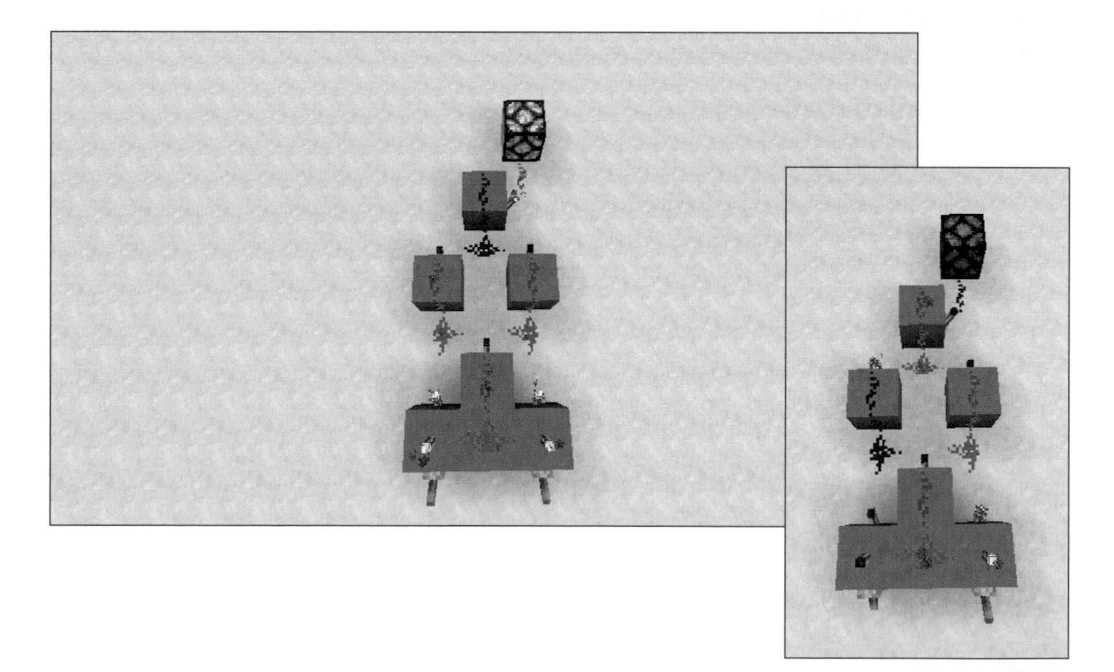

Figure 8-19: The XNOR gate.

Multicircuitous designs

To continue your experience in redstone engineering, replace the levers in the basic gates with redstone wire and hook the gates together. Figure 8-20 shows two different ways to build an advanced circuit, with a diagram of the circuit for comparison, as shown in Figure 8-21.

Figure 8-20: Advanced redstone design.

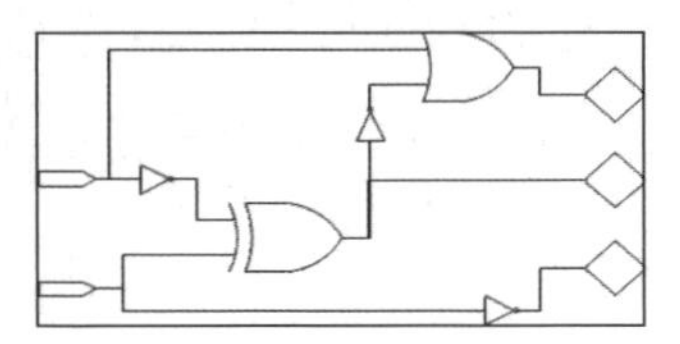

Figure 8-21: Circuit diagram.

In case you're interested, this circuit adds 3 to any 2-digit binary input, expressing the answer in binary form.

If you don't fully understand the concepts explained in this section but you still want to use redstone, simply copy the models we provide or study other people's designs on the Internet. Hide your mechanisms underground if you want them to function without being out in the open.

Counting Minecraft Ticks

Ticks in Minecraft are not bugs — they are specific lengths of time. Minecraft has three types of ticks: game ticks, redstone ticks, and block ticks.

- **Game tick:** A game tick lasts 1/20th of a second — for every second that goes by, 20 ticks are generated. On each tick, many things in the game happen; for example, mobs update their APIs, the sun moves, and hunger makes its scan. A full day in Minecraft lasts for 24,000 ticks, which is 20 minutes in real time. When you're using the `/time set` command, the numbers you enter indicate the equivalent number of game ticks in the regular version of Minecraft. Game ticks don't affect the number of frames per second (that cause lag).
- **Redstone tick:** A redstone tick lasts 1/10th of a second, making two game ticks for every redstone tick. Repeaters can control redstone ticks along with a few other redstone devices. Repeaters automatically have 1 redstone tick delay, but you can right-click to adjust to a 4-redstone tick delay. Someone who requests to put this repeater on two ticks or two ticks of delay is always referring to redstone ticks.
- **Block tick:** A *chunk* in Minecraft is a 16 x 16 x 16 block of cubes that separate Minecraft into sections. Chunks are sometimes given special properties, such as a slime chunk (a chunk that slimes can spawn in) or your spawn chunks (chunks near your world spawn that always are loaded). On every single game tick, 3 blocks are chosen at random in each chunk in 15 chunks that are centered on the player. Those 3 blocks in each chunk are given a random block tick. Though most blocks in Minecraft ignore this tick, a few blocks do something with it. For example, saplings may grow, leaves may decay, or ice may melt. You can change how many random ticks occur per section by using this command:

  ```
  /gamerule randomTickSpeed [Random ticks per section]
  ```

  Sometimes, blocks schedule ticks for the future. These scheduled ticks are scheduled for blocks that have a predictable pattern. A repeater has a scheduled tick to change its state from On to Off. Water also schedules a tick whenever it needs to flow.

Scheduled ticks and random ticks are two different types of ticks and follow separate sets of code, but they both involve ticks in blocks.

Nearly all video games are driven by one big, continuous loop. Every advancement in a video game synchronizes with this loop. One full cycle of this loop in a video game is a tick.

Activating Command Blocks

Command blocks (see Figure 8-22) are blocks that run commands that do not need the player to be present. Anything involving a tilda (~) uses the block's location to do whatever command is running. This capability is quite useful for minigames on servers and adventure maps, because a player can't be present all the time. You can activate command blocks with redstone and have multiple command blocks running at the same time, making it especially useful when you want multiple commands running and you have only one of you. Setting a command block on a superfast 1-redstone-tick clock makes it faster than you can run the command that many times.

Figure 8-22: Command blocks.

Creating Self-Sustaining Farms

Redstone — a big part of farming — lets you collect items automatically. Unlike the farming techniques we discuss in Chapter 5, redstone farming creates mechanisms that make the farm self-sustaining without much, if any, further input from you, the player.

Redstone farming can be done on crops, passive mobs (that is, farm animals), and even hostile mobs. As with most redstone concepts, searching the Internet for tutorials can be invaluable.

A basic type of wheat or sugar cane redstone farming involves activating a water supply (such as using a lever to open a dam and release the water), which pushes the crop into a holding area — automatic harvesting! When the signal is lost, the water supply turns off and the crop is left in one area, to be quickly picked up by the player.

One of Thomas's favorite redstone farms involves chickens. The contraption shown in Figure 8-23 is an automatic cooked chicken farm. Here's how it works: The chickens at the top lay eggs that get sucked up by a hopper and put into a dispenser. The dispenser then throws the eggs onto the half-slab, where a baby chicken is spawned. A baby chicken is about a half-slab tall, and an adult chicken is more than a half-slab tall.

When the chicken grows into an adult, it dies in the lava. Animals that die by fire (or lava) drop their cooked meat rather than their normal, uncooked meat. After the adult chicken dies, its food drops, gets sucked up by the hopper, and is placed into the chest, where it can be collected. By keeping loaded the chunks that Thomas's chicken farm is in, an endless supply of chicken meat is being continually created and gathered for his use.

Figure 8-23: Thomas's redstone chicken farm.

9

Progressing Through the Later Block Ages

In This Chapter

- Exploring the Iron Age, Agricultural Age, and Wealth Age
- Discovering the fun stuff
- Collecting loot and other items with big projects
- Getting from here to there with boats, farm animals, and minecarts
- Protecting your base

As you progress through Minecraft, the minerals you mine, the tools you build, and the livestock you catch can all change the game for you. As you discover new things in Minecraft you'll quickly start to find and discover new things you can do in the game, and take your game to new levels. Each "age" in Minecraft is opened up by the discovery of these items and minerals in the game.

Exploring the Iron Age

The Iron Age is key to opening up all sorts of advanced techniques in Minecraft. Once you have iron, you can build iron tools. Once you have iron tools, you can build cool things like minecarts, iron golems that protect your village, and even buckets, to get water, lava, and other useful fluids for your Minecraft world.

Using Tools of the Iron Age

After you've mined for a while or found a profitable cave, you may find iron ore. When you unlock iron, many more items become available, as described in Table 9-1. These items open an entire world of possibilities, including quality tools and weapons, minecart transportation, and buckets, which provide air underwater, allow you to gather milk (as shown in Figure 9-1), prevent food poisoning, and hold water or lava to fill cauldrons, heat furnaces, and do a variety of other jobs.

Table 9-1 Items in the Iron Age

Item	*Find or Craft?*	*Description*
Anvil	Crafted from 3 iron blocks, 4 iron ingots	This expensive item can repair, combine, and name other items. The anvil also inflicts massive damage if it falls on a mob.
Block of iron	Crafted from 9 iron ingots	This expensive decoration block is used for beacons, iron golems, and anvils.
Bucket	Crafted from 3 iron ingots	To pick up water or lava, right-click it while holding a bucket. Right-click a cow to obtain milk.
Cauldron	Crafted from 7 iron ingots	Fill a cauldron by right-clicking it with a bucket of water; throw dyed leather armor into a cauldron of water to wash it out. Right-clicking a cauldron while holding a bottle fills the bottle with water and drains the cauldron somewhat. Cauldrons can hold water in the Nether, where it would usually evaporate. A cauldron automatically fills if left outside in the rain.
Flint and steel	Crafted from 1 iron ingot, 1 flint	Right-click any surface while holding this tool to start a fire. You can also use it as a weapon, burning enemies by setting fire to the ground near them.
Iron axe	Crafted from 3 iron ingots, 2 sticks	This lumberjacking tool is fast and durable.
Iron bars	Crafted from 6 iron ingots (makes 16)	This transparent decoration block connects to adjacent blocks.
Iron door	Crafted from 6 iron ingots	An iron door cannot be opened unless it's powered (see Chapter 8 to learn about powering things with redstone).
Iron helmet, chestplate, leggings, boots	Crafted from 5, 8, 7, or 4 iron ingots, respectively	This strong armor set offers sturdy protection.

Item	*Find or Craft?*	*Description*
Iron hoe	Crafted from 2 iron ingots, 2 sticks	As efficient as a stone hoe, but it has even more durability.
Iron ingot	Iron ore cooked in a furnace; rarely dropped by zombies; crafted from 1 block of iron (makes 9)	It's the basic ingredient of most iron-based items.
Iron ore	Found underground	It's the gateway to the Iron Age.
Iron pickaxe	Crafted from 3 iron ingots, 2 sticks	This fast, durable pick can profitably mine any breakable block other than obsidian.
Iron shovel	Crafted from 1 iron ingot, 2 sticks	This strong shovel is efficient in providing lots of materials and building space.
Iron sword	Crafted from 2 iron ingots, 1 stick	This strong sword is an excellent resource for even the Nether.
Minecart	Crafted from 5 iron ingots	This vehicle rolls along minecart rails. Right-click rails to place the cart, and right-click the cart to hop in. Other mobs sometimes ride minecarts.
Powered minecart	Crafted from 1 minecart, 1 furnace	The powered minecart moves on its own when given fuel (right-click it while holding fuel), and it can push other minecarts.
Rail	Found in abandoned mine shafts; crafted from 6 iron ingots, 1 stick (makes 16)	Minecarts can travel along rails that slant upward on blocks and bend around corners. If a rail can bend in two different ways, give it redstone power (see Chapter 8) to switch the direction of the track.
Shears	Crafted from 2 iron ingots	Use shears to harvest leaf blocks, shear sheep, and break wool blocks faster.
Storage minecart	Crafted from 1 minecart, 1 chest	This mobile storage chest can travel along minecart rails.
Tripwire hook	Crafted from 1 iron ingot, 1 stick, 1 plank (makes 2)	Place two of these items on opposite walls, and connect them by laying string across the ground. If the string is touched or broken without shears, the hooks emit redstone power (see Chapter 8).

Figure 9-1: Milking a cow by using a bucket.

Playing with fluid dynamics

After you obtain buckets, it's time to start mastering the unique system that Minecraft uses to handle these two liquids:

- **Water:** Appears everywhere as waterfalls, oceans, and rivers
- **Lava:** Rarely seen but appears in large pools deep underground

Both fluids are made of these types of blocks:

- **Source:** Can be moved around by using buckets
- **Flowing:** Creates the unique texture of liquid blocks

Flowing blocks always flow down slants and form the common interpretation of waterfalls and slides; however, they can flow only a limited distance horizontally.

Flowing water can turn into source water, if its direction of flow stabilizes. You can make a renewable source of water by pouring it in a 2 x 2 square, making a small pool to fill a bucket. Lava is different because its source blocks are finite and nonrenewable — it's an important resource to find underground, until you reach the Nether.

When water and lava collide, interesting things happen. When a lava source block is watered down, it turns into obsidian, as shown in Figure 9-2; flowing lava turns into stone or cobblestone, depending on the direction of the collision. To get obsidian quickly, you can find a pool of lava and dump water into it or simply make your way to the End, which is full of obsidian.

Farming techniques are largely based on water and lava principles. Well-built farms (you can read about them in Chapter 5) have a water perimeter around them. More advanced farms push animals through lava to create instantly cooked meats.

Create a renewable source of obsidian. Every time you enter the End, an obsidian platform appears under you. You can break this platform and loot the obsidian and then break it again when you return to the End. (You can read about obsidian Chapter 11.)

Figure 9-2: Water and lava colliding to create obsidian.

Entering the Agricultural Age

Of course, the wide variety of tools at your disposal during the Iron Age is more than enough to start your transition to having all the tools and means to begin the Agricultural Age. You can obtain the (optional) items described in Table 9-2.

Table 9-2 Agricultural Items

Item	*Find or Craft?*	*Description*
Bread	Crafted from 3 wheat	This food item is easy to obtain in large quantities.
Cake	Crafted from 3 buckets of milk, 2 sugar, 1 egg, 3 wheat (buckets aren't consumed)	Place this large cake on the ground and eat it by right-clicking. It has 6 slices, as shown in Figure 9-3, so several players can share it.
Cookie	Crafted from 1 cocoa bean, 2 wheat (makes 8)	This food item is easy to make, but not effective.
Melon block	Can be farmed; crafted from 9 melon slices	This large fruit is split into slices when broken.
Melon seed	Found in treasure chests in abandoned mine shafts; crafted from 1 melon slice	The seed is used to farm melons, as described in Chapter 5.
Melon slice	Found when breaking melon blocks; sold by certain farmers (see Chapter 5)	Melon can be eaten, crafted into melon blocks and "glistering melons," or turned into more seeds.
Seed	Found by breaking tall grass or tilling land	Seed is used to grow wheat (see Chapter 5); right-clicking 2 chickens while holding seeds produces a baby chicken.
Wheat	Found by growing seeds (see Chapter 5)	Pigs, cows, and sheep react to wheat like chickens react to seeds; you can also use wheat to make bread, cake, and cookies.

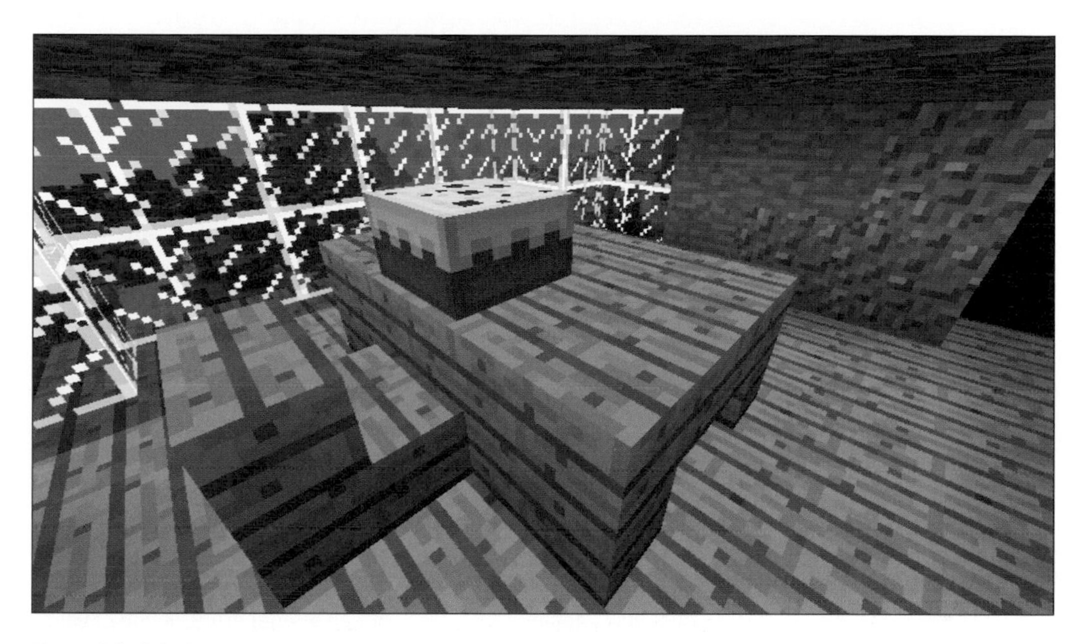

Figure 9-3: Cake!

Reaping the Benefits of the Age of Wealth

When you reach the Age of Wealth — the final age based on the main world you start with (also called "the overworld") in Minecraft — you have mined quite a bit and gathered such rare minerals as lapis, gold, redstone, emerald, and diamond. Tables 9-3 through 9-6 describe some of the most interesting items we suggest you should obtain.

This is when Minecraft becomes truly interesting, when you have gathered all the materials necessary to create large farms including hostile mob farms, build transportation systems, and secure your base (as discussed later in this chapter). You also have the materials necessary to go to the Nether and the End (a misleading term because the game progresses after you return from the End), as described in Chapter 11, or further your redstone skills.

Table 9-3 Gold-Based Items

Item	*Find or Craft?*	*Description*
Glistering melon	Crafted from 1 gold nugget, 1 melon slice	It's the necessary ingredient for potions of healing (see Chapter 10).

(continued)

Table 9-3 *(continued)*

Item	*Find or Craft?*	*Description*
Gold block	Crafted from 9 gold ingots	This beautiful but expensive decorative block can also be used to make powerful golden apples or store gold ingots efficiently.
Gold ingot	From gold ore cooked in a furnace; crafted from 1 block of gold (makes 9) or 9 gold nuggets	It's the base ingredient for gold-based items.
Gold nugget	Dropped by zombie pigmen; crafted from 1 gold ingot (makes 9)	This is a smaller version of the gold ingot; it can be used to make ingots or to craft glistering melons, golden apples, and golden carrots.
Gold ore	Found deep underground	It serves as a gateway to gold-based items, as shown in Figure 9-4.
Golden apple	Crafted from 8 gold nuggets, 1 apple	It functions like a normal apple but also regenerates some of your health over 5 seconds; it can be used to cure zombie villagers (see Chapter 7).
Golden apple (epic variant)	Crafted from 8 gold blocks, 1 apple	This variant of the golden apple will restore your health quickly for half a minute and gives you resistance and fire resistance for 5 minutes; it cannot cure villagers, however, and is made somewhat impractical by its incredibly steep cost.
Golden carrot	Crafted from 8 gold nuggets, 1 carrot	It's a moderately effective food item and the vital ingredient in potions of night vision and invisibility (see Chapter 10 to learn more about potions).
Golden helmet, chestplate, leggings, boots	Crafted from 5, 8, 7, or 4 gold ingots, respectively	Better than leather but worse than iron, golden armor primarily showcases your prestige. It tends to have better enchantments than other items, however (see Chapter 10 to learn about enchanting armor).
Golden sword	Crafted from 2 gold ingots, 1 stick	It's as powerful as a wooden sword and much less durable, making it mostly a prestige item.
Golden tools	Crafted from 1 (shovel), 2 (hoe), or 3 (pickaxe or axe) gold ingots; 2 sticks	Pickaxes, axes, shovels, and hoes are easy to break — but incredibly fast-working.

Figure 9-4: Gold ore mine.

Table 9-4	Redstone-Based Items	
Item	***Find or Craft?***	***Description***
Clock	Crafted from 1 redstone dust, 4 gold ingots	Roughly tells the time using its dial, even when placed in an item frame; like the compass, malfunctions in the Nether and the End
Compass	Crafted from 1 redstone dust, 4 iron ingots	Has a dial that points toward home, even when placed in an item frame (and points straight ahead if you're facing toward home); malfunctions in the Nether and the End
Detector rail	Crafted from 6 iron ingots, 1 stone pressure plate, 1 redstone dust	A special minecart rail that cannot round corners but provides a redstone current (see Chapter 8) when a minecart rolls over it

(continued)

Table 9-4 *(continued)*

Item	***Find or Craft?***	***Description***
Dispenser	Crafted from 7 cobble-stone, 1 bow, 1 redstone dust	Can store as many as 9 stacks of items; when powered (see Chapter 8), spits out one item from any of its 9 slots; can also shoot arrows, launch snowballs and fire charges, and hatch spawn eggs If a bucket of water or lava is placed in a dispenser, the dispenser empties the bucket in front of it, leaving the empty bucket inside. A dispenser with an empty bucket scoops up the liquid in front of it.
Map	Crafted from 8 paper, 1 compass	When blank and being held, can be right-clicked to start using it, and to produce a sketch of the area around you, along with a marker showing your location; can be placed in an item frame and displayed To zoom out on a map, place it in the crafting grid with 8 papers around it to expand its size. Explore while holding a map to fill out undocumented areas.
Note block	Crafted from 8 wooden planks, 1 redstone dust	When powered (see Chapter 8) or left-clicked, plays a musical note The instrument that's played depends on the block beneath the note block: A wooden block makes a bass guitar sound, a sandy block is for the snare drums, a glassy block makes a click, the stone-based block is for the bass drum, and all others produce a light piano sound. Right-clicking a note block tunes up its pitch by a half-note, remaining within one octave; you can use power-ful mechanisms to play complex melo-dies with many of these blocks.
Piston	Crafted from 3 planks, 4 cobblestone, 1 iron ingot, 1 redstone dust	When powered (see Chapter 8), extends a pusher a single block in any direction, pushing as many as 12 blocks with it These pushers retract when the power source ceases. Pistons always face toward you as you place them. Pistons don't push certain blocks, such as obsidian, bedrock, chests, furnaces, or powered pistons.

Item	Find or Craft?	Description
Powered rail	Crafted from 6 gold ingots, 1 stick, 1 redstone dust (makes 6)	A special minecart rail that cannot round corners but usually brings passing minecarts to a halt; when powered (see Chapter 8), however, becomes a booster rail, speeding up passing minecarts and allowing them to move without much initial momentum
Redstone dust	Found when breaking redstone ore	The basis for redstone items; can be placed on the ground as wire (see Chapter 8)
Redstone lamp	Crafted from 1 glowstone, 4 redstone dust	Lights up when given redstone power, as described in Chapter 8
Redstone ore	Commonly found deep underground	An underground ore that provides redstone dust when broken; glows when disturbed
Redstone repeater	Crafted from 2 redstone torches, 1 redstone dust, 3 stone	Creates a delayed current, as described in Chapter 8
Redstone torch	Crafted from 1 redstone dust, 1 stick	Provides weak light and continuous redstone power; can be crafted into redstone repeaters, as described in Chapter 8
Sticky piston	Crafted from 1 piston, 1 slimeball	A specialized piston that, when retracted, can pull a block with it; useful for building reusable mechanisms and hidden doors

PE Minecraft has neither redstone nor redstone blocks.

Table 9-5 Diamond-Based Items

Item	Find or Craft?	Description
Diamond	Found when mining diamond ore; crafted from 1 block of diamond (makes 9)	A valuable, must-have material for the later stages of the game; without diamonds, can trade with a blacksmith (see Chapter 7) for diamond merchandise

(continued)

Table 9-5 *(continued)*

Item	*Find or Craft?*	*Description*
Diamond axe	Crafted from 3 diamonds, 2 sticks	Can be used to raze entire forests and grant you lots of materials quickly (Trees replanted with saplings ensure a source of nearby resources.)
Diamond block	Crafted from 9 diamonds	A prestigious and valuable item that shows off your wealth; must be stored where it can't be stolen
Diamond helmet, chestplate, leggings, boots	Crafted from 5, 8, 7, 4 diamonds, respectively	The strongest and most expensive set of armor in the game
Diamond hoe	Crafted from 2 diamonds, 2 sticks	A durable tool that's as efficient as any other (and may not be the best use of diamonds)
Diamond ore	Found deep underground, but rarely	The best ore you can find underground, providing a diamond when broken; should be collected whenever you see it (while watching for lava)
Diamond pickaxe	Crafted from 3 diamonds, 2 sticks	A powerful pickaxe that is the only one that can mine obsidian productively
Diamond shovel	Crafted from 1 diamond, 2 sticks	A fast-digging tool that levels out an area for construction
Diamond sword	Crafted from 2 diamonds, 1 stick	The best sword in the game and an invaluable resource against bosses
Enchantment table	Crafted from 4 obsidian, 2 diamonds, 1 book	Enchants items and makes them more powerful; see Chapter 10
Jukebox	Crafted from 8 planks, 1 diamond	A prestige item that plays music when right-clicked while holding a record; can be difficult to obtain if you're new to the game
Obsidian	By pouring water on lava or finding it in the End	An extremely hard material, used to make nether portals and enchantment tables

Table 9-6 Miscellaneous Wealthy Items

Item	*Find or Craft?*	*Description*
Emerald	Obtained from emerald ore or by selling items to villagers (see Chapter 8); crafted from 1 block of emerald (makes 9)	A form of currency used in villages, and the ingredient to create blocks of emerald
Emerald block	Crafted from 9 emeralds	An ornate, bright green decoration block
Emerald ore	Found underground in Extreme Hills biomes (see Chapter 5)	An unreliable but helpful source of emeralds
Lapis lazuli	Found when breaking lapis lazuli ore; crafted from 1 lapis lazuli block (makes 9)	A soft gem (often simply called *lapis*) that can be used as blue dye and crafted into lapis lazuli blocks
Lapis lazuli block	Crafted from 9 lapis lazuli	A deep blue decoration block
Lapis lazuli ore	Found deep underground	Drops lapis lazuli, your source of blue dye in Minecraft

Finding the Nether and End

During the Age of Wealth, you may also reach the Nether and the End, unlocking the items described in Table 9-7 (see Chapter 11 for more details). Many players go to the Nether as early as gameplay allows in order to obtain brewing ingredients and fire charges. They then return to the Nether and eventually to the End to gather other useful items.

Table 9-7 Nether and End Items

Item	*Find or Craft?*	*Description*
Bedrock	Appears at the bottom of the overworld, the top and bottom of the Nether, and occasionally in the End	Prevents players from leaving the bounds of the Minecraft world; despite being known for its indestructibility, easily obtainable and breakable in Creative mode
Blaze powder	Crafted from 1 blaze rod (makes 2)	A powerful material for making strength potions, magma cream, eyes of ender, or fire charges

(continued)

Table 9-7 *(continued)*

Item	*Find or Craft?*	*Description*
Blaze rod	By killing Blaze	Can be used as furnace fuel or crafted into brewing stands or blaze powder, as shown in Figure 9-5
Brewing stand	Crafted from 1 blaze rod, 3 cobblestone	Can be right-clicked to brew potions after placing it on the ground (see Chapter 10)
Cobweb	Found in abandoned mineshafts and strongholds	Slows down everything that passes through it except for cave spiders; provides a lot of string, however, as you hack through it
Dragon egg	Appears on the return portal in the End	A useless block that can teleport when right-clicked, falling randomly to the ground
End portal frame	Found in the Stronghold	A block in which the end portal appears whenever eyes of ender are placed into each slot
End stone	Makes up the End	A building block souvenir from the End; also one of the only blocks that the ender dragon cannot destroy
Ender chest	Crafted from 8 obsidian, 1 eye of ender	A powerful, unique chest in which you can place items to make them available to you and no other players in every ender chest in the Minecraft world; can be broken and rebuilt and *still* stores your items Multiple people can use the ender chest network, with each chest storing separate 27-space inventories for each player. Breaking an ender chest yields 8 obsidian, so you lose the eye of ender.
Eye of ender	Crafted from 1 blaze powder, 1 ender pearl	Can be thrown by right-clicking while holding it; drifts in the direction of the nearest Stronghold If the eye drifts downward, the Stronghold is close. You also need eyes of ender to fill the end portal frame and unlock the End.

Item	*Find or Craft?*	*Description*
Fire charge	Crafted from 1 blaze powder, 1 coal, 1 gunpowder (makes 3)	Can be loaded into a dispenser and fired as a flaming projectile; surfaces can be right-clicked to set them on fire at the cost of one charge per ignition
Ghast tear	By killing ghasts	Can be difficult to obtain if you kill a ghast at long range, but used to brew regeneration potions (see Chapter 10)
Glowstone block	Appears as stalactites in the Nether; crafted from 4 glowstone dust	A brightly glowing block and a useful light source that drops glowstone dust when broken; can be used to make redstone lamps
Glowstone dust	Appears when breaking glowstone blocks	A material used to empower potions (see Chapter 10) and make glowstone blocks at a slight deficit
Magma cream	By killing magma cubes; crafted from 1 blaze powder, 1 slimeball	Used to brew fire resistance potions, which can be useful in the Nether
Monster spawner	Found in dungeons and Nether fortresses, and in the Stronghold	Repeatedly spits out enemies, unless it hits a limit; can spawn zombies, spiders, skeletons, Blaze, and silverfish, depending on how they're used in the world; drops experience orbs when broken
Moss stone	Found in dungeons and jungle temples	Used primarily for building; considered a prestige item because of its rarity
Moss stone wall	Crafted from 6 moss stone (makes 6)	The mossy equivalent of a cobblestone wall
Mossy, cracked, chiseled stone brick	Mossy and cracked found in the stronghold; chiseled found in jungle temples	Rare variants of stone bricks; can be used as prestige items or crafted like all stone bricks
Nether brick	Makes up fortresses in the Nether	A darkly colored building block that can be turned into fences and stairs
Nether brick fence	Crafted from 6 nether bricks (makes 6)	A dark equivalent of wooden fences

(continued)

Table 9-7 *(continued)*

Item	*Find or Craft?*	*Description*
Nether brick stairs	Crafted from 6 nether bricks (makes 4)	The nether brick equivalent of stairs
Nether wart	Found in Nether fortresses	A farmable dark crop that grows only on soul sand (see Chapter 5); a must-have item for brewing potions
Netherrack	Makes up most of the Nether	A soft material that's easy to break; caught on fire at the top, continues to burn until manually extinguished
Soul sand	Makes up parts of the Nether	Slows down anything that walks over it; used to grow nether wart and build the wither
Wither skeleton skull	Occasionally, by killing wither skeletons	A skull that can be worn as a hat, placed as a decoration, or used to build the wither

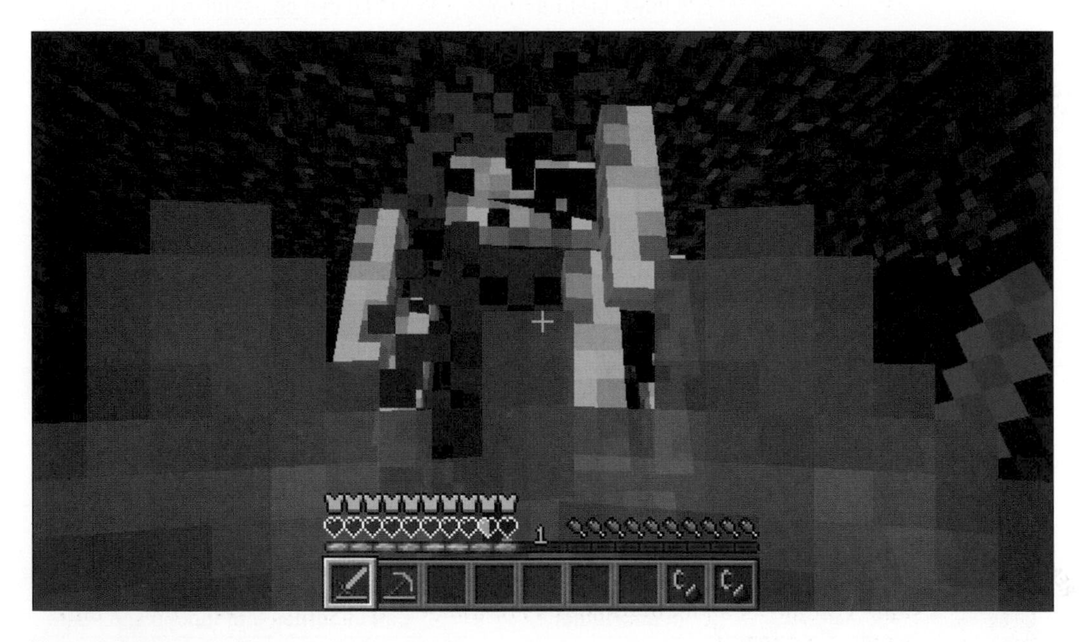

Figure 9-5: Fighting a blaze to gain blaze rod.

Coloring with dyes

To add a little color to your Minecraft world, experiment with the 16 dye colors described in Table 9-8. Dyes are largely decorative in Minecraft, but can also be helpful in contraption construction as a color code. Dyes are also applied to leather armor, banners, collars, wool, and directly to sheep. Carpets are commonly dyed and used in towering (see Chapter 19), as an alternative to a gate (see Chapter 5), and decoratively.

Table 9-8 Minecraft Dye Colors

Dye Color	*Dye*	*How to Get the Dye*
Black	Ink sac	Kill squids.
Blue	Lapis lazuli	Mine lapis lazuli ore.
Brown	Cocoa beans	Break cocoa bean pods.
Cyan	Cyan dye	Craft green + blue dye together.
Gray	Gray dye	Craft black + white dye together.
Green	Cactus green	Cook cacti in a furnace.
Light gray	Light gray dye	Craft white + gray or white + white + black dye together.
Light blue	Light blue dye	Craft white + blue dye together.
Lime	Lime dye	Craft green + white dye together.
Magenta	Magenta dye	Craft any of these combinations: purple + pink, red + blue + pink, or red + red + blue + white.
Orange	Orange dye	Craft red + yellow dye together.
Pink	Pink dye	Craft red + white dye together.
Purple	Purple dye	Craft red + blue dye together.
Red	Rose red	Craft it from 1 rose (makes 2).
White	Bone meal	Craft it from 1 bone (makes 3).
Yellow	Dandelion yellow	Craft it from 1 dandelion (makes 2).

When several dyes are combined in the crafting grid, the mixed dye has the same volume as all its ingredients combined. For example, red + blue + pink equals 3 magentas.

You can use dyes to paint these items:

- **Wool:** Place a block of white wool and a dye into the crafting grid to color it.

- **Leather armor:** Place a piece of leather armor, along with any number of dyes, into the crafting grid, to mix color into the armor and make clothing. Dye can be soaked out of armor by throwing the clothes into a cauldron of water. Ironically, you cannot dye leather, only leather armor.
- **Sheep:** Right-click a sheep while holding dye to color it! When two sheep breed, the baby will take on the color of the parents or a mixed color of the two parents. Sheep will also naturally spawn in black, white, gray, light gray, brown, and occasionally pink. Figure 9-6 shows the multicolored sheep farm we created.
- **Wolf collars:** Right-click a tamed wolf while holding dye to change the color of its collar.

Figure 9-6: Multicolored sheep farm.

Finding the Fun Stuff

Various other items appear in the game that don't logically fit elsewhere in this chapter. This is the fun stuff, which allows you to make your game more interesting, fun, and amusing. Play with a pig by dangling a carrot in front. Create your own cheats with command blocks. Dabble with fire. These are essentially the "toys" of the game! You may find the items described in Table 9-9 during your Minecraft adventure.

Table 9-9 Miscellaneous Items

Item	*Find or Craft?*	*Description*
Bottle o' enchanting	Occasionally available via trading	A potion that you throw by right-clicking (making it explode into a small amount of experience orbs when it hits the ground); can be fired from a dispenser
Carrot on a stick	Crafted from 1 fishing rod + 1 carrot	Can be used while riding a pig if you hold the right mouse button, causing the pig to charge in the direction you're facing; loses durability as the pig nibbles at it and eventually leaves the fishing pole empty when the carrot snaps off
Chainmail armor	Occasionally available via trading	Moderately powerful armor that's difficult to find for sale from a villager, making each piece a prestigious reward
Command block	Only obtainable via `/give`	The most technical block in the game; executes a cheat (see Chapter 12) when given redstone power (see Chapter 8); can be right-clicked to open the dialog box and set the cheat; usually used for custom maps and adventures
Fire	Found mostly in the Nether	A block, representing a burning surface, that can spread across blocks such as wood, leaves, and wool; often seen in the Nether, though trying to "break" it simply extinguishes it; can be created with flint and steel, fire charges, or the embers that bounce off lava blocks; can be added to the inventory, however, only via `/give` If you add fire blocks to the inventory and place fire in a crafting grid in the shape of armor, you can (oddly enough) craft chainmail.
Grass block	Appears on the surface of all grassy biomes	A separate block, available in Creative mode; spreads to other, nearby dirt

(continued)

Table 9-9 *(continued)*

Item	***Find or Craft?***	***Description***
Heads	Appears only in Creative mode	A quirky item that resembles the head of a mob; can be placed on the ground or worn as a hat to change the look of your head Creative mode offers five flavors: human, zombie, skeleton, creeper, and wither skeleton, though third-party programs can be used to retexture a head to look like anything you want. Only the wither skeleton skull is available in Survival mode (used to summon the wither).
Monster egg	Appears only in Creative mode, whenever a silverfish burrows into a block	A trap that contains silverfish waiting to pounce A silverfish that takes damage awakens nearby monster eggs, causing more to swarm; if you find a block of stone, cobblestone, or stone brick that seems breakable by hand, it has a silverfish inside.
Music disc	Yellow and green discs found rarely in dungeon chests; dropped when a skeleton kills a creeper	Can be used in the jukebox to play unique background music (except for the broken black disc, which holds a mysterious message); can be obtained by skilled players by luring skeletons into shooting creepers without exploding them Minecraft has 11 different discs at the time of this writing.
Mycelium	Makes up Mushroom Islands	A rare grass found in mushroom biomes (see Chapter 5); spreads onto grass and dirt Nothing can spawn on it except for mooshrooms.
Saddle	Found sometimes in dungeon chests; occasionally available via trading	Allows you to ride on the pig whenever you want by right-clicking it (while holding a saddle) If the pig dies, you can pick up the saddle to use later. The pig still follows its own interests while you're riding it, however, unless you have the next item in this list.

Item	Find or Craft?	Description
Spawn egg	Found only in Creative mode	One of many different types, each of which holds a different mob; causes a creature to spawn on a surface when you right-click while holding one; can also be placed in dispensers, causing mobs to pop out when the dispenser is powered To spawn a baby animal, right-click an animal while holding its corresponding spawn egg.
Sponge	Creative mode only	A decorative block that serves no purpose, but was used to soak up nearby water and lava (while Minecraft was still in the early development stage)

Starting Big Projects

As you progress through the game, you start to gain the resources you need to create bigger and bigger projects. Farming mobs or golems or farming other projects may be tasks that you focus on. The more time you spend on these bigger projects to collect loot and other items, the more advantage you have within the game.

Farming hostile mobs

A hostile mob is anything that attacks you without you interfering with them. Endermen, zombie pigmen, and wolves aren't hostile mobs. Considered neutral mobs, they attack you only if you attack them — or in the endermen's case, only if you look at their faces. Farming hostile mobs can be quite useful.

By containing certain mobs, you can spawn and kill them to collect their loot. Hostile mob farms work in two ways:

- A dark area where mobs spawn
- A type of killing system, often a steep drop causing hostile mobs to fall to their deaths

Other killing systems include drowning mobs, or using redstone contraptions — especially doors and pistons or hoppers, cacti, and a variety of other imaginative creations.

Mob farms can be created effectively on the surface, below ground, and in the ocean, as shown in Figure 9-7. Creating mob farms in the sky or the Nether is impractical. The exception to this rule is wither skeletons, ghasts, Blaze, and magma cubes, which can be farmed only in the Nether. Consequently, the Nether mobs are uncommon to farm.

Figure 9-7: Mob farm.

This list describes the most frequent types of hostile mob farms we have encountered:

- **Slime:** Slimes are special because they spawn only in certain chunks and swamp biomes. Slime farms, which are complicated to create, are best explained using web tutorials (you can find these by searching for "slime farms" on your favorite search engine, or on Youtube). Advanced players create slime farms (assuming that they can even find a slime chunk) to harvest slimeballs. Slime farms are becoming less common as slime abilities have increased in the latest Minecraft update.
- **Skeleton:** Skeletons are commonly farmed for their bones, to create bone meal used as fertilizer in crops. Some players use a dog (or even dog army) to exterminate skeletons.
- **Creeper:** The creeper is another difficult mob to farm. However, it drops gunpowder and is often farmed with another mob (either intentionally or unintentionally).

- **Zombie:** In a traditional farm, zombies drop only rotten flesh. Many players then trade that flesh for emeralds via a cleric villager. Consequently, you should create a zombie farm close to a village *or* bring a cleric villager next to your zombie farm. If you kill a zombie, you may also gather a wide array of items, including iron swords, ingots, and shovels, armor, carrots, and potatoes.
- **Zombie pigmen:** Technically a neutral mob, this valuable mob can be farmed for gold nuggets (and occasionally gold ingots or swords). This mob is farmed later in the game because it requires the presence of Nether portals.
- **XP:** Many players create mob farms to gain experience points, which are necessary for enchantments and anvil work (see Chapter 10). The only difficulty in this type of farm is that you have to kill mobs manually. A good design is to create a farm that causes some damage to the mob, weakening it so that the player can easily finish the job.
- **Other hostile types:** Include the nether monsters, enderman, witch, spiders, cave spiders, and silverfish. Witches are particularly useful because they can drop valuable potions, which you can normally create only after visiting the Nether (see Chapter 10).

Many mob farms are created by monster spawners, a cage-like block found in structures such as dungeons, abandoned mineshafts, Strongholds, and the nether fortress. Spawners create mobs in a surrounding area, assuming that the area is suitable for the mob. Spawners cannot be moved (without cheats), so you must create the mob farm where the spawner was found. Many players create this type of area and wall it off using water or torches and even encasing the top, allowing the mob to spawn in the dark middle but not escape.

Spawners can create other mobs using the `/setblock` command. For example, the following command creates a cow spawner:

```
/setblock <x> <y> <z> mob_spawner 0 replace {EntityId: "Cow"}
```

Farming golems

Some mobs appear only when you build them yourself, by stacking blocks on top of each other in a particular order. Minecraft has the three constructs described in this list (and shown in Figure 9-8):

- **Snow golem:** Spreads snow as it walks, throws snowballs at nearby hostiles, and explodes into snowballs when killed. Used in the snow farm; snow golems create an infinite amount of snow. If you encase the snow golem but make it so that you can access the snow on the ground, you can get infinite snow. You can then collect the snowballs by using a shovel.

Snow golems are created by placing 2 snow blocks on top of each other and then placing a pumpkin (or jack-o'-lantern) on top, creating a pumpkin-headed snowman.

- **Iron golem:** Lumbers after hostile mobs and blasts them into the air. This powerful golem can naturally spawn to protect villages and their inhabitants. But beware: It can attack you if angered. It drops poppies and iron when killed. To have one naturally spawn, you need at least 10 villagers, 21 houses, and no other iron golems in a 62 x 62 x 12 area. If the criteria are met, one spawns about every six minutes. The number of villagers (and the number of doors) doesn't affect the spawn rates.

  To create an iron golem farm, you can build an artificial village, causing iron golems to spawn. Start by building a 6 x 6 platform. Punch a 2 x 2 hole in the middle of the platform. Then build three high walls around the platform. On top of the three high walls, place at least 21 doors. Build another 6 x 6 platform on the top half of the doors. Make another three-block-high wall around this platform. Create another 2 x 2 hole in the middle of this platform. Make sure that the 2 x 2 holes are aligned. On the blocks next to the 2 x 2 hole, place 4 signs. Do this on both platforms, to stop the water from flowing into a death trap. Place water source blocks at the corners of both platforms. Then create a killing chamber, at least 4 blocks below the first spawning platform.

  Iron golems take no fall damage, so height isn't an issue. Create a little 1 x 4 x 2 pocket for villagers to stand on. It should be 1 block below the bottom part of the door. Finally, place two or more villagers into the pouch. After they're in, they begin breeding after you either trade with them or toss bread on the ground for them to pick up. Eventually, you get as many as ten villagers and can have the iron golems spawn naturally.

  Many players instead simply craft an iron golem by placing 4 blocks of iron into a T shape and then placing a pumpkin on top. Having enough iron for multiple projects (including iron weapons, tools, golems, and more) is necessary in the Iron Age in Minecraft gameplay.

  The iron and snow golem can be constructed only by placing the pumpkin last. If you place it earlier, the construct doesn't come to life.

- **Wither:** Appears as a boss and fights and attacks everything around it, including you. If you manage to defeat it, however, you can get a powerful item, the nether star. The nether star is used to craft the powerful beacon. (You can read more about beacons in Chapter 10.) Fighting the wither is relatively easy when it's in an enclosed area. While in an enclosed area, the wither cannot fly up, making it easier to defeat with a sword. The simplest enclosed area is a cave.

You create the wither by placing soul sand (an ingredient that's in short supply) in a T shape and then placing 3 wither skeleton skulls on top in a horizontal row. The wither isn't farmed in large quantities like other mobs, but is created exclusively by you.

The wither is harmful to the landscape around it. Fight the wither far away from your house, or summon it in the Nether or the End for extra safety.

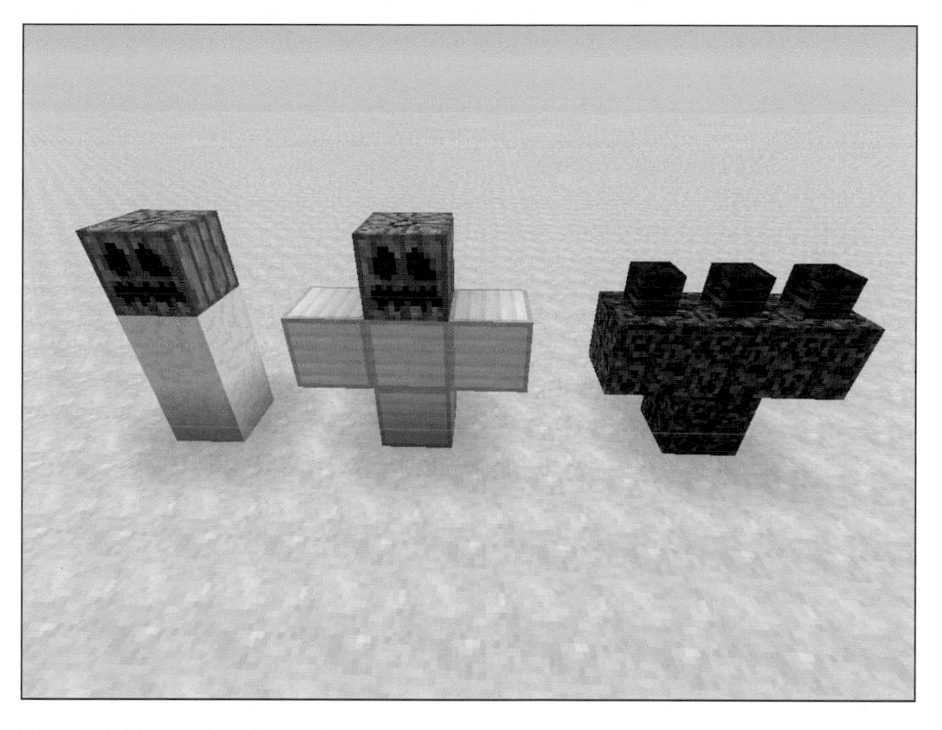

Figure 9-8: Snow golem, iron golem, and wither.

Exploring the block ages in Minecraft PE

The PE version of Minecraft progresses through these block stages a little differently from the PC version. Many blocks are simply unobtainable, including all redstone, saddles, and End items. The Iron Age is critical, as are the golden and diamond stages of the Age of Wealth.

Hunger doesn't exist in Minecraft PE, so farming is unnecessary except to collect ingredients such as wool from sheep.

Mob farming is almost unheard of, because XP farms don't exist. There are also no golem constructs. This chapter points to the reason that many players upgrade to the PC version eventually.

Building Transportation Systems

Transportation systems are critical in getting you from here to there quickly within the game of Minecraft. These systems can often be automated or even farmed (in the case of pigs and horses) to accomplish specific tasks automatically for you as you play the game.

Building boats

Boats move significantly faster than you can walk (yes, you can walk through water in Minecraft, but you must come up for air now and then or you'll drown), allowing you to move across large distances. Boats are invaluable in the ocean biome for this reason. Boats can be controlled by either water currents or you. Occasionally, you may store items in a boat, allowing the current to transport those items. Some players build elaborate canals or water elevators, often using doors as locks. However, most players favor minecarts or horses because they are faster. Boats also tend to be fragile and crash easily. Fortunately, a boat can always be broken back into oak wood by hitting the boat (regardless of what wood was used to craft it) and used.

Riding pigs and horses

Though pigs were once ridden for transportation, pig riding is now done almost exclusively for entertainment because the horse has become a much better option. To ride a pig, you must first saddle the pig and then craft a carrot on a stick. To obtain a saddle, you must find one in a chest (commonly, in a dungeon or blacksmith's shop), trade for one, or find one fishing. After you climb onto the saddle, the pig begins to eat the carrot and starts to run. Eventually, the carrot is completely eaten (shown as its Durability bar depletes). You can even access Boost mode, by right-clicking the carrot on a stick, though the carrot depletes faster. Because this sight is comical, players often race each other or even battle while mounted on their pigs in MultiPlayer mode.

The horse is the most common mode of transportation. It's faster than a minecart, without the hassle of gathering resources to create rail lines. Horses are complex and wild. First, you must tame one by right-clicking while empty-handed on the horse and mounting it repeatedly. You must then saddle the horse (pig and horse saddles are the same) in order to ride it.

Horses also have to be fed — usually wheat or apples — to maintain health points. The speed of the horse is determined by its own "genetic" ability. Because it's impossible to tell from the outside, many players continue to breed horses until they discover a fast one. Horses can also have armor, as shown in Figure 9-9. In addition to running, horses can jump. (Again, their jumping ability is genetic.)

Figure 9-9: A horse with saddle and armor.

Regular horses are faster than minecarts and can run faster when splashed with a speed potion. Horses are afraid of water, and they wander if they aren't tied with a lead when left unattended. Also, horses spawn only in plains and savannas. Still, the horse is considered the single best mode of transportation.

The donkey and mule, which are considered types of horses, cannot be ridden, but can carry chests filled with items, as shown in Figure 9-10. Many players therefore ride a horse and pull a chest laden donkey (or mule) using a lead. A donkey's chest has only 15 inventory slots.

Donkeys also need to be fed like horses.

Figure 9-10: A mule with a chest.

Transporting by way of minecarts

Minecarts are much faster than walking and are used to transport players and blocks (including mobs) over long distances. However, finding resources to build enough rails in Survival mode can be challenging. Many players switch to Creative mode to build their systems and then return to Survival mode. Also, minecarts are now commonly built as elaborate roller coasters. In Figure 9-11, Joseph (Thomas's brother) has built a roller coaster.

Minecarts lose speed over time and require booster rails that are created from redstone. (Redstone is described in depth in Chapter 8.) Minecarts can be connected to form a train. Also, special minecart cars can be created, including chest minecarts (with storage abilities), powered minecarts (which work like engines being fed coal and don't require booster rails), and TNT minecarts (portable bombs).

The minecart can be particularly useful underground as part of a major transportation system. It's also used to transport mobs easily, especially if you want to relocate a mob farm. You can also use minecarts in a complex redstone system either as a trap or to activate different contraptions.

Many players find that creating rail systems in mountainous terrain is somewhat difficult. Again, switching to Creative mode lets you experiment with different rail designs, to ensure that your minecart can safely navigate around curves and even fall off drops without causing damage.

Figure 9-11: Joseph's rollercoaster — note the minecart in midair!

PE Transportation

In Minecraft PE, the only modes of transportation are walking (not even sprinting) and minecarts, though the rail system is significantly simpler than the one in the PC version. Consequently, PE players often become minecart experts as they build practical transportation systems using traditional and powered (booster) rails. Unlike PC-powered rails, which can be powered on and off, PE-powered rails are always on, creating a booster effect to passing minecarts and increasing their speed.

Securing Your Base

As your base (once a simple house or hut) expands, you may want to protect it from other players (in MultiPlayer mode) or from hostile mobs. You can use a variety of methods.

To prevent hostile mobs from spawning, simply provide enough light at all times — commonly by using torches. Another method is to create a fence of cacti in a 2-row checkerboard pattern, as shown in Figure 9-12. Iron golems also make excellent patrol guards. Cobblestone is a better material than the highly flammable wood when building your base. To prevent spiders, create a lip at the top of the wall surrounding your base. Hide from skeletons using translucent blocks such as glass or fences. Because zombies can break down doors (in Hard mode), create doors that open and close with pistons (as discussed in Chapter 8).

Figure 9-12: Cacti fence.

To secure it from other players, you can try to hide your base by using terraforming (see Chapter 19). Another common technique is the booby trap, usually created from a pressure plate connected to TNT. More advanced players will try to build in extreme locations like at the bottom of the ocean or in the sky.

10

Powering Up

In This Chapter

- Enchanting weapons, tools, and armor
- Brewing potions
- Creating beacons

One of the most exciting parts of playing Minecraft is your ability to power up weapons, tools, armor, and even yourself. This chapter explores the complex but rewarding side of enchantments, brewing, and beacons.

Many of the items in this chapter can be achieved only after a player has collected resources in the Nether (see Chapter 11) and has earned a significant number of experience points (the little green bar above your inventory, earned by progressing through the game, killing mobs, collecting orbs, and other things). Alternatively, many players may find items already enchanted in chests, dungeons, or other structures (as shown in Chapter 7) or even find potions dropped from a witch, but cannot gain other powers until overcoming many obstacles in the game (like building a beacon). But don't get discouraged: After you have gathered all necessary resources, you will likely find enchantments and brewing to be rewarding experiences in Minecraft.

Enchanting Weapons, Tools, and Armor

To *enchant* means to add special powers to an item, making it more effective. For example, you can make a pickaxe mine faster or make a pair of boots that mitigates the damage inflicted by falling.

Enchantment tables, which are used to enchant items, are crafted from diamond, obsidian, and a book, as shown in Figure 10-1. (Each of these ingredients is somewhat rare and takes time to gather, unless you switch to Creative mode.) You generally need only one of these tables, which you place on the ground to begin enchanting. Don't worry about losing diamonds — enchantment tables are much too durable to be destroyed by creepers or other hazards.

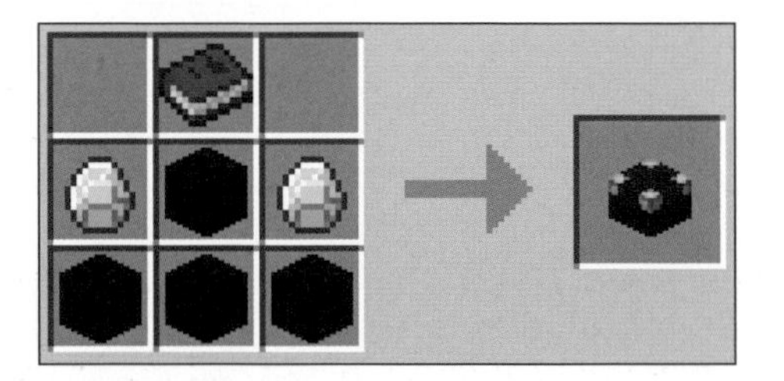

Figure 10-1: Enchantment table recipe.

Enchanting an item

After you create an enchantment table, follow these steps to enchant an item:

1. **Right-click the enchantment table to open the Enchant menu.**

   The Enchant menu, shown in Figure 10-2, consists of a square (where you can place the tool, weapon, or armor to enchant) and three tablet slots that show available enchantments.

   Figure 10-2: Enchant menu.

2. **Place in the square the item you want to enchant.**

   If the item can be enchanted, three tablets appear, each showing a green number (with the largest in the bottom row). This is the level of the enchantment — the green number above the Experience bar represents the number of levels you have to spend on enchantments. Tablets appear grayed-out when you don't have the necessary points to use them.

3. **Click an available tablet to ascribe (or place an enchantment upon) the selected item with a random enchantment.**

   The higher the number on the tablet, the higher the chance of getting a powerful enchantment!

Tablets can reach Level 30 to provide especially strong enchantments. Unfortunately, if the enchantment table is placed without bookshelves, you can't surpass Level 8. If you have a lot of experience orbs and want the best of the best, you have to power up the enchantment table.

To improve the enchantment table, you have to place bookshelves nearby. When a bookshelf is near an enchantment table, the table absorbs information from it and produces higher-level tablets. However, bookshelves have to be arranged in a certain way: As many as 32 of them can be placed around a single enchantment table, as shown in Figure 10-3.

Figure 10-3: Powerful enchantment table.

Only 15 of these bookshelves are required in order to access a Level 30 tablet, and you can subtract more if you lack experience orbs. However, to get 15 bookshelves, you have to harvest 135 sugar canes and kill approximately 45 cows. Ascribing low-level enchantments to some items while you get more bookshelves can be worthwhile.

Many players build houses large enough to hold their bookshelves and enchantment tables. Though enchantment tables are durable, bookshelves are not. Be a savvy player and build a house using quality materials, or build it underground (refer to Figure 10-3).

Using enchantments

When an item is enchanted, it shows the names of all its enchantments under the item label. Some enchantments are followed by Roman numerals (such as I, II, III, IV, or V), representing the level of that particular enchantment. Enchantments are passive and take effect when you use the enchanted item. Available enchantments are detailed in Tables 10-1 through Table 10-4.

Table 10-1 Enchantments: Pickaxe, Axe, Shovel

Enchantment	*Possible Levels*	*Effect*
Efficiency	I, II, III, IV, V	The tool breaks blocks much faster than a normal tool.
Unbreaking	I, II, III	The tool is more durable and can break more blocks before it shatters.
Fortune	I, II, III	Any block that cannot be replaced when broken, such as diamond ore and melon blocks, has a chance of giving up extra loot. Gravel has a better chance of providing flint when broken.
Silk touch	I	This special enchantment lets you obtain any block you break as an item, even if it would normally drop another item, such as coal ore or stone. A silk touch item cannot be enchanted with fortune at the same time, and it cannot harvest certain blocks such as monster spawners.

Table 10-2 Enchantments: Sword

Enchantment	*Possible Levels*	*Effect*
Sharpness, smite, bane of arthropods	I, II, III, IV, V	These enchantments boost the sword's damage and cannot be active at the same time. Smite deals extra damage to the undead, and the bane of arthropods deals extra damage to bugs. Sharpness inflicts slightly less extra damage.

Enchantment	*Possible Levels*	*Effect*
Knockback	I, II	Attacking an entity with this enchantment knocks it backward much farther than in a normal attack.
Looting	I, II, III	Enemies you slay with this sword can drop more items, and have a higher chance of rewarding you with rare items.
Fire aspect	I, II	Enemies you hit with this sword are lit on fire and take constant damage over time.

Table 10-3 Enchantments: Armor

Enchantment	*Possible Levels*	*Effect*
(Fire/blast/projectile) protection	I, II, III, IV	Only one protection enchantment at a time can be used, and it increases the defensive capacity of the armor. Four types of this enchantment can guard you against burning, explosions, or ranged weapons — the classic "protection" enchantment protects against all damage.
Respiration (helmet only)	I, II, III	You can hold your breath underwater much longer while wearing this helmet.
Aqua affinity (helmet only)	I	Normally, you break blocks much more slowly while underwater. You can mitigate this effect by wearing this helmet.
Feather falling (boots only)	I, II, III, IV	These boots let you take less damage from falling.

Table 10-4 Enchantments: Bow

Enchantment	*Possible Levels*	*Effect*
Power	I, II, III, IV	Arrows fired by this bow inflict bonus damage.
Punch	I, II	This bow is extra strong, knocking its targets backward.
Flame	I	Arrows fired by this bow are ignited and can set targets on fire, inflicting damage over time.
Infinity	I	This bow doesn't consume ammunition, so you can use it as long as you have at least one arrow. You can't retrieve arrows fired by this bow.

Some powerful enchantments have several of these effects. For example, you might obtain a pickaxe with Efficiency IV, Unbreaking II, and Fortune I. You can combine enchanted items using an anvil if you didn't get the enchantment you want and you want to improve it.

Repairing things on the anvil

The anvil can repair, combine, and name items. You can always place two damaged tools in the crafting grid to combine their durability, but the anvil can do a lot more. Place an anvil on the ground and right-click it to open the menu, as shown in Figure 10-4.

To repair a tool, weapon, or piece of armor, place it in the leftmost slot on the menu. In the middle slot, you can add base materials. (To repair wood, you need planks; similarly, you can use leather, cobblestone, iron ingots, gold ingots, or diamonds.) In exchange for some experience levels (indicated by the green number that appears at the bottom of the screen after you find a certain number of experience orbs), you can increase the durability of a damaged item. Each material can repair only 25 percent of the durability of the item. Enchanted items remain enchanted.

In addition, you can place a second item of the same type in the middle slot on the screen to "combine" the items. This action deducts more experience orbs than the normal repair action, but it can combine enchantments and make them even more powerful. Also, certain items cannot be repaired using a raw material, including bows and shears. They can be repaired only by placing a sacrifice item in the second slot. The sacrifice item must match the target item exactly. For example, an iron sword cannot be repaired with a golden sword. Unlike raw materials, which can increase durability by only 25 percent, combining two items using an anvil adds the durability of the two items together and then adds a 12 percent bonus. However, the durability can never reach more than 100 percent. Unless a player is seeking primarily to combine enchantments, it would be a poor use of resources to combine items with durability over 50 percent.

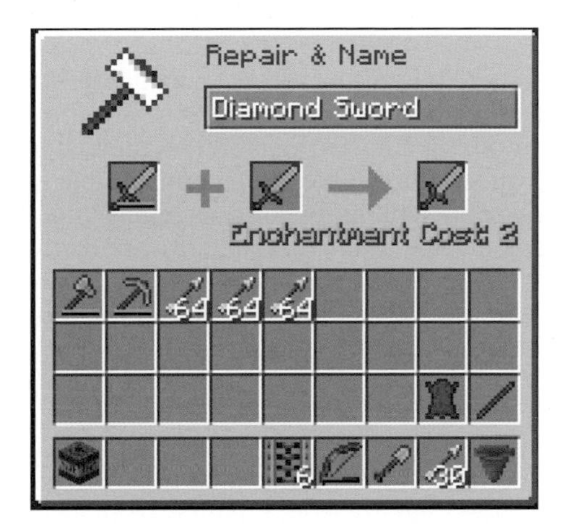

Figure 10-4: The Anvil menu.

To determine what a final repaired (or combined) item will look like, simply place the target item in the first slot and the sacrifice item (or material) in the second slot. The final item is displayed on the far right end, assuming that you have enough experience levels (or are playing in Creative mode). If you choose to complete the repair (therefore giving up the sacrifice item and experience points), simply place the final item into the inventory slot, finishing the anvil repair.

Rather than place a raw material or sacrifice item, you can place an enchantment book in the sacrifice slot, transferring enchantment to the target object. Two enchantment books can also be combined to create a higher-level enchanted book.

Not all enchantments can be combined. Those that are considered contradictory or too similar cannot be combined, such as fortune with silk touch.

Anvils lose durability over time by repairing items (or by taking fall damage). Intentionally dropping anvils, though effective in killing mobs and producing a comical sight in Creative mode, is generally not a good use of iron in Survival mode. An anvil can repair approximately 25 items before losing durability.

Crafting an anvil requires 31 iron ingots. A complete set of iron armor requires only 24 iron ingots.

Finally, when you place any item in the leftmost slot, its name appears at the top — you can change it to whatever you want at the cost of a level. Your diamond sword can become Excalibur, for example, or a stack of saplings can become Minitree 6000s.

The name tag, a special item in Minecraft, works with an anvil. Name tags are found in dungeon chests, from fishing, or by trading with librarians. Name tags are fairly rare. After you obtain a name tag, you can place it into the anvil and give it a name (similar to renaming an item). The name tag can then be applied to a mob. In addition to naming mobs for amusement, named mobs don't despawn, even when a player is some distance from the mob.

Only hostile mobs despawn, so the name tag advantage is limited to hostile mobs. All mobs — even villagers — can be named except ender dragons and players.

Be on the lookout for a few Easter egg name tags. The two most common are Dinnerbone and Grumm, which make a mob turn upside-down, as shown in Figure 10-5. When naming a sheep Jeb, its wool changes from a single color into a rainbow. A rabbit named Toast changes its skin texture to a white-with-black spotted bunny.

Figure 10-5: The name tag Grumm creates a horse that runs upside-down.

Brewing Potions

Brewing potions is another faculty available to you as you progress in Minecraft. After you obtain a blaze rod, a difficult item achieved in the Nether (see Chapter 11), you can craft it with cobblestone to make a *brewing stand,* as shown in Figure 10-6. This item is used to mix and set potions, which you can drink or throw to cause various effects.

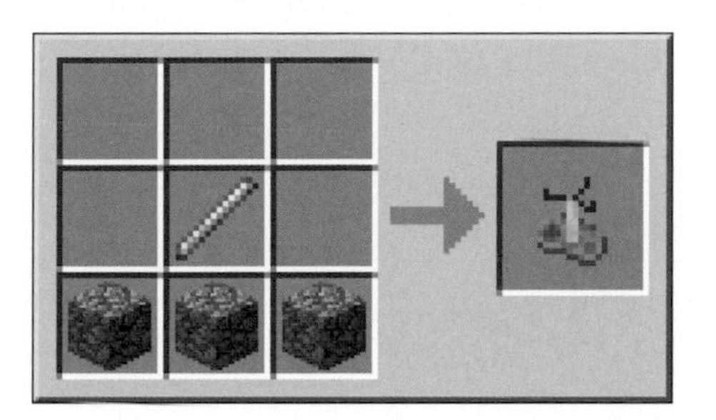

Figure 10-6: Brewing stand recipe.

To create a considerable number of potions, you need a good supply of glass blocks, a water supply, and nether wart. You can craft glass by smelting sand in a furnace, and you can find nether wart in nether fortresses and farm it, as explained in Chapter 5. If you place the brewing stand in the Nether, you should take buckets of water in the inventory. Glass bottles filled with water do not stack.

Build the brewing stand near your nether wart farm so that you can get all the nether wart you need while you need it.

If you're brewing negative potions, you need a large supply of fermented spider eyes. It takes time in the game to defeat enough spiders (or cave spiders) to gather this ingredient.

Brewing basic potions

Each potion begins by making a base potion and then adding an ingredient to create an active potion. Additional ingredients can be added to make a potion more intense, last longer, or turn negative. Finally, gunpowder can be added to create a splash potion.

To brew potions, follow these steps (and see Figure 10-7):

1. **Craft glass into bottles, and then right-click a water source or a cauldron to fill them with water.**

   These bottles can be brewed into potions. Craft enough bottles to make all the potions you want. A cauldron runs out of water quickly — a more effective option is a water block or buckets of water.

2. **Right-click the brewing stand and place some water bottles in the slots.**

   Because each ingredient yields 3 bottles worth of potion, a savvy brew master always brews in groups of 3, for maximum efficiency.

Figure 10-7: Brewing menu.

3. **Add the base ingredient.**

   You usually add nether wart as the base ingredient, but you can add a fermented spider eye if you want to make only a potion of weakness (described later in this section). When nether wart is added to water bottles, the result is an awkward potion.

4. **Add the secondary ingredients.**

   If you used nether wart, the water bottles turn into awkward potions, which have no effect. However, you can keep these potions on the brewing stand and add more ingredients to give them the characteristics you need; see Table 10-5.

Table 10-5 Basic Potions

Ingredient	*Potion*	*Effect*
Glistering melon	Potion of healing	Some health is restored.
Blaze powder	Potion of strength	You inflict more damage under this effect.
Ghast tear	Potion of regeneration	Your health rapidly regenerates.
Sugar	Potion of swiftness	You can run much faster.
Magma cream	Potion of fire resistance	You take much less damage from fire. This potion is a good one to use while fighting Blaze.
Golden carrot	Potion of night vision	You can see much better in the dark.
Spider eye	Potion of poison	Damage is dealt to you over time; it's useless for now.
Fermented spider eye	Potion of weakness	Your attack power is reduced temporarily; it's useless for now.
Pufferfish	Potion of water breathing	You do not lose oxygen bar points when underwater.
Rabbit's foot	Potion of leaping	You can jump half a block higher.

Some of the figures in this book were produced by using the night vision potion (brewed from a golden carrot). To see how this effect looks, refer to Figure 7-10, over in Chapter 7.

Using potions

To use a potion, select the potion and hold down the right mouse button to drink it. Though potions of healing have an instantaneous effect, others can last for a couple of minutes. Any potion effects that you might have are shown when you open the inventory screen.

If you're afflicted with an effect such as wither or weakness, which can be dangerous, drink a bucket of milk to cleanse all potion effects. You can obtain milk by selecting a bucket and right-clicking a cow.

Modifying potions

After you brew some potions, you may want to modify their effects. You can brew four different ingredients into the potions to modify them:

- **Redstone dust:** Increases the duration of a non-instantaneous potion, allowing you to retain its effects for a long time. It cancels out the effects of glowstone, described in the next bullet.
- **Glowstone dust:** Makes potions stronger and more effective, if possible. It cancels out the effects of redstone (see Figure 10-8).

Figure 10-8: Potion of strength.

- **Gunpowder:** Turns potions into *splash potions*, which have a differently shaped bottle, and you can throw these potions by right-clicking. When a splash potion hits an object, it explodes, applying the potion's effect to everything nearby. If you have a harmful potion such as poison, turn it into a splash potion and throw it at your enemies! Unfortunately, throwing a splash potion destroys the bottle. See the "Brewing splash potions" section, later in this chapter, for more information.
- **Fermented spider eye:** Used on a potion with a positive effect, reverses it, as explained in the next section.

Brewing negative potions

In addition to the helpful potions described earlier in this chapter, Minecraft has a whole class of negative potions, which generally have a negative effect. You can make and use negative potions by adding a fermented spider eye to potions, as described in Table 10-6. Fermented spider eyes are crafted by placing a spider eye, sugar, and a brown mushroom anywhere on the crafting grid.

Table 10-6 Brewing Negative Potions

Negative Potion	*Reagent*	*Effect*
Potion of slowness	Potion of swiftness or fire resistance	You walk much slower.
Potion of harming	Potion of healing or poison	This potion instantly deals damage.
Potion of weakness	Potion of strength or regeneration or leaping	This potion reduces your attack power. However, you can brew it by simply adding a fermented spider eye to a water bottle.
Potion of invisibility	Potion of night vision	You become invisible, and you cannot be seen by anything unless you're wearing armor.
Potion of poison	Awkward potion	You are poisoned, damaging your health hearts.

As with other potions, you can modify these potions with redstone, glowstone, or gunpowder. As Tables 10-5 and 10-6 show, Minecraft has more types of positive potions than negative ones. To achieve a certain negative potion such as weakness, you can choose from more than one brewing recipe. Players should determine which ingredients are easiest and brew accordingly.

The potion of invisibility is considered desirable by many players. It's considered a negative potion only because it's the *corrupt* version: It's brewed by adding a fermented spider eye to a positive potion, of the night vision potion. When the invisibility potion is used, the player becomes invisible to other players and mobs. Beware: If you're wearing armor, you can still be seen.

You can brew a potion of weakness by simply placing a fermented spider eye into the top of the brewing stand with water bottles below, creating an active potion with no additional ingredients.

Brewing splash potions

Of course, some potions seem fairly useless because their effect on you is negative. When you use a splash potion, you can instantly apply potions to anything you want. Simply brew gunpowder into any potion and it becomes a powerful projectile that you can throw by selecting it and right-clicking.

Splash potions are useful for a number of reasons, including these:

- If you craft splash potions of healing, you can throw them on the ground to instantly heal yourself (and everything around you).
- You can throw splash potions of slowness into a group of enemies to make a quick escape or use potions of harming to bring them down.

All undead mobs, such as zombies and skeletons, are immune to poison, and potions of harming only heal them. If an undead is nearby, use a splash potion of healing to hurt the undead and heal yourself.

Splash potions can also be thrown using a dispenser (see Chapter 8).

Reverting potions

When you revert a potion, you downgrade a strong potion into a weaker version of that potion. Because glowstone and redstone cancel each other out, a simple way to revert many potions is simply to add either glowstone or redstone, or whichever ingredient was not used in the creation of the potion.

Brewing order

The order of ingredients in Minecraft matters significantly. If nether wart is not added as the first ingredient to the water bottles, the only potion that can result is ultimately a potion of weakness (created after a fermented spider eye is added).

Fighting witches and potions

You can clearly see the effects of potions when you fight witches. These enemies, who are difficult to beat, live in huts in the swamp (see Figure 10-9). When they take damage, they drink potions of regeneration, and they use potions of fire resistance to avoid burning. They also throw an assortment of splash potions at you to weaken, poison, slow, and damage you. However, if you defeat a witch, she drops an assortment of potion reagents, including the occasional nether wart. Witches are detailed in Chapter 5.

Figure 10-9: A witch, outside her hut.

Building the Beacon

One of the most powerful items in Minecraft is the beacon. It can be created only after defeating the wither, which yields a *nether star.* A player must first go to the Nether, as shown in Chapter 11, and then create and defeat a wither, as shown in Chapter 9. To make a beacon (see Figure 10-10), you need these items:

- 3 obsidian
- 5 glass
- 1 nether star

After placing the beacon on the ground, make a solid pyramid of metal blocks (blocks of iron, gold, diamond, or emerald) beneath it; though the simplest one is a single 3 x 3 square, various other setups are shown in Figure 10-10. When you finish, the beacon automatically sends a light beam into the sky. The beam is white unless you used stained glass, which changes the light to the color of the glass. The larger the pyramid, the greater the power of the beacon. The largest pyramid is built from 164 blocks with a 9 x 9 layer on the bottom, a 7 x 7 layer next, a 5 x 5 later after that one, and then a 3 x 3 layer on the top. However, unless you're playing in Creative mode, it's nearly impossible to find enough gold, diamond, or emeralds to create the largest pyramid.

Figure 10-10: Setting up a beacon.

The cheapest way to build a beacon is by using iron blocks, but you can use gold, diamond, or emerald if you're feeling artistic. At the time of this writing, you gain no advantage by using more powerful minerals. Minerals can be mixed to create the pyramid. Players with vast resources often create pyramids using an alternating pattern for added aesthetics.

The purpose of the high-end and powerful beacon is to provide bonus powers to all nearby players. For example, a beacon might allow all players within a radius to run faster or to absorb less damage.

To make the beacon work, right-click it to open the Beacon menu. You see five primary power icons and one secondary power icon. You can select only one primary power and one secondary power, and you can select a power only if you have built a large enough pyramid beneath the beacon.

The required size of the pyramid is shown in the image next to each icon, as shown in Figure 10-11 and described in Table 10-7. The icons and powers on the Beacon menu are explained in Table 10-7.

After you have selected a primary power (and a secondary power, if the pyramid is large enough), place an iron ingot, a gold ingot, a diamond, or an emerald in the slot provided, and click the green check mark. The beacon constantly powers you as long as you're in its range (from 20 to 50 blocks, depending on the size of the pyramid). If you want to switch powers, a new gem (iron or diamond, for example) must be fed into the beacon using the GUI.

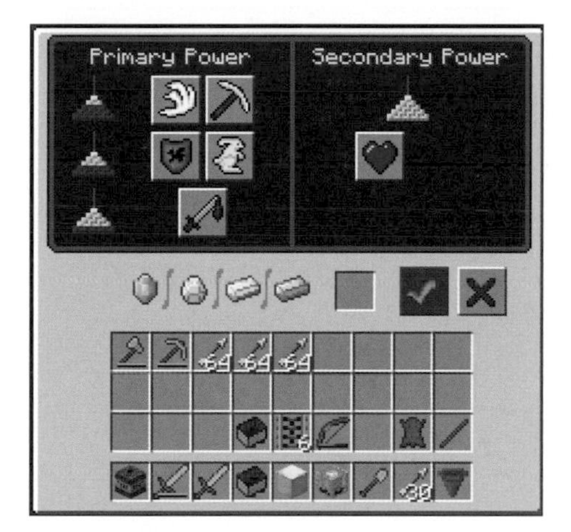

Figure 10-11: Using the Beacon GUI menu.

If you want your beacon to rest on the ground, build your pyramid underground.

Beacons require an unobstructed view of the sky above them (or they can have transparent blocks above beacons in the Nether). The beacon beam fades as it reaches higher into the sky and is practically invisible in the Nether. More commonly, a beacon beam is strong enough to create a large landmark and is highly visible.

Table 10-7 Beacon Icons and Powers

Icon	*Name*	*Ability*	*Pyramid Level*
	Speed	Increased movement	Level 1
	Haste	Increased mining speed	Level 1
	Resistance	Increased armor rating	Level 2
	Jump Boost	Increases jump height and distance	Level 2
	Strength	Increased melee damage	Level 3
	Regeneration	Regenerates heart health	Level 4 and can be combined with any one other power

Beacons can be powerful in MultiPlayer mode because more than one player can benefit from the powers of a single beacon. Also, players can share resources in constructing a larger pyramid beacon, as shown in Figure 10-12.

Figure 10-12: Two players with haste power from the same beacon.

11

Advancing to the Nether, the End, and Beyond

In This Chapter

- Surviving the Nether
- Conquering the End
- Exploring Hardcore mode

As you pursue your own, open-ended goals, eventually you will want to use the ingredients and resources found only in the Nether. Some players come to the Nether as quickly as possible and return later, as their skills improve. Others stay in the overland world to build, mine, and farm and only visit the Nether much later in the gameplay. Beyond the Nether lies the End, and then more difficult survival modes such as difficult and hardcore. Even experienced players can take a while to complete the tasks outlined in this chapter.

Reaching the Nether

A major step in Minecraft is building the portal that transports you from the classic overworld into the *Nether* dimension — a dangerous place with an interesting new set of blocks and monsters. To unlock more items — and reach the next stage of the game — you have to reach the Nether.

Building a portal

Building your first nether portal requires a source of water and lava, as well as a flint and an iron ingot. Follow these general steps to build one, as shown in Figure 11-1:

1. **Get at least 10 obsidian blocks, which are formed by pouring water over still lava (as explained in Chapter 9).**

   The incredibly hard block of *obsidian* is breakable only by a diamond pickaxe. To mix some obsidian, select one of these options:

   a. *Craft a bucket by using iron ingots.*

   b. *Right-click water or lava to pick it up.*

   c. *Right-click to replace a liquid; place both liquids on top of each other to make obsidian.*

   d. *Mine the obsidian with a diamond pickaxe or simply mix it directly into the frame (as detailed in Step 2).*

Figure 11-1: The Nether and its portal.

2. **Build an obsidian frame that encloses a rectangle 2 blocks wide and 3 blocks high or greater.**

   This step requires 14 obsidian blocks (or 10, if you skip the corners).

3. **Light the interior.**

   Now you have only a hollow black rectangle. To turn it into a portal, you give the interior a little spark. The easiest way to do so is to craft flint and steel from an iron ingot and a flint (sometimes dropped from gravel blocks). Right-clicking surfaces with flint and steel lights them on fire, but reduces the lighter's durability. Right-click the interior of the frame with the flint and steel to fill it with purple smoke. This smoke is a portal to the Nether.

To use the portal, stand inside the frame until the screen fades into purple. You will soon appear in the Nether next to a second portal that can take you home.

Surviving the Nether

The *Nether* is a huge, cave-like landscape made mostly of *netherrack*, a weak reddish stone. *Soul sand,* a block that slows your avatar, is found in large patches along with gravel. The floor of the Nether is covered in a huge lava lake, and the ceiling contains shining stalactites made of glowstone. Clusters of nether quartz are mixed with the netherrack, and it's the only ore found in the Nether.

During your visit to the Nether, try to find a *nether fortress* — a giant structure, made of red bricks, that resembles a broken castle. Powerful enemies appear in the fortress, but these enemies are also the key to the Stronghold, the next stage of the game.

The following list describes enemies you may confront in the Nether:

- **Zombie pigman:** Despite its frightening appearance, this creature wants nothing to do with you. If you attack one, however, every other zombie pigman in sight will rush toward you, inflicting a considerable amount of damage with their swords. Killing a zombie pigman yields rotten flesh, gold nuggets, and occasionally, other gold items.

  How to fight it: Ensure that the group cannot surround or corner you, and try to defeat them one at a time.

  TECHNICAL STUFF

  If you kill a zombie pigman in a single hit, the others will not turn on you. However, you can kill a zombie pigman in a single blow only by using a diamond sword enchanted with Sharpness V and with a Strength II beacon. Both items are extremely difficult to acquire. See the official Minecraft wiki for more details on killing zombie pigmen.

  Though not common, a variant of this mob spawns the pigman chicken jockey — a baby zombie pigman riding a chicken. If the pigman rider is killed, the chicken acts as a normal chicken that lives only in the Nether. This mob is not immune to fire.

- **Ghast:** This airborne, white jellyfish is dangerous. It tries to elude you while spitting explosive fireballs. A single battle with a ghast can turn a patch of netherrack into a burning wasteland. Ghasts drop both gunpowder and ghast tears. Gunpowder is necessary to make TNT, but is commonly acquired from creepers, whereas ghast tears are used in potions (described in Chapter 10) and can be obtained only from a ghast.

  How to fight it: Attack its tentacles with a bow and arrow, or hit the fireballs to reflect them back at the ghast. Also note that ghasts cannot destroy hard blocks such as cobblestone.

- **Magma cube:** This fiery, red cube hops after you, inflicting damage on impact. Step back after killing a large one — it splits into smaller magma cubes. Only tiny cubes drop items, and they provide magma cream, which is used in brewing potions (see Chapter 10). The magma cube is something like a fiery version of a slime.

  How to fight it: Attack it immediately after it jumps to outmaneuver it.

- **Wither skeleton:** This darker version of the skeletons outside the Nether patrol nether fortresses with their stone swords. Don't let one of them reach you! Its sword causes you to *wither* for a short time, which slowly drains the Health bar and (unlike poison) potentially kills your avatar. Wither skeletons can sprint (unlike most mobs) and are immune to fire. They commonly drop bones and coal, but the real treasure is the rare drop of their wither skeleton skull. (It's used to summon a wither that, when defeated, provides the nether star that's used to craft the powerful beacon.) Occasionally, regular skeletons spawn in the Nether, and they are not fireproof.

  How to fight it: Because the wither skeleton appears mostly in nether fortresses, be sure to fight it in a long passageway, where it can't corner you. A bow and arrow work well. Also, because a wither skeleton is 3 blocks high (remember that a player is only 2 blocks high), you can trap it by escaping through a door that's 2 blocks high.

  A spider and a wither skeleton may spawn (though rarely) in close proximity, and a wither jockey is created. This extremely rare mob is a wither skeleton riding a spider — try defeating that!

- **Blaze:** This floating, fiery construct surrounds the watchtowers of the nether fortress. The watchtowers have burning, metal grates that constantly create new Blaze. This block is a type of spawner. You can break this spawner with a pickaxe, but you need Blaze in order to obtain certain items. When a Blaze begins to emit fire, it is preparing to throw a triple-fireball attack that's incredibly dangerous. Upon death, it drops useful blaze rods, needed in creating a brewing stand, and when converted to blaze powder, is used to craft the eye of ender, brew potions, and craft a fire charge.

  Blaze are used in Blaze XP farms because Blaze drop double the amount of experience of other mobs, such as zombies (see Chapter 9).

  How to fight them: Kill Blaze as fast as possible and don't let them trap you under heavy fire. You can hurt Blaze by throwing snowballs at them! You can also resist them by using fire-resistance potions (as mentioned in Chapter 10).

Other mobs can walk into the Nether using the same portal you used. Also, you can build iron golems and summon the wither in the Nether, though snow golems melt within seconds after being created.

Finding the Stronghold

After you're familiar with the Nether, you may go back and forth between the Nether and the overworld, gathering resources to continue building, mining, farming, trading, brewing, and undergoing other adventures in Minecraft.

When you're back in the overworld, your next major step in Minecraft is to head toward the Stronghold. This huge, underground structure, which appears in the overworld, contains the end portal — the passage to the final dimension.

Unfortunately, the Stronghold is generally difficult to find — you need resources from the Nether to detect it. Follow these steps to find the Stronghold:

1. **Collect ender pearls.**

   These items are dropped by endermen, and used for teleportation. You may have to explore during the night to find some. It's hard to tell how many ender pearls you need, so collect a few and complete these steps, and then go back for more pearls if you don't have enough to teleport where you need to.

2. **Collect blaze powder.**

   Kill some Blaze in the Nether to obtain blaze rods, which can be crafted into powder. You need at least as much blaze powder as ender pearls.

3. **Craft the blaze powder and ender pearls into eyes of ender.**

   Place one of each item on the crafting grid, in any order.

4. **Select an eye of ender and then right-click to throw it.**

   The eye of ender drifts into the sky, angled in the direction of the Stronghold. If the eye moves forward, for example, the Stronghold lies ahead.

5. **Follow the eye of ender to move toward the Stronghold. Continue to throw eyes until they begin floating down instead of up.**

   After the eye of ender has hovered for a while, it either drops back down to be used again or shatters. Craft several eyes and follow them toward the Stronghold. It may take a significant length of time to gather enough blaze rods and ender pearls to craft multiple eyes of ender.

6. **When the eyes begin floating down, dig, dig, dig to find the Stronghold.**

After you reach the Stronghold, you fall into a ruined stone chamber with a white-and-green frame in the center. The room also contains a fiery grating that spawns silverfish (an ugly bug that's described in Chapter 5). Use a pickaxe to break this grating and then approach the green frame. (It would contain the end portal, but it's broken.) To repair and activate the end portal, use 12 more eyes of ender to fill in each empty slot in the frame, as shown in Figure 11-2.

Figure 11-2: End portal.

Playing PE Minecraft — the Nether

The PE edition of Minecraft has no Nether, but it does have an alternative — the nether spire. The nether spire is the unofficial name of what is often thought of as simply the Nether in Minecraft PE, though it differs greatly from the PC version.

To create (rather than transport) the nether spire, you need to build the nether reactor: It involves 4 gold blocks, 1 nether reactor core, and 14 cobblestone.

1. **Place 5 cobblestone blocks to create a T shape. Then place 4 gold blocks, 1 on each corner.**
2. **Place a nether reactor core in the center square (crafted from diamond and iron ingot). Then place 4 cobblestone blocks, 1 on each corner.**
3. **Place 5 cobblestone blocks on the top, forming another T shape that's identical to the one on the bottom layer.**

After the nether reactor core is built, simply right-click the nether reactor core, and the nether spire will generate. The reactor turns to obsidian (with the exception of the core). It begins to spawn an amazing number of blocks, so have the inventory empty and ready.

If you build the reactor too high, it won't work. If you're playing with multiple players, all players must be near the reactor core in order to activate.

You also need to be at or above ground level and build the reactor at least 3 blocks above water (if you're building it above water). If the conditions of building are successfully met, the word: "Active!" displays on the chat screen.

Instantly, the nether spire is generated, destroying any blocks in its path, in addition to the blocks that spawn and drop to the ground. The spire is composed of nether rack, with multiple levels and floors. Inside, zombie pigmen spawn (if the difficulty level is set high enough in Survival mode). These zombie pigmen are always hostile, unlike in the PC version, where they are a neutral mob. Also, the zombie pigmen in PE mode get hurt in sunlight. When killed, they drop valuable gold and feathers.

After the reactor is active, the reactor core changes to red. The whole process of activating the reactor lasts for 45 seconds. Then the reactor turns into obsidian, and the reactor core burns out. You can mine out the core and it gives you a fresh reactor core. Additionally, the spire crumbles and breaks leaving gaps between the nether rack spire. To prevent it from crumbling, you can mine out the reactor core and gold blocks. If you interrupt the reactor, you're cursed with eternal nighttime. Luckily, no hostile mobs spawn in the night. Sleeping in a bed turns your world to daytime, but after 20 seconds pass, nighttime starts to fade in again. To fix this problem, just log out and log back in.

The spire is a huge structure — do not activate the reactor in your house or else it will destroy your house!

Conquering the End

If you're playing in PC mode, you should have by now found the end portal by digging into a Stronghold using ender peals as a guide. Don't jump into the end portal just yet — you face a battle when you enter, and you must be prepared for it. Explore the Stronghold and find items in treasure chests. Get a sword, a bow with sufficient ammunition, and some blocks. Also, take safety precautions by placing a storage chest and bed near the portal. Many players enchant their weapons and armor before entering the End (see Chapter 10). You also need to bring a variety of less common weapons, including a pumpkin to use as a mask, snowballs, and eggs (especially if arrows are in limited supply).

Drop off any unnecessary valuables before entering the End so that you don't lose them, and don't be afraid to delay your entry for a while.

When you're ready, you can jump into the portal. You're immediately transported to *the End* — a dimension, smaller than the Nether, that consists of a few floating platforms, as shown in Figure 11-3.

Figure 11-3: The End.

You immediately notice these elements of the End:

- **Endermen:** The place is full of these creatures, as mentioned in Chapter 2. You don't want a swarm of them on your heels, so don't look at any of them — an enderman attacks you if your crosshair passes over it.

  If you can't seem to avoid looking at endermen, place a pumpkin in the Helmet slot of the inventory. You can wear the pumpkin on your head like a Halloween mask. It makes seeing difficult but also lets you look at endermen without angering them.

- **Ender dragon:** If the dragon is nearby, the Boss Health bar appears at the top of the screen to represent the ender dragon. This huge, black dragon flies around the stage and tries to run you down.
- **Pillars:** Many obsidian pillars dot the End, and each one holds a crystal. If you cause damage to the ender dragon, it can fly to a crystal and heal itself. You have to destroy these crystals to bring down the dragon.

To defeat the dragon, consider these suggestions:

- **Destroy the ender prisms.** These vulnerable crystals explode when touched. You can destroy most of them by hitting them with arrows, snowballs, or eggs. If you simply can't reach one, use blocks to *pillar-jump* (jump and place a block under you) until you reach the top of the pillar. Be careful when smashing the prism: The explosion causes damage and may knock you off the pillar.

  Keep an eye on the dragon — it can inflict a lot of damage if it charges you. It destroys any block it touches except for the ones appearing in the End. Turn away the dragon by attacking it.

- **Attack the ender dragon.** The rest of the fight is fairly straightforward. When the dragon charges you, attack it with everything you have. Shoot arrows at it if you want, and don't worry about the arrows hitting any endermen — they teleport to avoid the projectile and don't pursue you.

Unlike in the Nether, where snow golems simply melt, the snow golem is an effective weapon in the End. Simply bring plenty of snowballs and pumpkins in the inventory, and construct some golems (see Chapter 9) after entering the End. These items throw snowballs at the endermen, who simply teleports, keeping the fight ongoing while you're free to take on the ender dragon (as shown in Figure 11-4). Eventually, the End slowly and comically fills with snowballs.

Figure 11-4: Snow golems fighting enderman.

After the ender dragon is defeated, it slowly drifts into the air, where it breaks apart and explodes in a shower of experience orbs. Collect as many as you can! The dragon also drops a gray fountain with an egg on top. The egg is decorative, and it teleports when you right-click it. Jump into the black depths of the fountain to view a cut scene and then return to the overworld.

Congratulations! You have now survived the End and lived to tell the tale.

Staying busy in the afterglow of completing The End

The End is somewhat of a misnomer — even after you beat the dragon and leave the End, the game is far from over. You have the orbs necessary to perform powerful enchantments (detailed in Chapter 10), and the End provides a good source of obsidian and ender pearls.

Your house and resources are still there — now it's time to fulfill your own goals. Build giant bases, collect loads of diamonds or emeralds, craft new items including the rare ender chest, and explore the biomes. You can also fight the wither, which is an optional boss that's detailed in Chapters 5 and 9. Perhaps you want to try your hand at more redstone contraptions or build an intricate rail system. Many players continue to journey between the Nether, End, and overworld, collecting resources as they go. Your choices are unlimited.

Some players are ready now to start a new game using customized settings or play in a multiplayer game with their friends (see Chapter 12 and 13). Others like to start from scratch with a higher difficulty level. The rest of this chapter is devoted to anyone who wants to test their skills in the ultimate version of survival that Minecraft has created.

Surviving Hardcore Mode

At this point, you may have been using either Survival mode or Creative mode (or both). You may enjoy increasing the difficulty level in Survival mode and want to set it to Difficult. Or you may want to play in Hardcore mode for an intense survival challenge.

When you open the world-creation screen, one difficulty setting for a new world is Hardcore mode, as shown in Figure 11-5.

Figure 11-5: Starting a Hardcore world.

Hardcore mode resembles Survival mode (covered in Chapters 1 through 10) but has these differences:

- **The game difficulty is set to Hard.** You cannot change the game difficulty. Zombies break down doors, mobs inflict extra damage, and you can die from the lack of food. Creepers are incredibly dangerous in this mode, and they can generally bring you down with a single blast.
- **Your world is deleted when you die.** Don't dwell on elaborate building procedures, because you have only a single life in Hardcore mode. Stay alive any way you can. If you're on a Hardcore server and you die, you're banned from the server until someone pardons you and lets you try again.
- **The hearts on the Health bar look different.** The "angry eyes" on the Health bar indicate that you're in Hardcore mode and that you should preserve your health.

Your experience in Hardcore mode can be rather different from Survival mode. To succeed in Hardcore mode, follow these principles:

- **On your first night, find protection and food.** Craft a wooden sword — or a stone one, if you have time. Farming is a useful long-term strategy for growing food, but first obtain effective short-term sustenance, such as meat or mushroom stew. Cows are useful because they provide lots of food and makeshift leather armor.
- **Find shelter quickly.** The easiest way to find shelter is to find 3 sheep as fast as you can and then craft a bed. If you use this bed as soon as night falls, you can sleep through the night and not be interrupted by a wandering monster. Alternatively, build a simple house with a light source and fill it with food.
- **Start a farm.** Maintaining a consistent food source is essential to thriving in Hardcore mode. (See Chapter 5 for more on farming.)
- **Obtain armor.** Find a ravine or a cave with a lot of coal, and craft iron armor as quickly as possible. Wearing armor lowers the chance of being defeated by a few surprise skeletons.
- **Avoid creepers.** In Hardcore mode, creepers can kill you with ease, even when you wear armor. Always look around for creepers, to prevent them from following you, and use sprinting attacks to knock creepers away from you. If a creeper manages to sneak up on you, move as far as possible from the explosion radius.

  Add windows or other features to your house to be able to check for creepers hiding around bends.
- **Advance carefully and always have an escape route.** Use lots of torches and scaffolding to navigate caves and obtain high-end minerals, such as redstone or diamond. Use cobblestone to build bridges in the Nether and avoid the danger of falling into lava.

In Hardcore mode, carry flint and steel with you in the Nether — in case you need to reactivate your portal home. One of the worst things that can happen in the Nether is for a ghast to hit your portal home with a fireball, deactivating it. If all else fails, you can obtain the reagents for a fire charge (see Chapter 4) from wither skeletons, Blaze, and ghasts. Use the fire charge on the portal frame to reactivate it.

Part IV
Expanding Your Minecraft Experience

Visit `www.dummies.com` for more great *For Dummies* content online.

In this part . . .

- Get into multiplayer games and cheats
- Customize your experience
- Visit the Minecraft YouTube channels
- Get the scoop on Minecon

12

Playing in Multiplayer Worlds and Cheats

In This Chapter

- Playing in multiplayer worlds
- Understanding LAN and public servers
- Using the Chat menu
- Using cheats
- Playing mini games

Because Minecraft rewards creativity and progression toward your own goals, a large part of the accomplishment you may feel during the gameplay stems from being able to share this creativity and progression with friends. In MultiPlayer mode, multiple avatars explore the same world — all online — and collaborate with or battle with other people.

Starting or Joining a Multiplayer World

Playing on a Minecraft server has several benefits. For example, you can

- Build collaboratively, as shown in Figure 12-1.
- Embark on adventures as a team.
- Create a town.

- Gather and trade resources.
- Duel other players.
- Chat and hang out.
- Use customized gameplay. Some servers use third-party programs that improve their content but don't have to be downloaded.

Figure 12-1: Two players, building a house.

Minecraft offers several ways to place multiple people in the same world. This section describes them in order of difficulty.

Setting up a LAN server

On a local area network server — or *LAN* server, as it's commonly known — friends who share the same Internet connection send their avatars into the same world in which you're playing.

Starting your LAN server

To start a LAN server, follow these steps:

1. **Start or continue a world in Minecraft.**
2. **Press Esc to open the Game menu.**
3. **Click the Open to LAN button.**
4. **Select the settings you want and click Start LAN World.**

   Now people who share your network connection can join your server.

Joining another LAN server

If you want to join a LAN server started by someone else, follow these steps:

1. **Select Multiplayer from the main menu.**

   The server list appears. It should be empty if you're just starting in MultiPlayer mode. At the end of the server list, you see the message `Scanning for LAN Worlds.`

2. **Wait for your friend's LAN world to appear.**

   After a short time, the server list should display a LAN server with your friend's Minecraft username and world name.

3. **Click the server name and then click the Join Server button.**

   Alternatively, simply double-click the server name.

The LAN feature lets you play online in any world that normally is single-player.

If the LAN server doesn't appear or you cannot log in, check your Internet connection — you or the server host may have a network problem, or you may be using a different network.

Joining a public server

Of course, you may want a server that can run even when you aren't online, and one that's accessible by people using a different Internet connection. A server of this kind is defined by an IP address or a web address, which is, loosely, a string of characters used to access a port and play online.

Learning the steps to join a public server

To join a public server, follow these steps:

1. **Select Multiplayer from the main menu.**

   The server list appears. It should be empty if you're starting out in MultiPlayer mode. You can add servers to this list to access them quickly, and you can delete them when you no longer use them or when you want to add them again later.

2. **Click the Add Server button.**

   The Add Server menu appears.

3. **Choose a name and fill out the address.**

   In the Server Name text box, name the server so that you can identify it when it appears on the server list. The Server Address box holds the IP address of the server, which can be shared manually or online. Some servers have websites you can visit to get the address.

4. **Click Done.**

   The server list returns and automatically tests your connection to the server.

5. **After the connection is established, click the server name and then click the Join Server button to start playing.**

The five bars next to a server on the server list monitor your connection to that server. If the bars are crossed out and a red error message appears, your connection may not work, or the server may simply be down temporarily.

A server may not work because it hasn't been updated to the latest version of Minecraft. To continue using a server or an add-on after the game is updated, select the Not Now option when asked whether you want to update Minecraft. This query appears every time you start the game, unless it's already up to date.

Creating your own public server

Creating your own server is more difficult than completing other multiplayer options, and you need to know how to open the 25565 port on your router to run it; this topic is beyond the scope of this book, however. You can find instructions for downloading the server launcher at `www.minecraft.net/download` — port forwarding instructions depend on your router or any third-party program you might use.

Joining regular and bukkit servers

A regular server simply hosts the original Minecraft game, allowing multiple players. A bukkit server changes and customizes the game format but does not require you to download anything. Many of our favorite multiplayer experiences are on bukkit servers and function around mini games. (See the section "Playing Mini Games," later in this chapter.) Mods (discussed in Chapter 13) require you to download the mod.

Many parents are more comfortable with bukkit servers instead of mods because the risk to the computer is significantly less. Bukkit servers require no new downloads on the computer to play, so the risk of viruses, Trojans, or malicious worms is significantly less.

Some of our favorite bukkit servers are described in this list:

- **The Hive (`hivemc.com`):** The Hive is known for its extremely popular mini games, including Hide and Seek, Hunger Games, and Block Party.

- **Mineplex** (`mineplex.com`)**:** This site offers mini games and reward gems along with super smash mobs.
- **SuperCraftBros** (`minecade.com/SuperCraft/Bros`)**:** This advanced game blends Super Smash Bros (from Nintendo) with Minecraft.

Playing PE MultiPlayer Mode

Most players in the PE edition use a LAN server when in MultiPlayer mode (found in the settings) to connect siblings and friends using devices on the same Internet connection, as shown in Figure 12-2. The connection is less stable when playing devices that are not of the same brand in the same LAN game, such as the iPad and the Kindle.

Figure 12-2: Playing on a PE LAN server.

A handful of public multiplayer servers exist but do not have customized names, making it quite difficult for players to find and connect to these servers.

Using the Chat Menu and Cheats

You can both communicate with other players and use *cheats* (which cause instant alterations to the world) by pressing T, typing a message, and pressing Enter. Note that if you hide the chat log by using the Options menu, you cannot chat.

Parents should beware about what their kids are saying, and whom they are chatting with in Minecraft, because the Chat menu has no parental controls. Some parents simply turn off the chat function altogether; others choose to monitor it. Many players rarely use chat, because they're engrossed in the game. On LAN servers, players are likely to know each other because they are using the same Internet connection, so chat should not be a problem.

When friends (or family members, like us) want to chat only with each other but are playing on a public server, they can use Skype (or another medium) while they play and simply turn off the Chat menu.

The Chat menu also lets you use cheats if the server or world allows it. A cheat is preceded by a slash (/) when you enter it on the Chat menu. If you're running a public server, the slash is not used.

Use cheats by entering the commands described in the following sections.

Entering commands that can be used by all players

Any players who are connected to the world can use these commands:

- `/help`: Display all cheats available to you. If you can't view them all, type **`/help 2`**, **`/help 3`**, and so on, to see more. If you're using a public-server launcher, type **`help`** to view the commands that are accessible from the launcher.
- `/kill`: Your avatar dies.
- `/me`: In this third-person form of talking, you type **`/me`** followed by an action to indicate that your avatar is emoting. For example, someone named Isometrus would type `/me wants cake` to make the chat log display `* Isometrus wants cake.`
- `/seed`: View the world seed, mentioned in Chapter 13.
- `/tell`: Send a private message that only the target player can read — for example, `/tell Isometrus Don't tell anyone, but I hid my diamonds in the basement.`

Using operator-only commands

An *op* is a person on a public server who has exclusive rights to certain cheats. Ops can be assigned by the server administrator or by other ops. Anyone who is an op and connected to the server can use these commands:

- `/difficulty`: Changes the difficulty of the server — typing `/difficulty 0` turns on Peaceful mode, and 1, 2 and 3 refer to Easy, Normal, and Hard, respectively.
- `/clear`: Clears the target player's inventory — for example, `/clear Isometrus`. You can also add the name of a minecraft item and a damage value (see the appendix, available for download at `www.dummies.com/go/minecraftfd`) to remove only a specific item from a player's inventory. For example, `/clear Isometrus minecraft:dirt` removes any dirt blocks from Isometrus's inventory, whereas `/clear Isometrus minecraft:stone_sword 0` removes all unbroken stone swords.
- `/gamemode`: Changes a player's game mode. You can enter Survival mode by typing `survival`, `s` , or `0`. (Creative is `creative`, `c` or `1`, Adventure is `adventure`, `a`, or `2`, and Spectator is `spectator`, `sp`, or `3`) For example, `/gamemode 1 Isometrus` sets Isometrus to Creative mode. If you don't enter a player's name, the command targets you.
- `/defaultgamemode`: Changes the initial game mode when you log in. For example, `/defaultgamemode s` sets all new players to Survival mode.
- `/gamerule`: Changes a game rule. You can further customize the server by entering `/gamerule`, followed by a rule, followed by either `true` or `false`. For example, you can enter `/gamerule keepInventory true`. The rules that can be changed by using this command are listed in Table 12-1, at the end of this list.
- `/give`: Gives the target player an item. You must know the minecraft:item of your specific item (see the appendix). The full syntax of the `/give` command is

  ```
  /give <player> <item> [amount] [data] [dataTag]
  ```

  You can skip the last three options, if you want. For example, `/give Isometrus minecraft:dirt 32` places 32 dirt blocks in Isometrus's inventory.
- `/say`: Loudly broadcasts a message, such as `/say Server going down in 15 minutes`. Typing `say <message>` into the server launcher sends the message under the username `[CONSOLE]`.
- `/spawnpoint`: Sets a player's spawn point to your current location so that his avatar appears there whenever he dies or joins the world. For example, `/spawnpoint Isometrus` sets Isometrus's spawn point

to your current location. You can also enter coordinates such as /spawnpoint Isometrus 300 60 400 to manually set a spawn point. Coordinates are in the form <x> <y> <z>, where the positive y-axis points toward the sky; press F3 to view your current coordinates.

- /time: Changes the time and can be used in many different ways — for example, /time set day and /time set night cause a forced sunrise or sunset. Also, /time set # sets the time manually, where # is a number measured in 20ths of a second and 0 is sunrise. You never have to enter a number larger than 24000, which also forces sunrise. The command /time add # adds the value of # to the current time. Finally, /time query allows you to see how long you or other people have been playing in this world (/time query gametime "Name of Player") or how long the day/night cycle has been running (/time query daytime "Name of Player").
- /toggledownfall: Turns rain on or off.
- /tp: Followed by two player names, teleports one to the other; for example, /tp Alice Bob teleports Alice to Bob. If you enter only one name, you teleport to the target player. You can also use coordinates such as /tp Isometrus 300 60 400 to teleport a player to a specific point.
- /weather: Changes the weather to clear, rainy, or stormy by giving the command /weather clear, /weather rain, or /weather thunder. You can also use a number such as /weather rain 30 to change the weather for a set number of seconds.
- /xp: Grants experience orbs to the target player. For example, /xp 500 Isometrus gives Isometrus 500 experience orbs, enough to bring him to Level 19. If no player name is given, the orbs are given to you. You can also type the text /xp 500L Isometrus (or similar) to grant 500 levels rather than 500 orbs. Additionally, using a hyphen (–) subtracts levels until it reaches 0. Just type the chat /xp -500L Isometrus (or similar) and your 500 levels are gone. You cannot give a negative amount of orbs, only levels.

Table 12-1 Game Rules

Rule	*Default Setting*	*Effect*
commandBlock-Output	True	Operators can view the effects of redstone command blocks on the Chat menu. Turn off this setting if you begin receiving spam. These blocks, which activate cheats when given redstone power, can be obtained only by using /give minecraft:command_block.

Rule	*Default Setting*	*Effect*
doDaylightCycle	True	Toggles on or off the cycle between night and day.
doFireTick	True	Fire spreads, destroys certain blocks, or dies out.
doMobLoot	True	Mobs that are killed can drop items.
doMobSpawning	True	Mobs (described in Chapter 9) appear in the world naturally. When this setting is False, the spawn egg may still be used.
doTileDrops	True	When this setting is False, blocks that are broken cannot produce items.
keepInventory	False	Players who die keep their items.
logAdminCommands	True	When this option is set to False, any commands that are used are not put on the server launcher. (If many commands are being run constantly, it might make Minecraft run faster.)
mobGriefing	True	Blocks are destroyed or moved by creepers, ghasts, endermen, the wither, and the ender dragon.
naturalRegeneration	True	When this option is set to False, you can regenerate your health only by using potions or golden apples. A full Health bar doesn't regenerate health.
randomTickSpeed	3	This option determines how often a random tick occurs (such as grass spread or leaf decay). It can be set only to a number greater than or equal to 0.
reducedDebugInfo	False	This setting determines whether the debug screen is reduced or normal.
sendCommandFeedback	True	This setting determines whether the commands from the player show feedback in the chat log. (For example, when you change the game mode, the chat log says, "Your game mode has been updated."
showDeathMessages	True	The messages indicate when the player dies.

Using operator-only, public-server-only commands

Anyone who is an op can use these commands, though they don't work on LAN servers:

- `/op`: Followed by a player's username (such as `/op Isometrus`), makes her an operator (or *op*) and allows her to use more cheats. If nobody on the server is an op, type the command (without the slash) into the server launcher. To use cheats on a LAN server, click the Allow Cheats button after clicking Open to LAN.
- `/deop`: Removes a player's operator status; the opposite of `/op`.
- `/ban`: Followed by a player's username (such as `/ban Isometrus`), bans the player from the server until another op issues a pardon. This technique controls malicious players who damage other players' work or cheat to get ahead. If you want the player to know why he was banned, you can add a reason to your ban, such as `/ban Isometrus As an example to the others.`
- `/ban-ip`: Bans a specific IP address, preventing a certain computer from connecting to the server. You can't ban offline players with this command.
- `/banlist`: Shows a list of all banned players. Type `/banlist ips` to list all banned addresses.
- `/debug`: Lets you use `/debug start` and `/debug stop` to control debug profiling, if your server behaves erratically.
- `/kick`: Temporarily boots a player from the server. Uses the same syntax as `/ban` but allows the player to log on again.
- `/list`: Lists all players on the server; however, you can do this easily by pressing the Tab key.
- `/pardon`: Pardons a banned player, allowing him on the server again, using the same syntax as `/ban`. You can also use `/pardon-ip` to pardon a banned address.
- `/save-all`: Saves the world in case you have to shut down the server. You can also use `/save-off` and `/save-on` to toggle automatic saving. If you're about to make a significant change to the world, you can use `/save-off` to prevent the world from saving so that you can recover your old world if something goes wrong.
- `/stop`: Saves and shuts down the server.
- `/whitelist`: Produces an optional list of all players who are allowed on the server. (The list of banned players is often known as a *blacklist.*) The command `/whitelist on` prevents anyone from joining unless

she's an op or a member of the whitelist; `/whitelist off` turns off the whitelist, so anyone can join the server.

You can type a command such as `/whitelist add Isometrus` or `/whitelist remove Isometrus` to change who's allowed on. The command `/whitelist list` lets you view the whitelist, and `/whitelist reload` lets you refresh the whitelist to see whether a banned player can get on the server.

Using nonspecific parameters

Many commands ask for the name of a player, such as `/tp` or `/give`, but you can instead use a parameter from Table 12-2. For example, the command `/tp @a 0 60 0` teleports every player to the center of the map.

Table 12-2 Extra Parameters

Parameter	Whom It Targets
@p	The nearest player (in a redstone command block, the player closest to the block targeted)
@r	A random player
@a	All players (repeated for every player online)
@e	All entities

Playing Mini Games

Many of the public servers on Minecraft are based around mini games. Mini games cover a wide range of games where players compete against each other in a relatively short game. These games often have custom reward items not found in traditional Minecraft, such as reward gems or other achievements.

Mini games, like the one shown in Figure 12-3, often spoof other types of games, including kart racing and PacMan, or sports such as baseball and archery. Other mini games are based on players fighting each other either in a boxing ring or an obstacle course. Others offer a warfare scenario where players build bases and try to defeat each other (known as faction games).

Figure 12-3: The mini game "spleef" encourages players to break blocks and cause other players to fall through. The last player standing wins!

We describe some of our favorite mini games in this list:

- **Spleef:** Try to knock off other players by breaking the blocks below them. The blocks are usually blocks that you can break instantly, like TNT. In many versions, like Fire TNT, you light leaves or another flammable block on fire and try to survive without falling or dying from the fire.
- **Block Party:** This fun and exciting game features a pattern of clay or wool on the floor, and all players are assigned a specific color. Try to stay on that color until the next pattern of clay or wool pops up. If you don't make it in time, the floor that is not that specific texture of clay or wool disintegrates, making you lose. After the floor disintegrates, a new pattern appears if you've made it to the next round. The last player standing wins.
- **Sky Battle:** Try to defeat other players to be the last one alive. There's one island per player and at least one chest to get you geared up for the battle; often, one main island at the center contains multiple chests so that you can get more gear. The game also has other islands — usually, a 3 x 3 platform — and almost always has only one chest somewhere around the middle.

Avoiding trolling

Trolling occurs whenever someone intentionally annoys another player, often by stalking, or following someone around, destroying their property, or stealing their items. Outside of faction servers which encourage such activity as the main purpose of the game, players compete in certain game scenarios, including fighting sequences, but are not allowed to destroy or steal from each other's houses.

Though a practical joke among friends might be acceptable, trolling often ruins the fun for another player. Common trolls include using TNT to blow up another player's structures and stealing items from another player's chest. Administrators aggressively monitor for trolls and ban players.

Don't be a troll. Just don't do it!

Hacking occurs whenever a player downloads a hack that alters her own player but not the other players within the game. A common hack is to increase the amount of damage a player inflicts with a single blow. If you think a player has enhanced an avatar by using a hack, be sure to report it to a server administrator.

13

Customizing Your Experience

In This Chapter

- Implementing additional world options
- Managing the Minecraft folder
- Exploring Adventure mode and custom maps
- Discovering mods and texture packs
- Using apps

After players discover the incredible diversity that's offered in multiplayer games and public servers, they often want to customize their own gameplay and become creators as well. This chapter can help you examine the many custom options that are available, explore Adventure mode in Minecraft, and create your own modifications to the Minecraft game.

Implementing Additional World Options

In addition to its various game modes, Minecraft has several minor features you can use to further customize your world. When you open the world-creation screen, click the More World Options button, to access these features. When creating a world, you can customize it in these five ways (as shown in Figure 13-1):

- **Seed for the World Generator:** Seeds allow you to customize the terrain of your world rather than spawn in randomly (see the next section).
- **Generate Structures:** Click this button to specify whether structures such as villages (see Chapter 7 for a full list) appear in your world.
- **World Type:** Click to toggle the world type between Default, Superflat, Large Biomes, Amplified, Customized, and Debug mode (all of which are discussed later in this chapter).

- **Allow Cheats:** Click to allow the world cheats specified in Chapter 12. The default setting is On in Creative mode and Off in other modes. You can also enable or disable cheats after converting a world to a LAN server.
- **Bonus Chest:** Click this button to make a bonus chest appear next to you when you start creating the world. This storage chest contains useful starting materials.

Figure 13-1: Additional world options.

Using seeds

Seeds are Minecraft's way of generating terrain. Each biome you spawn in is determined by the seed. With a custom seed, you can have a desert biome right next to a mesa biome. You can have 8 diamond ore directly underneath. There are many, many Minecraft seeds out there. If you see a world you like, you can create a new, identical world. Use the `/seed` cheat (explained in Chapter 12) to view the world seed, and then insert it in the text box at the top of the screen. Use the seed code (generally, a very large number) as the template for building a world.

You can share the seed code with other players and look up seed codes online. Simply search online for the feature you want. For example, searching *seeds with a jungle temple* quickly yields an appropriate seed code. We recommend that you type *DUMMIES* and *Test123* into the text box to see what world spawns. Remember that if you produce an interesting-looking world, share the string with others so that they can reproduce it.

One of our favorite seed codes came from `minecraft.forum.net` and produces every biome within 2100 square blocks. The code is 35267400. Go try it!

Customizing a superflat world

Superflat worlds are simply worlds made of stacked layers of blocks. The default flat world is composed of a layer of grass, two layers of dirt, and a layer of bedrock — and, occasionally, structures such as dungeons or villages. The flattened, single-biome superflat world allows for easier building at the cost of a less natural feel. And if you just want to design something without much getting in the way, this biome is perfect.

After selecting Superflat as the world type when creating a world, you can then choose the type of superflat world by clicking the Customize button and selecting the world. Click the Presets button to view detailed options for customizing your world, as shown in Figure 13-2.

Figure 13-2: Selecting a preset.

The text box at the top of the Select a Preset screen shows the code for your world; click the Use Preset button at the bottom of the screen to implement the code. You can also replace it with the code for an interesting world that another player has created and shared.

To customize your own superflat world, go to `http://chunkbase.com/apps/superflat-generator` for guidance.

Alternatively, you can select one of the eight default worlds available to you, as described in Table 13-1.

To delete a section of a superflat world, select any section on the Superflat Customization screen and click the Remove Layer button.

My favorite preset world is Redstone Ready, but I play it only in Creative mode. Animals don't naturally spawn in, so they don't annoy me. And because it's a desert, I don't have to deal with rain, either.

Table 13-1 Preset Worlds

Name	*Biome*	*Description*
Bottomless Pit	Plains	Similar to Classic Flat but with no bedrock layer (so that you might fall through the earth!)
Classic Flat	Plains	A simple, grassy expanse with some villages
Desert	Desert	A desert with villages, pyramids, wells, and underground structures
Overworld	Plains	A flat re-creation of the default Minecraft world, with many of its features
Redstone Ready	Desert	A visually and mechanically perfect world for trying out redstone creations, with villages
Snowy Kingdom	Ice Plains	A cold world that experiences snowfall occasionally
Tunnelers' Dream	Technically Extreme Hills (different grass color, sparse trees)	A grassy plain with a sparse number of trees, on top of a huge underground with dungeons, mine shafts, and strongholds
Water World	Technically Plains	A deep ocean, home to several interesting villages

Choosing large biomes and amplified worlds

Large biomes are 16 times the size of traditional biomes in Minecraft. Otherwise, they share the same seeds as the default mode. If you like biomes with a lot of space, large biomes is the right option for you. This biome prevents you from moving quickly from one biome to the next, allowing you to conquer and live within a few biomes. Many players mix seed codes (discussed later in this chapter) with the large biome to create a large space of their favorite biome. Perhaps you want a vast savanna or a giant flower forest, for example.

Amplified (often written as AMPLIFIED) has become a favorite among serious Minecraft players. Amplified means big — big mountains, chunks of land just floating in midair, big spikes of ice that reach to the build height. It's so big that these mountains tower over the default hill biomes. See Figure 13-3 for an example.

Figure 13-3: Amplified world.

Players will find this mode to be extremely challenging, with few caves and a high chance of falling. Despite villages needing a flat place to spawn, they generate in this world in strange configurations. Finally, not all biomes are affected by this setting — oceans, for example, remain untouched.

An Amplified world requires significantly more RAM memory in your computer than do default worlds. You must have a strong PC (one that has lots of memory) to play in this mode.

Playing in Customized mode

Customized mode lets you customize all parts of the generation. Most of the options are confusing, but if you take the time to see how to do it, you can complete amazing feats. As with the superflat world type, Mojang has (thankfully!) added presets for you to get the idea of how the customization works.

In Customized mode, players can change the terrain in 16 ways, choose the type of 11 ores, and decide the 18 types of structures and environmental factors that will spawn. The number of combinations and complexity is almost endless.

Most players simply choose from the preset list, detailed in Table 13-2.

Table 13-2	Customized Mode Presets
Preset Name	***Description***
Water World	A deep ocean filled with underwater palaces
Isle Land	A world filled with floating islands
Caver's Delight	A digger's paradise (and quickly becoming a favorite among mining fans)
Mountain Madness	An alternative to Amplified mode but with the same basic feel
Drought	Provides Water Scare biomes and is more than just a desert
Caves of Chaos	Takes Caver's Delight and twists the caves into unique and dangerous designs
Good Luck	Named because of its lack or resources; has plenty of lava (see Figure 13-4)

Figure 13-4: The customized world preset Good Luck.

Playing in Debug mode

Debug mode, shown in Figure 13-5, is used to test block configurations and is similar to Creative mode for developers (such as resource pack for developers, as discussed later in this chapter). Though the average player may never use this mode, it is an interesting place to visit.

Figure 13-5: Debug mode.

To access this hidden world, you have to hold down the Shift key while clicking the World Type option; eventually, you see the text *Debug Mode*. All options are disabled. You're forced to enter this world only in Spectator mode, but luckily Mojang allowed players to use cheats. When a world is generated like this, it shows every block and block state in the game. Ten blocks below all the blocks in the game is a barrier block floor. When switched to a game mode such as Creative mode, changing anything is impossible. When you break something, it reappears instantly. When you try to place anything, it's immediately destroyed.

PE Old World Type

PE also allows for an Old World Type, which is a finite world surrounded by an invisible layer of bedrock — perfect for older devices because it takes significantly less memory.

Using the Profile Editor

The Profile Editor allows you to create or edit a profile in the Minecraft launcher. To get to the Profile Editor, simply open the Minecraft launcher and then click either Edit Profile or New Profile. At the top is the Profile Name section. The only common element that anyone uses is the profile name, which is the name of your profile.

Then you see the Version Selection section. (We use this section quite often.) The first check box enables the *snapshots,* or experimental development versions, that show off what's in the next update. To prevent corrupting your worlds, create new ones in Minecraft.

The second check box is for the old, *beta* versions of Minecraft. This was Minecraft in 2010 and 2011. Don't forget to create new worlds in the beta version. Loading a single-player mode without creating a new world deletes data that comes after the beta.

The third check box is for the even older, *alpha* versions, developed in 2010. Everything that applies to the beta version applies to this version. The final section, Java Settings (Advanced), is for advanced users, and you probably will never have to touch this area of Minecraft.

Lastly, you see three buttons at the bottom. Clicking the Cancel button closes the window. The Open Game Dir (Dir stands for Directory) button opens the game directory or, by default, the `.minecraft` folder (mentioned at the beginning of the following section). Click the Save Profile button to either save an existing profile or create a new profile.

Managing the .minecraft Folder

If you want to download maps or texture packs, duplicate or export worlds, reset statistics, or manage screen shots, you use the `.minecraft` folder. This set of files on your computer contains information about your personalized version of Minecraft, and it appears in the Users⇨*Username*⇨AppData⇨Roaming folder on your PC. The AppData folder may be hidden, so you can simply search your computer for the phrase *.minecraft*. You can locate the `.minecraft` folder in two simple ways. One you can do while Minecraft is up, and the other one is on the launcher.

Clicking the Options button when the game is paused or you're at the title screen opens the Options screen. You have many options to choose from; to go to the `.minecraft` folder, you click the Resource Packs button. This action shows you a list of the resource packs that are, and are not, running. Click the Open Resource Pack Folder button and backtrack your way to the `.minecraft` folder. That's all there is to it.

While you're in the Minecraft launcher, click either the Edit Profile or New Profile button. That should pop up the Profile Editor dialog box, shown in Figure 13-6. Click the Open Game Dir button. That pulls up the .minecraft window. Then you can exit out of the Profile Editor window and close out of the Minecraft launcher window.

Figure 13-6: Profile Editor.

Do not edit the files in the `.minecraft` folder if you don't know what you're doing. If the source files are damaged, you may have to purge Minecraft and download it again. The same advice applies to using the `saves` folder — at the worst, you may corrupt or lose some of your worlds, rendering them unplayable.

You usually have to close the Minecraft window to be able to make changes to files.

Using .minecraft

You can use the `.minecraft` file system to further customize your experience, by editing files in a way that's unavailable from within the game. Some of the folders you can edit are described in this list:

- `saves`: When you open this folder, you find more folders, each one corresponding to one of your worlds. The names of your folders may not correspond with the names of your worlds, especially if either was renamed, but the world-selection screen in Minecraft also displays your folder names in gray under the world names.

By copying, uploading, or downloading the files (usually in a `.zip` file) inside these world folders, you can obtain and share custom maps, duplicate worlds, or store backups. To copy a world into `saves`, simply create a new folder and put the world files in the `saves` folder.

- `screenshots`: In this folder, you can find all your screen shots. (Press F2 to take a screen shot.)
- `resourcepacks`: Insert resource packs (previously called texture packs) into your game by placing them here. These groups of folders, images, and other types of files can be imported in a single folder or Zip file. To select a resource pack, click the Resource Packs button on the Options menu and change the general look of the game by giving new images to the surfaces of blocks and entities. Resource packs can be shared by graphical designers — if a pack requires a third-party program to work, follow the extra download instructions that are provided.

Recovering .minecraft

If Minecraft crashes while you're managing the file system, you can try one of these methods to recover your content:

- **Backtrack to look for conflicts.** Delete any recently downloaded third-party software from the `.minecraft` folder.
- **Start over.** Back up your worlds, screen shots, and other game elements, and then completely uninstall Minecraft and download it again.
- **Search for your specific error online.** For example, if Minecraft displays an error message when you continue a world, you can search for the error message online and see what other players have to say.

Exploring Adventure Mode

Adventure mode — which adds another layer of difficulty to Minecraft — was created to allow players to follow a player-created map, often through a series of challenges and obstacles.

It resembles Survival mode in that players can interact with mobs, trigger mechanisms, and make trades. Players cannot break or place blocks without the NBT tags canDestroy or CanPlaceOn, respectively. That means no punching wood or mining.

You can start a game in Adventure mode when creating a new world, or you can use the `/gamemode` cheat (described in Chapter 12) to switch to Adventure mode from any world.

Adventure mode is used almost exclusively for interacting with custom maps, discussed in the later section "Playing Custom Maps."

Playing Custom Maps

With the explosion of online Minecraft players, a new genre of Minecraft was born: custom maps (see Figure 13-7). *Custom maps* are games created inside the Minecraft world. Rather than play in a world of survival, these games take the biomes, blocks, and mobs of Minecraft to create new games, puzzles, and challenges. Customs maps are often divided into the categories CTM maps, adventure maps, and game maps.

Figure 13-7: Custom map.

Using CTM maps

CTM, or Complete The Monument maps, ask players to collect resources, such as wool, and then complete the monument, like a puzzle, placing each block correctly.

Exploring adventure maps

An Adventure map is based on a quest. Players follow a series of instructions and conquer obstacles along the way. They often have a storyline that goes along with the game. Players often play in Adventure mode during these maps to prevent a player from breaking blocks pertinent to the game.

Creators of adventure maps (of any custom maps, really) are master command block designers. Command blocks (as discussed in Chapter 8) allow the creator (or admin) of a map to place nearly indestructible blocks in the game that will execute specific commands when triggered.

Using game maps

Game maps are often similar to the mini games discussed in Chapter 12. However, these maps are often generated using command blocks rather than bukkit servers. They're also often more advanced and take longer to play than a common mini game.

Navigating the Escape Key Window

When in a game, pressing the Escape key opens the Game menu (not to be confused with the title screen). As shown in Figure 13-8, this screen is also called a pause screen, because when you're using the screen the game pauses for your individual player.

Figure 13-8: Game menu.

The game pauses and gives you a list of options you can choose. The options on the Game menu are explained in Table 13-3.

Table 13-3 Game Screen Options

Option	*Description*
Back to Game	Returns you to your game to continue fighting hostile mobs and other activities
Achievements	Shows a list of achievements, how to unlock them, and other advice
Statistics	A list of information about what you have done in your world, including but not limited to Distance Swum (that is not a typo), Distance by Pig, and Talked to Villagers
Options	Displays a list of advanced options (see Table 13-4)
Open to LAN	Opens a LAN server after choosing the LAN options
Save and Quit to Title	Saves the game and takes you to the title screen

Earning achievements

Achievements are awards given in Minecraft for completing certain tasks. Achievements are found in both the PC and Console editions (but, sadly, not in PE). Many of the achievements have names based on movies, video games, or common phrases.

The PC version has 33 achievements. Xbox 360 offers 20, and PS3 offers 29. The Console edition has a trophy feel when a player earns an achievement. A handful of achievements are unique to the Console edition, including MOAR tools (constructing one of each type of tool) and Leader of the Pack (befriend 5 wolves). Other achievements have slightly different names in the Console edition compared to the PC edition.

The PC achievements are listed in Table 13-4. You can see what they look like in Figure 13-9.

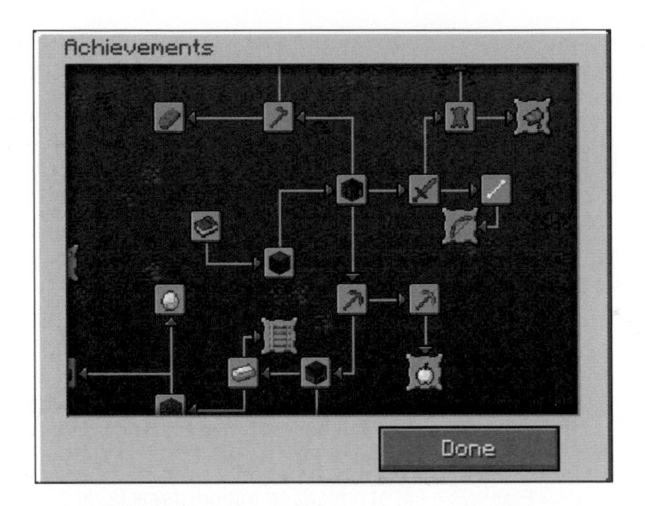

Figure 13-9: Earning an achievement.

Table 13-4 Achievements in Minecraft PC

Name of Achievement	*In Game Description*	*Previous Achievement Requirement*	*Action to Get Achievement*
Taking inventory	Press E to open the inventory.	None	The E changes depending on how you set the inventory button.
Getting wood	Attack a tree until a block of wood pops out.	Taking inventory	Pick up the wood block from the ground.
Benchmarking	Craft a work-bench with 4 blocks of planks.	Getting wood	Craft a crafting table in your inventory or a crafting table.

From here, the achievements split into three sections, mining, farming, and fighting. Table 13-5 lists the farming achievements; Table 13-6 lists the fighting achievements; Table 13-7 lists the mining achievements.

Table 13-5 Farming Achievements

Name	*Description*	*Requirement*	*Action*
Time to Farm!	Use planks and sticks to make a hoe.	Benchmarking	Craft any type of hoe.
Bake Bread	Turn wheat into bread.	Time to Farm!	Craft bread.
The Lie	Collect wheat, sugar, milk, and eggs.	Time to Farm!	Craft a cake.

Table 13-6 Fighting Achievements

Name	*Description*	*Requirement*	*Action*
Time to Strike!	Use planks and sticks to make a sword.	Benchmarking	Craft any sword.
Monster Hunter	Attack and destroy a monster.	Time to Strike!	Kill any hostile mob as long as it isn't a baby.
Cow Tipper	Harvest some leather.	Time to Strike!	Grab leather from the ground
Sniper Duel	Kill a skeleton with an arrow from more than 50 meters.	Monster Hunter	Shoot a skeleton or wither skeleton with a bow and arrow from 50 or more blocks away horizontally.
When Pigs Fly	Fly a pig off a cliff.	Cow Tipper	Saddle up a pig and make it take more than 2 hearts of fall damage while riding it.
Repopulation	Breed two cows with wheat.	Cow Tipper	Breed two cows or two mooshrooms.

Table 13-7 Mining Achievements

Name	*Description*	*Requirement*	*Action*
Time to Mine!	Use planks and sticks to make a pickaxe.	Benchmarking	Craft any type of pickaxe.
Getting an Upgrade	Construct a better pickaxe.	Time to Mine!	Craft any pickaxe that is not a wooden pickaxe.
Hot Topic	Construct a furnace out of 8 stone blocks.	Time to Mine!	Craft a furnace; the description states from 8 stone blocks but all you need is 8 cobblestone blocks.
Overpowered	Build a notch apple.	Getting an Upgrade	Craft a notch apple (an enchanted golden apple).
Acquire Hardware	Smelt an iron ingot.	Hot Topic	Smelt and grab an iron ingot from the furnace.
Delicious Fish	Catch and cook a fish.	Hot Topic	Smelt and grab an iron ingot from the furnace.
On A Rail	Travel by minecart at least 1 km from where you started.	Acquire Hardware	Travel at least 1000 blocks from where you got into your minecart; the distance, measured in a straight line, resets how many blocks are traveled if there are any curves in the track.
DIAMONDS!	Acquire diamonds with your iron tools.	Acquire Hardware	Grab a diamond from the ground.
Diamonds to you!	Throw diamonds at another player.	DIAMONDS!	Throw diamonds at a player or a mob that can pick up items; only the original owner gets the achievements, and the diamond must also create a new stack in the other players' inventory.

Name	Description	Requirement	Action
Enchanter	Use a book, obsidian, and diamonds to construct an enchantment table.	DIAMONDS!	Craft an enchantment table.
We Need to Go Deeper	Build a portal to the Nether.	DIAMONDS!	Go inside the nether.
Overkill	Deal 9 hearts of damage in a single hit.	Enchanter	As long as you kill a mob with a 9-heart damage sword, it gives you this achievement even if the mob doesn't have 9 hearts.
Librarian	Build some bookshelves to improve your enchantment table.	Enchanter	Craft a bookshelf.
Return to Sender	Destroy a ghast with a fireball.	We Need to Go Deeper	Kill the ghast with its own fireball.
Into Fire	Relieve a Blaze of its rod.	We Need to Go Deeper	Grab a blaze rod from the ground.
Local Brewery	Brew a potion.	Into Fire	Brew a potion; putting in and taking out a premade potion gives you the achievement.
The End?	Locate the End.	Into Fire	Go to the End.
The End	Defeat the ender dragon.	The End?	Return to the overworld in the End.

(cotinued)

Table 13-7 *(continued)*

Name	*Description*	*Requirement*	*Action*
Adventuring Time	Discover all biomes.	The End?	Visit the Beach, Birch Forest, Birch Forest Hills, Cold Beach, Cold Taiga, Cold Taiga Hills, Deep Ocean, Desert, DesertHills, Extreme Hills, Extreme Hills+, Forest, ForestHills, FrozenRiver, Ice Plains, Jungle, JungleEdge, JungleHills, Mega Taiga, Mega Taiga Hills, Mesa, Mesa Plateau, Mesa Plateau F, MushroomIsland, MushroomIslandShore, Ice Mountains, Ocean, Plains, Savanna Plateau, River, Roofed Forest, Savanna, Swampland, Stone Beach, Taiga, and TaigaHills biomes; keeps track of how many biomes you've been in, even before you get the achievement at the End.
The Beginning?	Spawn the wither.	The End.	Spawn the wither.
The Beginning	Kill the wither.	The Beginning?	Kill the wither.
Beaconator	Create a full beacon.	The Beginning.	Place down a beacon with a 4-level pyramid.

Adjusting your options

The Options button (on the Game menu) provides its own list of advanced settings. Here's where you can add skins and resource packs and choose from a large variety of other customized settings, as described in Table 13-8.

Table 13-8 Customized Settings

Setting Name	*Description*
FOV	Stands for *field of view*; adjusts your normal avatar's vision
Difficulty	Defines the difficulty level (Peaceful, Easy, Normal, Hard)
Skin Customization	Toggles on and off the outer layers of your Minecraft skin
Super Secret Settings	Plays a random sound when clicked and adds a shader that alters your Minecraft screen to include a realistic feel, including shadows
Music & Sounds	Defines how loud or quiet the music and sounds are in-game
Broadcast Settings	Settings that work with twitch when broadcasting on Minecraft
Video Settings	Complicated settings that edit how blocks behave and other types of screen-related things
Controls	Allows you to edit the controls; for example, a left-hander might choose the PL;' keys to move instead of the classic WASD keys
Language	Changes the English language to another language; includes most languages from Spanish to Pirate
Multiplayer Settings	Settings that control capes, chat, and visual effects
Resource Packs	Where you can add and take off resource packs and add new resource packs by opening the Resource Packs folder
Snooper Settings	A list of performance information about your copy of Minecraft and about your computer
Done	Returns you to the screen where you pressed Options

Customizing Skins

In addition to the customization menus on the World Generation screen, Minecraft can be customized using outside resources, as discussed in the remainder of this chapter.

One of the easier additions to Minecraft is skin customization. It lets players change the look of their avatars. If you don't like the default Steve or Alex skin, you can change it. An easy way to change your Minecraft skin is to go to the website `https://minecraft.net/profile`. You might be asked to log in. If so, log in and then you should be admitted to the site. If you read the page, it gives you instructions on what to do to upload a picture from your computer.

A few helpful apps and online programs can help you create your own Minecraft skin. I would use a search engine or the app store for your device to search for a Minecraft skin editor. These apps offer an extensive library of looks. Some provide a quick selection of complete skins, and others let you modify your features pixel by pixel, if you want.

As the Minecraft community has expanded, looks have included hoodies and jeans, mob type skins, mob hunters, business suits, and even a Mario skin. But the options are limitless. Thomas's skin, as shown in Figure 13-10, is modeled after a space commander.

Sadly, PE edition does not allow skin customization.

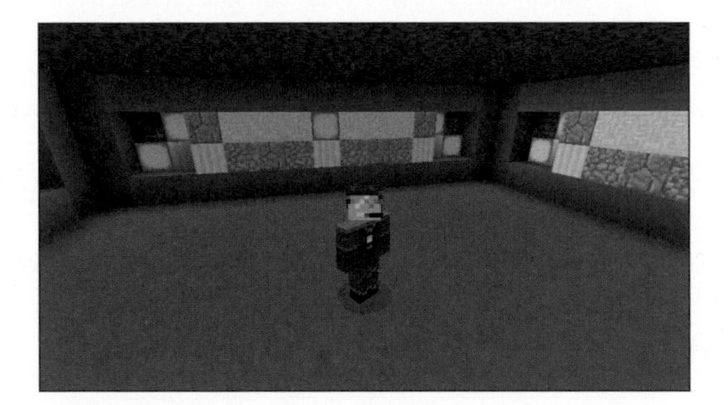

Figure 13-10: Thomas, with customized skin.

Installing Resource Packs

A *resource pack* changes the look and sounds of Minecraft without modifying the code. Previously, resource packs were called *texture packs* and only changed the look of Minecraft. Resource packs are created by Minecraft players. Both terms are commonly used interchangeably. The process can be fairly difficult, though some apps can simplify the process enough that even a teenager can do it. (Simply search the app store for a resource pack editor.)

Common resource packs change the look by adding more pixels per block than in regular Minecraft, making the textures look nicer by changing the blocks to HD-quality textures.

To add resource packs to your Minecraft world, follow these steps:

1. **Click the Resource Packs button.**

   It's on the Options screen (shown in Figure 13-11, as discussed in Table 13-3 and accessed via the Game menu). It opens the Select Resource Packs screen, where you can enable and disable resource packs.

   To get a resource pack into this window, you need to find and download a resource pack.

   When you download and open the resource pack, it should contain the Assets folder at the top.

2. **If it doesn't, open folders until you see that screen.**

   Keep only the folder that holds the Assets folder. You can delete the rest.

3. **In Minecraft, click the Open Resource Packs button.**

   The window that opens is the `resourcepacks` folder in the `.minecraft` folder.

4. **Drag the newly downloaded resource pack into the `resourcepacks` folder. In Minecraft, click the Done button and then click the Resource Packs button again to sync the resource pack window with Minecraft.**

5. **To see the new resource pack in action, hover the mouse cursor over the resource pack's picture and click the arrow. Then click Done. You're all set.**

Figure 13-11: The Select Resource Packs dialog box.

In addition to letting you change textures, resource packs are now changing the languages, music, and even end credits.

One of our favorite resource packs changes the look of Minecraft to that of a comic book. Another popular resource pack simplifies the redstone portion of Minecraft by changing the redstone dust to a wiring effect, making it easier to see the circuitry. Spoof resource packs also exist, including a *Star Wars* pack that was designed to interact with a custom adventure map.

Installing Mods

A mod in Minecraft is a plugin you add to Minecraft that modifies the game by changing the game code, usually adding new items to the game. Unlike bukkit plugins that are used on bukkit servers (see Chapter 12), which also modify the game code, mods are downloaded by players.

A few common mods help the performance of Minecraft. One such mod boosts the frames per second (FPS) of the game. Another one makes items easy to obtain and to spawn in items without using confusing commands.

The mods that are the most fun to use are the ones that add to the game. Think of new mobs that can teleport and blow up, new blocks that work like a spring, new swords that kill new bosses, and new bosses that blow up new types of bombs. That is just the tip of the iceberg.

Installing mods can be difficult. You can use two strategies: Move stuff around in the `.minecraft` folder, which you have to search for on your computer (it's in different places on the Mac and PC) or (an easier method) download and install forge. We recommend the second route, as the first route can be complicated and difficult to accomplish, involving some computer administration skills we didn't include in the "Foolish Assumptions" part of this book. We'll explain how to install Forge next.

Follow these steps to choose the second option, installing forge:

1. **Go to `http://files.minecraftforge.net/minecraftforge/new`.**
2. **In the Promotions section, find the latest version.**

   It should look something like this: `1.8-Latest-New`. You should see a bunch of words next to it, though we only want you to click the (Installer) link.

   This step should send you to AdFly, which is just an ad for malware – DO NOT CLICK ON THE MIDDLE OF THE SCREEN!

   Clicking on AdFly may download a virus.

3. **Rather than click anywhere on that site, go to the upper right corner of the screen that should start counting down.**

   You're instructed to wait 5 seconds.

4. **After 5 seconds, click the Skip Ad button where the text used to be. If you then see the words Click Here to Continue, click and you should see the proper page.**

   After you click the Skip Ad button, the download begins.

5. **When the download is complete, open the file. When the Mod System Installer window opens, click the Install Client button and then click OK.**

   You should see a message about successful installation.

6. **Click OK.**

   If you don't see the message, follow the directions in the window that tells you what to do next.

7. **Open the Minecraft launcher.**

   Create a new profile (that's our recommendation) or edit a profile instead. After you click either profile, the Profile Editor window opens.

8. **Click the Use Version list and scroll to the bottom.**

   You should see the message Release 8-Forge <a string of numbers>.

9. **Click on the option, Release 8 Forge in the version list.**

10. **Click the Save Profile button. Press Play to start running the forge.**

Now that forge is running, to install a mod, download one and make sure it matches your current forge. Then go to your .minecraft folder. You may notice that the files in the .minecraft folder are not all the same as they were before. Don't worry about any of it. Just open the mods folder and drag the mod to that folder. When you start up your modded Minecraft profile, the mod should be installed.

AdFly is a dumping ground for malware and computer viruses. However, many creators of mods have such long URL tags that they are forced to use AdFly to shorten their links. Be sure to install strong antivirus software on your computer.

Installing Mod Packs

A *mod pack* is a group of mods that are used in Minecraft to produce a different Minecraft experience. Most mod packs can be found in mod pack launchers, or launchers (like the Minecraft launcher) that hold multiple mod packs. The most common ones are Technic and Feed The Beast (often referred to as FTB). They have a variety of different packs and usually are one or two updates behind Minecraft. For example, Minecraft at the time this book was written is at 1.8, but most mod packs are played in Minecraft 1.7.10 or 1.6.4. The reason is that most mods cannot update quickly.

Hands down, my favorite mod pack is Feed The Beast. It has both jetpack and energy quarries.

Some mod packs are for computers that have less RAM memory, usually referred to as *lite packs* (as in FTBLite). Some launchers even have custom resource packs in which to play the mod pack. All mod pack launchers require a Minecraft account, just like the Minecraft launcher. When you start up a launcher and choose a mod pack to play, you usually have to wait quite a long time because it is downloading tens to hundreds of mods.

The PE version of Minecraft does not have an open game code system. Consequently, mods and resource packs aren't generally available.

Some hackers have jailbroken mobile devices and created limited external customization of the PE Minecraft version. However, this is extremely difficult and uncommon.

Customizing Gameplay Through Apps

As discussed throughout this chapter, many players use apps to customize their gameplay. Seed apps for your mobile device provide a list of seed codes with descriptions and pictures to help you choose the seeds you want, and they're the simplest of the external Minecraft apps (that we could find). Other common apps include skin customization apps and resource pack apps. Though these apps are used on mobile devices, they do not usually work in the PE version of Minecraft. Instead, data from the app is uploaded to the PC version to be used. To download apps for Minecraft, search for *skin creator* in your mobile app store of choice. We show you an example in Figure 13-12.

Seed codes are not identical across Minecraft platforms. Players need different seed codes for the PC, PE, and Console editions. Many apps, though accessed via a PE device, are actually used to customize the PC game.

Your Minecraft game should now have taken on a whole new life — new modes, new types of worlds, new custom uploads. The sandbox just got a whole lot bigger.

Figure 13-12: App store.

14

Minecraft in the Larger World

In This Chapter

- Using external sites and resources
- Exploring YouTube and beyond
- Visiting Minecon

After you've been through the Nether dimension and into the End game, what happens next? Many resources are available to help you continually make Minecraft a fun and addictive experience. From YouTube to the Minecraft wiki to even saving up your money and visiting Minecon each year, you can find plenty to do that's related to Minecraft — outside of the Minecraft experience itself.

Checking Out External Sites and Resources

The Minecraft community has found many ways to connect Minecraft with real life, by building famous architectural structures in Creative mode and using Minecraft as an educational tool and a supplemental resource. As long as you have an Internet connection, you have an outlet to a vast and creative educational community.

Some truly amazing websites — such as the Minecraft forums (`www.minecraftforum.net/forum`) and Minecraft wiki (`www.minecraftwiki.net`) — focus on Minecraft, by providing information, discussion, and downloads of third-party programs. You can use various Minecraft websites to complete the tasks in the following list:

- **Ask for help.** Many people offer their helpful opinions on the more advanced concepts of Minecraft.
- **Discuss ideas.** Share your Minecraft passion with others.

- **Play custom maps.** Lots of people build maps that add extra challenge to the game or create a whole new way of playing. Maps generally require extra third-party programs to play.
- **Download mods and resource packs.** These items greatly change the look and feel of Minecraft and allow you to alter the game in exciting ways.
- **Customize your character's skin.** Change your avatar's look by downloading a skin or making your own in an image editing program. You can find instructions at `www.minecraft.net/profile`.
- **Build and share.** Connect to the community via forums, servers, or ask questions on social media (like our Facebook Group at `www.facebook.com/groups/minecraftfordummies/`) to optimize your Minecraft experience.

Take precautions, such as installing an anti-virus program, when visiting websites and downloading items, to avoid infecting your computer with a nasty virus or another type of malware. Thomas learned firsthand about downloading mods to his computer, because once one of those mods included malware, and Jesse had a doozy of a time getting rid of the mess.

Parents should apply an antivirus and protection solution, such as Norton Internet Security, to protect the computer — and their kids — from the harmful content and apps that are sometimes found on malicious sites. Kids should always ask their parents before downloading any apps, games, skins, mods, or programs from the Internet. In our house, asking for permission is a condition for being able to play (or even to write about Minecraft).

Watching YouTube

One of the best resources online is YouTube — it has thousands of Minecraft-related YouTube channels and videos. Many of them offer tutorials on everything you need, from building to surviving and from building redstone contraptions to downloading mods — and, of course, so much more.

Many players watch Minecraft YouTube channels largely for entertainment purposes, to see what crazy or amazing structures, customs maps, or mining systems have been created. We often watch Minecraft music videos and spoofs and share them around the dinner table. In fact, for us, Minecraft-themed YouTube videos are the new Saturday morning cartoons!

When you subscribe to your favorite YouTube channels, you'll definitely want to subscribe to the YouTube channels we've made — Minecraft For Dummies (shown in Figure 14-1) and Minecraft Recipes For Dummies — to get access to all the great recipes and tips you see in this book, and more. Come say Hi at

```
youtube.com/minecraftdummiesbook
youtube.com/minecraftrecipesfd
```

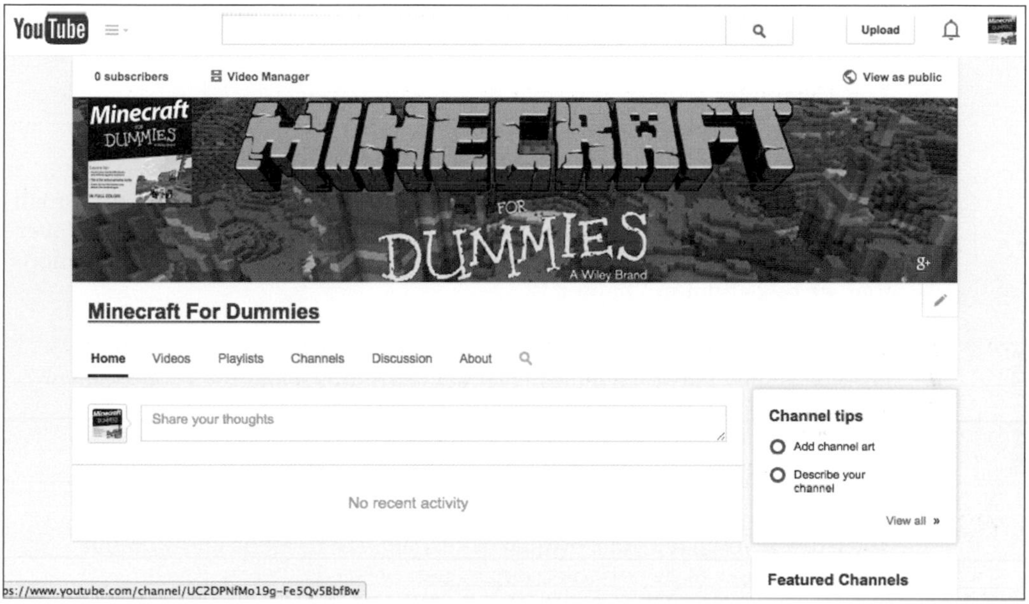

Figure 14-1: The Minecraft For Dummies YouTube channel.

Subscribing to Redstone YouTubers

The Redstone YouTubers (also known as *redstoners*) are channels on YouTube that focus primarily on redstone. Here are our favorites:

- **Sethbling (**`www.youtube.com/user/sethbling`**):** Works mostly with command blocks, usually to create new concepts. Sethbling (who is also a MindCracker, or member of the special MindCrack community of Youtubers) and has worked on a few bukkit plugins (for altering Bukkit servers) and MCEdit (a program for editing worlds in Minecraft) filters. He has created many minigames.
- **Mumbo Jumbo (**`youtube.com/user/ThatMumboJumbo`**):** Working primarily with redstone contraptions that are survival friendly, Mumbo Jumbo creates outstanding redstone tutorials, including the Batman equipment pole, a 2 x 2 hidden storage area, and a variety of other contraptions. He has made a few minigames and is a member of Hermitcraft, another community, or guild of YouTubers.

- **ACtennisAC (**youtube.com/user/actennisac**):** Makes working models in Minecraft from real-life objects. Famous for his fully functional Minecraft printer, fully functional iPhone, fully functional escalator, and his texture pack based on the Minecraft LEGO sets, ACtennisAC has made a couple of minigames, including Wii Sports in Minecraft, Angry Birds in Minecraft, and snowboarding in Minecraft.

Finding Minecraft YouTube groups

Minecraft YouTubers often create multiple entertainment video series at a time. The most common series for Minecraft YouTubers are single-player survival series, multiplayer survival series, and modded Minecraft single-player series. Often, the modded series is played in modpacks, which provide mods that we talk about in Chapter 13.

You can find multiple Minecraft YouTube groups. The members of these groups usually play on a multiplayer server that is *whitelisted:* Only player profiles listed on the whitelist are allowed to join.

Following Minecraft YouTube groups

The following are our favorite Minecraft groups to follow and watch on YouTube; if you have your own favorites, be sure to let us know on our Facebook Page, at facebook.com/minecraftfd:

- **Mindcrack (**youtube.com/user/MindCrackNetwork**):** This official YouTube group is so popular that the Mojang staff (the creators of Minecraft) are an unofficial part of the group. The Mindcrack team even has their own booth to themselves at Minecon.
- **Hermitcraft (**youtube.com/playlist?list=PL9188F5316A0720BB**):** A few members of this official YouTube group (it has 25 members) are related to Mindcrack in some way.

Watching other YouTube entertainment channels

Outside of the larger group channels, check out some YouTube channels created by individuals. Here are some of our favorites:

- **Ethoslab, by Etho (**youtube.com/user/EthosLab**):** Etho has vowed to make his channel, Ethoslab, kid friendly. Jesse likes Ethoslab because he doesn't like to hear swearing in videos. Etho has one of the longest single-player Minecraft YouTube video series of all time, with more than 350 episodes. His longest-lasting video series is his map-making series, where he makes a map named Battlebane.

  Etho makes only one or two episodes of his map-making series per year and is a member of the Mindcrack network.

- **YouAlwaysWin, by Metius and BrotherGUNNS** (`youtube.com/user/YouAlwaysWin`)**:** This channel is led by two friends — Metius and BrotherGUNNS — who do almost everything together. They often refer to themselves as Dumb (Metius) and Dumber (BrotherGUNNS), and they play adventure maps and mod packs together.
- **Ssundee** (`youtube.com/user/ssundee`)**:** SSundee *loves* mods and creates daily episodes — usually, one episode of a series per week. He usually has two or three modpack series and an additional mod review series, and he has an additional multiplayer server series.

JOSEPH'S CORNER

Especially during the summer, I watch too much Minecraft YouTube, so my mom limits me to 30 minutes a day. That still gives me enough time to watch my favorite tutorials without spending too much time on YouTube. She also has to approve the channels I watch, to make sure that they're kid friendly.

Watching building-focused YouTube channels

If you're interested in finding better ways to build in Minecraft, check out the work of these hosts of channels on YouTube:

- **BdoubleO100, by BdoubleO100 and Generikb** (`youtube.com/user/BdoubleO100`)**:** This channel is often about building rather than survival. Together, BdoubleO100 and Generikb (who have a Mindcrack relationship) have created the B Team, where they create businesses. The B team's favorite item in Minecraft is emeralds. Their businesses often involve payment with emeralds. BdoubleO100 is a member of Mindcrack.
- **TheRealMegaMiner** (`youtube.com/user/TheRealMegaMiner`)**:** This guy is someone who can help get *anyone* started with building. His simple tutorials show you how to build a simple castle, watchtower, tavern, pvp/spleef arena, and various other creations. This channel can definitely help you start building.
- **AlanBeckerMinecraft, by Alan Becker** (`youtube.com/user/AlanBeckerMinecraft`)**:** Alan Becker created Animator vs Animation 1, 2, 3, and 4 (one of our favorite YouTube channels). As part of his Minecraft channel on YouTube, he built a replica of the Japanese animated fantasy film *Spirited Away.* He also has a few redstone inventions.

Learning about plugins

In this section, we describe our two favorite YouTube channels that show you how to create Minecraft bukkit plugins. Just search for *Minecraft plugins* on YouTube to find many more!

- **StormCoreFilms (**youtube.com/user/StormCoreFilms**):** This simple plugin writer also teaches you how to create HD texture packs. The StormCoreFilms tutorials, though few in number, are excellent.
- **TheBCBroz (**youtube.com/user/TheBCBroz**):** This experienced plugin maker has a total of 82 tutorials, covering everything from sign teleportation to kits. He's working on the series Bukkit Minigame Tutorial, where he creates a minigame using Bukkit.

Finding map makers

As you progress in Minecraft, you'll eventually want to start making your own maps. These two mapmakers on YouTube can help you with the process:

- **SimplySarc (**youtube.com/user/SimplySarc**):** SimplySarc thinks of the coolest and most random concepts in Minecraft, including the telltale bomb (a bomb that talks when it blows up), sheepstone (redstone turned into sheep), and cracking an egg. He usually creates only fragments that can be implemented into an adventure map.
- **Dragnoz (**youtube.com/user/dragnoz**):** Dragnoz finds new ways to implement new features for his maps. He has created elemental arrows, lasers, player mind control, and much more. Some of his maps are Bouncy Steve, Face your RAGE, TRON Fire, and Packman.

You can find many more mapmakers by simply searching for *Minecraft map makers* on YouTube.

Listening to Minecraft music on YouTube

All sorts of fun Minecraft-focused songs are on YouTube. One of our favorite YouTube channel hosts is ZexyZec, who has partnered with popular YouTube music artists to produce catchy music video parodies that combine Minecraft with popular songs. Another one, Blue Monkey, has partnered with similar artists for parodies, as described in this list:

- **"Running Out of Time" (**https://www.youtube.com/watch?v=awv8REl5_BQ**):** This parody of the song "Say Something" (by A Great Big World) is performed by Peter and Evynne Hollens.
- **"Mine With Me" (**https://www.youtube.com/watch?v=ed88MqPh--c**)**: Performed by Lindee Link, this song is a parody of Taylor Swift's "You Belong With Me."
- **"Promise" (**https://www.youtube.com/watch?v=kPtWVYzC2vU**):** Also performed by Lindee Link, this song is a parody of Christina Perri's "A Thousand Years."
- **"Minecraft" (**https://www.youtube.com/watch?v=SSlxrE03DBo**):** This video was produced by Blue Monkey in conjunction with Peter and Evynne Hollens, as a parody of Pink's "True Love."

Going Beyond YouTube

Because of the popularity of Minecraft, contests and clubs have formed in local communities. (Even the authors' local library had a Minecraft contest to find the teenager with the best building construct.) Other groups focus on redstone or plugin development. To find a group near you, check your local library or ask around at your school.

Merchandise (see Figure 14-2) has also become part of the game. One of the most popular Halloween costumes from Minecraft is a creeper (and many moms still aren't even sure what it is). Because the game is often compared to LEGO, it's no surprise that you can now find an entire series of LEGO Minecraft sets (and more are already scheduled). After you add stuffed animals, shirts, lamps, toys, and kitchen items, Minecraft items bring the game to life for younger players and are part of the collection for fans. And now, with the possibility of a major motion picture being made, Minecraft mania will only continue to grow.

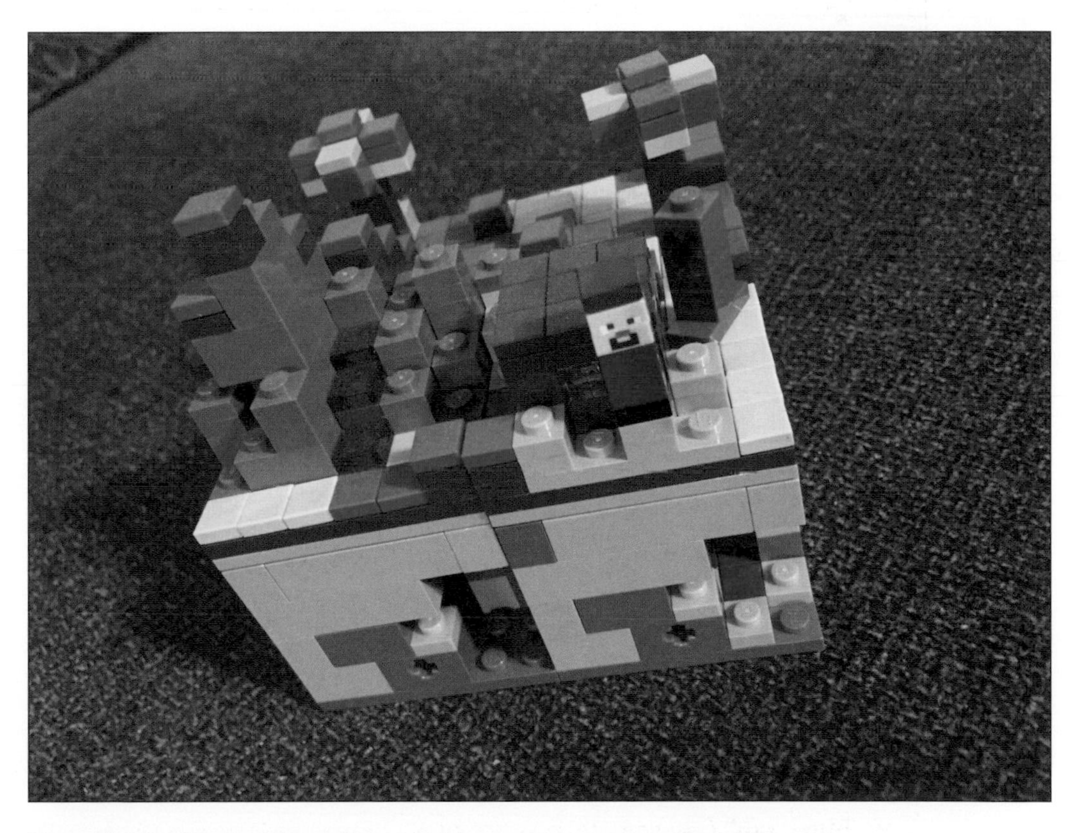

Figure 14-2: Our favorite Minecraft merchandise — can you guess what it is?

Going to Minecon

So what can a fan do to properly show their Minecraft passion? In addition to playing the game, becoming an expert at mod development, playing with friends on multiplayer servers, buying the merchandise, and reading this book, it might be time to consider making the trek to Minecon.

This weekend convention, officially sponsored by Mojang, attracts thousands of fellow Minecraft fans. It has been held in both the United States and Europe. One cool bonus is that attendees receive unique capes in their Minecraft accounts, which they can wear on their characters in the game. Unfortunately, it's almost impossible to buy tickets (they sell out in seconds) and the event is difficult to attend, often because it is not close by most players of Minecraft. Consequently, many other types of conventions, particularly Comic Cons, which are held in more locations, often have unofficial Minecraft sections (which is perfect for wearing one of those Halloween creeper costumes).

Part V
Making Minecraft a Family Affair

Visit `www.dummies.com` for more great *For Dummies* content online.

In this part . . .

- Choose between Minecraft PC and Minecraft PE
- Get to know the available platforms
- Experiment with Minecraft game modes
- Helpful information for parents

15

Choosing the Platform That Works for You

In This Chapter

- Picking the right platform: PC or PE
- Playing Minecraft on the Xbox 360, Xbox One, and PS3
- Getting Minecraft for Raspberry Pi
- Preparing for future editions of Minecraft

Your first major decision in Minecraft is to pick a gaming platform. Choosing the platform can be tough: You have to decide how much of the game you want to play and how much you're willing to pay.

In this book, we primarily discuss the platform Minecraft PC/Mac/Linux (or Minecraft PC or just PC Edition). We also show you what you need in order to play all other versions — notably, the PE (Pocket Edition) version for the iPhone, iPad, and Kindle. The Minecraft platforms listed here will likely expand in the next couple of years, including, we hope, a Nintendo Wii version:

- Minecraft PC
- Minecraft PE
- Minecraft Xbox 360 and Xbox One
- Minecraft PS3
- Minecraft Raspberry Pi

Playing Minecraft PC

Minecraft PC (which stands for Personal Computer), shown in Figure 15-1, is the edition built for computer desktops, including Windows, Mac, and Linux. Minecraft PC is the most updated Minecraft version to-date, and it's the most expensive. Though the game can be downloaded for free, it cannot be played without an account. Consequently, if you want to play with someone else simultaneously, you have to buy an account for each person.

Figure 15-1: Playing Minecraft in the PC Edition.

This situation can be a headache for parents with multiple children who want to play at the same time. However, each person can share an account by playing in different worlds. That's what the authors' family does — with seven kids. Using this approach, no one interrupts another person's game.

Minecraft PC has more features than any other Minecraft platform, and it was the first platform to be created. At the time this book was written, the PC version cost $26.95. The PC version goes beyond the four main mobs and also offers enderman mobs and nether creatures.

Developing Minecraft

You can find a brief history of Minecraft PC at www.minecraft.net. The original version of Minecraft was called Cave Game (shown in Figure 15-2) and is now labeled Minecraft Pre-Classic. In Pre-Classic, the name changed from Cave Game to Minecraft: Order of the Stone, but was later changed to Minecraft to avoid confusion with the comic book series *Order of the Stick.*

Next, Minecraft got to a period where it was just called Minecraft. This period is called Classic. Then Minecraft went into a stage called InDev (or in Development). Two months later InfDev (Infinite Development) was created. Later Alpha began followed by Beta. After Beta you get Minecraft 1.1 which is now ever changing as it rapidly grows to 1.2, 1.3 and even 1.8 and beyond!

At the time of this writing, Minecraft PC requires an Intel Pentium D or AMD Athlon 64 (or K8) 2.6 GHz or greater CPU. (An Intel I3 or AMD Athlon II chip is recommended, though.) It requires a minimum of 2GB of RAM, and a graphics processor (GPU) with either Intel HD or an AMD (or ATI) Radeon chip with OpenGL 2.1. (A GeForce 2xx series or Radeon HD 5xx series card is recommended.) You need at least 200MB of hard drive space, though 1GB is recommended. In addition, you need at least the Java 6 release 45 installed (which should be automatically prompted upon installing the game). Mojang recommends Java 7 or greater for the most optimum gameplay, however. To see all the latest requirements from Mojang, see the Help web page at

```
https://help.mojang.com/customer/portal/articles/
325948-minecraft-system-requirements
```

My favorite version is the PC version because you can join other people's servers more easily and start LAN worlds. PC also has the most advanced mobs, items, and things you can do in the game making it a much more interesting experience to play in.

Exploring Minecraft PE

Minecraft Pocket Edition (or Minecraft PE) is Minecraft for your pocket. It operates on your smartphone or tablet, and it's available — for only $6.99! — in the iTunes App Store (for iOS devices) and on Google Play (for Android devices). Minecraft PE lags behind Minecraft PC in development and won't catch up any time soon, but the price is still quite a bargain. You can access Minecraft servers and play with your friends easily on other Minecraft PE devices. You can also download it on multiple devices for the iPhone/iPod/iPad as long as all of the Apple products share the same Apple ID. Rather than log in by account, you can save your game progress on the device you're playing on.

More PE versions have been purchased than PC versions. In addition to the game's low price, people love being easily able to take the game with them wherever they go. (Both kids and adults frequently play the game when they have a long wait or even a few minutes of free time.) By statistics alone, there's a good chance you're playing Minecraft PE on a mobile device (and that's okay). As on the PC version, have each person in your family play in a different world so that no one alters what another player has done.

More than one player can play simultaneously without making multiple purchases (unlike in the PC version). In our family, one kid plays on the iPad and another on the iPhone, each having their own game, but I purchased the app only once because both devices share an Apple ID.

The PE version lacks some of the more advanced areas of Minecraft, such as redstone, commands, villager trading, and the End. Ultimately, most gamers who start with this version will want to eventually purchase the PC version, to get the best experience out of the game.

Interestingly, however, the PE version has a few unique items that the PC version does not. The stonecutter block, not found in the PC version, is central to PE gameplay. Other unique features include the beetroot crop (though it's rumored to be featured in the next update of PC) and baby animals, which follow adults instinctively. Figure 15-2 shows Minecraft PE in action.

Figure 15-2: Playing Minecraft PE.

For new players and younger players, Minecraft PE is the best platform. It's user friendly for multiplayer experiences, offers fewer settings, and is inexpensive. Its biggest drawbacks are that it has no commands, no skins or texture packs (without hacking), and no major redstone.

Minecraft PE requires Android Gingerbread or later, or iOS 5.0 or later. Any device that can run these operating systems should be capable of running Minecraft. To read more about the latest system requirements for Minecraft PE, see the Minecraft wiki at

```
http://minecraft.gamepedia.com/Pocket_Edition#System_
requirements
```

Using Minecraft on the Xbox 360, Xbox One, and PlayStation 3

Minecraft for Xbox 360, Xbox One and PS3 (or "console edition") costs $20. It's hard to figure out unless you first complete the demo. The disc holds custom-made worlds and skins, but you have to buy texture packs separately.

In our opinion, you're better off paying the extra $7 for the PC version, which includes texture packs, instead of buying the Xbox version and texture packs separately. If you're used to playing games on a gaming console, however, this version may be for you.

The console edition mimics the PC version and includes the extra mobs, bosses, and nether creatures that you don't see in the PE edition. The only major difference is that it doesn't feature infinite worlds, but still offers a large number and variety of worlds. If your computer has limited memory or you would prefer to play on a gaming system rather than on a computer, this format gives you the nearly full PC experience without having to use a PC.

Parents should turn off the purchase ability of the Xbox to prevent the little hands in their households from being able to purchase texture packs. Jesse learned this lesson the hard way when his 5-year-old bought a few at his father's expense!

You need to complete the demo before starting game play.

Using Minecraft for Raspberry Pi

If you've purchased the extremely portable mini computer named Raspberry Pi, you're in luck — you can also play Minecraft on your new device. Minecraft for Raspberry Pi (or Minecraft Pi, for short) is in the alpha stage (it will have plenty more updates) and has only two options: Start Game and Join Game. On top of that, Minecraft Pi has only one game mode: Creative. Most Minecraft players spend at least some (if not most) of their time playing in Survival mode, so Pi is for testing redstone and building creations. In fact, it was built to encourage kids to learn how to program, and hack, Minecraft. The best part of using Minecraft Pi is that it's *free*. You can download the Minecraft Pi edition on your Raspberry Pi device at `http://pi.minecraft.com` using the browser on your Raspberry Pi and following the instructions you find.

Anticipating Future Editions of Minecraft

So many devices and so many platforms! You can only wonder how difficult it is for Mojang (the creators of Minecraft) to keep up with it all. A frequent request — and likely the most anticipated version of Minecraft — is for the Nintendo Wii U. Unfortunately, the company has no plan to even develop it. By the time you read this chapter, a version for Xbox One and PlayStation 4 should recently have been released. You can probably expect future upgrades to those as well.

16

Understanding the Minecraft Game Modes

In This Chapter

- Understanding the types of Survival mode
- Playing in Creative mode
- Exploring Adventure mode
- Surviving Hardcore mode
- Exploring Spectator mode
- Understanding dying and respawning

One of the most exciting parts of Minecraft is that it can be played in different modes for different purposes. That way, the game not only increases in difficulty (or decreases, if necessary) but also allows the game to be played in a new way. This chapter focuses on understanding the different modes, choosing the right mode for your game, and switching between modes as your game progresses. Later in this chapter, Table 16-1 describes the different modes and how they compare against each other.

Entering Survival Mode

Survival mode is the most-often-played, most-often-viewed, and most exciting mode of Minecraft. Unless you activate cheats, you cannot switch between modes, but you can switch between difficulty levels. In the PC version of Minecraft, you can click to select a difficulty level; whereas in the PE version, you use a slider to select the difficulty level.

The four options within Survival mode are based on the game's level of difficulty.

- **Peaceful:** We recommend Peaceful mode (or just Peaceful), which is the easiest difficulty level, for new or younger players who are starting a survival world, because the Hunger bar never depletes. The Health bar regenerates quickly (even if you're not at full hunger), and no hostile mobs will spawn, much less attack.

If you enter a more difficult mode, a mode other than Peaceful mode, the enderdragon can still be a small threat.

TIP

To start a survival world, begin in Peaceful, and switch to a higher difficulty level as you get geared up.

- **Easy:** The Easy difficulty level (or just Easy) is the easiest level that spawns monsters. In Easy mode, hostile mobs do less damage, and creepers cancel their explosions from a short distance. The Hunger bar depletes, and when it is empty, will hurt you until 5 full hearts remain. In Easy mode, cave spiders don't poison you, and the wither doesn't wither you, though wither skeletons do. Easy mode is a great place to start out if you still want to fight and kill.

I play in Easy mode because I like dealing with the challenges of the game, such as gathering food and avoiding mobs, without losing.

- **Normal:** In Normal mode (or just Normal), hostile mobs can spawn, and hostile mobs deal the standard amount of damage value. Also, if the Hunger bar is empty, you continue taking damage until you eat or the inventory decreases to half a heart. This is the medium-level mode in of Minecraft. It's not too easy and not too hard — it's in the middle. This mode is designed for traditional gameplay, balancing survival, building, crafting, gathering resources, and farming. Starting at this level can be difficult, especially if you want to explore the game rather than focus on survival.

Hard: In Hard mode, hostile mobs, often called *monsters,* can spawn and dish out more damage, and you have to put quite some distance between you and the creeper to escape from a creeper blast. You must keep an eye on the Hunger bar and find food. Even worse, zombies break down doors, and spiders have a chance to spawn with potion effects.

I rarely play in Hard mode because I rarely make it through more than a couple of nights. The number of monsters, the damage they incur, and the speed at which you go hungry is just too difficult at times for me! It's a fun challenge sometimes, though.

Turn on cheats to switch between modes.

Practicing with Creative Mode

Creative mode is the test-and-practice mode, the build mode, and the ultimate mode for building just about anything you like. In Creative mode, you have unlimited blocks to work with. In this mode, you can get most blocks and items, hostile mobs don't attack you, and you don't have to worry about food or dangerous items such as cactus or lava. Ironically, you can still die as a result of the `void` and `kill` commands. Figure 16-1 shows the extent of what you can do in Creative mode.

Figure 16-1: Survival mode difficulty setting.

You can switch between modes in the same game, so many players spend some time playing in Creative mode, even when they largely play in the more adventurous Survival mode. When you activate cheats (see the later section "Implementing cheats"), you can use Creative mode to manipulate gameplay in Survival mode. Newer players can defeat bosses in Creative mode more easily and then switch back to Survival mode to gain rewards. They can also spawn animals and items to further their Survival mode game.

Creative mode is largely used to try to build all sorts of structures because you have an unlimited number of items at your disposal. You can experiment to see what works, design elaborate houses, try redstone contraptions, and more, as explained in Chapters 8 and 9).

The best thing we have ever created in Creative mode is a portal for use in multiplayer servers. We regularly use Creative mode to test out command blocks, which you cannot do in other modes. When we cannot get our redstone to work, for example, we use Creative mode to troubleshoot the problem.

The best thing I have ever made in Minecraft is a roller coaster. (You can see it in Figure 16-2.) The coaster toured the highlights of the island, including an 8-bit art gallery and a volcano. Then it took “riders’ across the ocean to another island and made crazy, wild turns that wound into a lava pit. I put water below it so that as the lava burns the mine carts, you safely drop into the water without catching on fire. The ride ends when the water drops you into a room and you simply walk out.

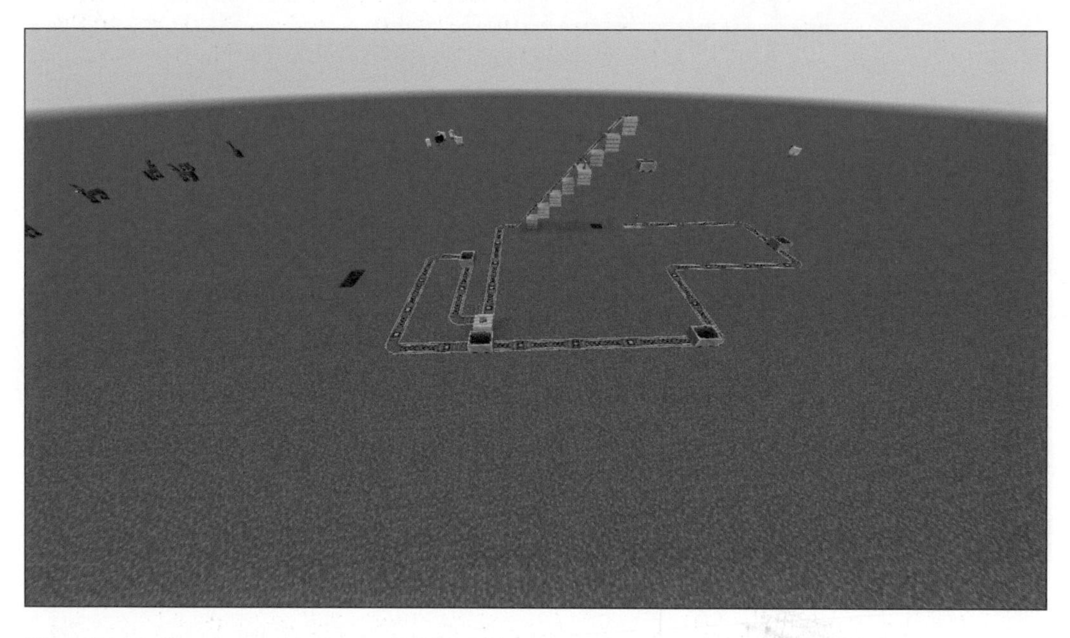

Figure 16-2: In Creative mode, you can build anything to your heart's content, like this roller coaster.

Navigating Adventure Mode

This mode is largely for playing adventure maps or quests. (See Chapter 13 to find out more about them.) If you like end goals, this is the mode for you. But you have few building opportunities, which makes this our least favorite mode. Though adventure maps don't come with the PC version, many maps are available to download for free.

I never play in Adventure mode unless I'm in a multiplayer game that my friends want to play.

Torturing Yourself Through Hardcore Mode

Some players would consider Hardcore mode to be cruel and unusual punishment for Minecraft. Hardcore mode is an adventure, where you're always aware of the forces of the night — one slip can cause devastating disasters. As you play Minecraft in Hardcore mode, you'll believe that you should have died three times already. Trust us: This is an exciting, risky, edge-of-your-seat adventure, and in this section, we explain why.

In Hardcore mode, you have only one life — when you die, you have no option to respawn. Hardcore mode is set to the most difficult survival level, and you can't change it. To top all that off, when you die and go back to the title screen, your Hardcore world gets deleted. What a cruel thing to do!

The creators of the game obviously wanted you to have no infinite lives in Hardcore mode. Even the cheats don't work. You can easily tell when you're playing in Hardcore mode by looking at the number of hearts in the inventory — they have angry-looking "eyes," as shown in Figure 16-3. Only hardcore players use this mode — it isn't available in the PE edition.

Hardcore mode is always set to the Hard difficulty level, but differs from Hard Survival mode.

Figure 16-3: In Hardcore mode, the hearts have angry-looking eyes, a symbol of the frustration you'll feel as you play.

Seeing the World Through Spectator Mode

The fun-to-play Spectator mode lets you play Minecraft as an observer, flying (you can only fly, not walk) throughout the world and viewing it from a birds-eye view. You can also play from the third-person point of view, through the eyes of the different mobs in the game. This feature gives you an interesting perspective: For example, you'll see as the creeper sees the world, with green-tinted vision (or *creeper vision*), as shown in Figure 16-4. Spiders have quintuple vision, showing the world five times in the same screen, whereas endermen have all the colors as opposites of their normal colors. To play as a mob, just left-click to take on their frame of reference and then press the Shift key to go back to flying over your spectator world.

Figure 16-4: Playing as a creeper in Spectator mode shows you the world through green-tinted vision.

Playing in Spectator mode also has a few other benefits, such as being able to explore the world without interacting with it. For example, in Spectator mode, you can fly right through blocks without having to break them.

Additionally, pressing any number on the keyboard displays a teleport system. Pressing any number, pressing 1, and then pressing 1 again shows you all the players you can teleport with. Pressing a number while viewing that teleport menu teleports you to the player corresponding to the number you pressed. Pressing 9 exits from that screen. Pressing a number, pressing 2, and then pressing 2 again displays the team's teleport system. While in that system, press a number to bring up the team corresponding to that number.

After that, pressing it brings up all players on the team. Pressing one of the numbers listed next to the players teleports you to the player corresponding to that number. However, you cannot craft or enchant. This mode is also not available in the PE version.

Table 16-1 Modes in Minecraft

Feature	*Survival*	*Creative*	*Adventure*	*Hardcore*	*Spectator*
Unlimited blocks	Partial	Yes	Partial	Partial	No
Smelting	Yes	Yes	Yes	Yes	No
Respawning	Yes	Yes	Yes	No	Yes
Preset difficulty	No	No	No	Yes	No
Multiplayer	Yes	Yes	Yes	Partial	Yes
Inventory	Yes	Yes	Yes	Yes	Partial
Hunger	Partial	No	Partial	Yes	No
Health	Yes	Hidden	Yes	Yes	Hidden
Enchanting	Yes	Yes	Yes	Yes	No
Crafting	Yes	Yes	Yes	Yes	No
Cheats	Changeable	Preset to Yes	Changeable	No	Changeable
Phasing through blocks	No	No	No	No	Yes
Brewing	Yes	Yes	Yes	Yes	No
Block placing	Yes	Yes	Partial	Yes	No
PE	Yes	Yes	No	No	No

Dying and Respawning

At some point, all players die during a game of Minecraft. Unless you're playing in Hardcore mode, your player will respawn back into the game. You respawn near the original spawn point or near a bed where you last slept. (Lying in a bed changes your spawn point.)

As morbid as it sounds, sometimes in Minecraft, you actually want to die and respawn in order to give yourself a second chance in the game. Dying in and of itself can be a solid strategy within the game.

One strategy is to die near your house, where your bed is, allowing you to respawn there. First off, when you die, you lose all your stuff. And by that, we mean that *all* your stuff falls on the ground. Then you have 5 minutes until they disappear forever. (That's a long time!) All your experience points also drop on the ground. If you pick the orbs back up, you notice that you seem to have lost a few experience points. If you're near your house, you can quickly gather your items without having to start the game over.

Another strategy is to die in an unloaded portion of the game. (This portion, or *chunk,* is a 16 x 16 area that loads dynamically as you move throughout new areas of Minecraft). If a chunk in your world is not loaded, it keeps the data it had when it was last loaded. If you died in an unloaded chunk, your items remain in that chunk because when you died, your items were the last bit of data it saved to that chunk, enabling you to find your stuff quickly.

Many players who realize that they're lost may want to keep going in a single direction until they realize that they're in an unloaded chunk, and then use this strategy.

When you die, the screen tint turns red and displays the phrase "You died!" (See Figure 16-5.) You also see your score and these two buttons:

- **Respawn:** Spawns you back into the game.
- **Title Screen:** Opens the title screen.

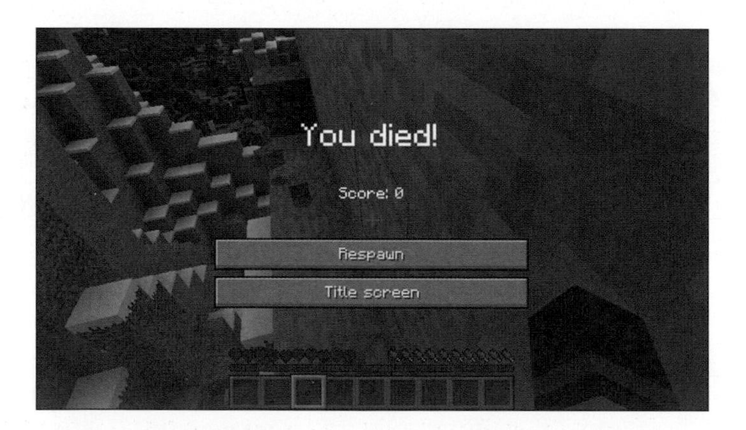

Figure 16-5: The screen you see when you die in Minecraft.

Dying in Hardcore and Peaceful mode

If you're playing in Hardcore mode, *don't die* — you don't have the option to respawn. You only have the Title Screen option. When you try to return to your world, you may notice that you have no world left — when you play in Hardcore mode, Minecraft deletes your world.

A player can die even in Peaceful mode. This happens from touching a cactus, by drowning or suffocating (in sand, for example), falling from a great height, falling into lava (see Figure 16-6), being struck by your own arrow, or being struck by lightning.

Death by lava or cactus destroys the items in the inventory (rather than causes them to drop to the ground).

Figure 16-6: Dying by lava destroys all items in the inventory.

To preserve your items in case of your death, place as much of your inventory into chests (or ender's chests) as you can. Any items in the inventory are dropped when your character dies, but everything in your chests will still be there when you respawn. Unfortunately, there's no way to preserve your experience points.

Implementing cheats

Cheats give you access to all commands in Minecraft. When creating your world, don't forget to turn them on, as seen in Figure 16-7. You can change from Creative mode to Adventure mode to Survival mode by using only two simple words. By using cheats, you can turn the time to daytime, for example, or give items to other players by using the `/give` command. Minecraft becomes a whole new ballgame with cheats enabled, but it also drains the challenge from a stand-alone survival world. It's up to you to decide whether cheating is for you! For a table of cheats, see Chapter 12.

Figure 16-7: The Enabling Cheats screen.

Understanding Game Modes in Minecraft PE

Minecraft PE has only Survival mode and Creative mode. Additionally, the difficulty level in Survival mode is indicated by a sliding bar that you can only slide all the way to the left (Peaceful) or all the way to the right (Hard), as seen in Figure 16-8.

There are no cheats in the PE edition, which means no switching from Survival mode to Creative mode and back to Survival mode. The main reason that the creators of Minecraft don't allow cheats in Minecraft PE is that it has no commands. There's no point to having cheats if you can't specify commands. Even though cheats don't exist in PE, some external apps let you edit the files to do similar types of tasks that a cheat would allow (see Chapter 13).

Figure 16-8: PE Survival Mode bar.

17

Understanding What Every Parent Needs to Know about Minecraft

In This Chapter

- Teaching with Minecraft
- Understanding ways to keep kids safe while playing Minecraft
- Learning proper Minecraft etiquette
- Playing with children

This chapter was written entirely by Jesse, Thomas's dad and someone who's familiar with the concerns of parenting a Minecraft "Steve!" (the character name everyone assumes when they play Minecraft).

If you're a parent, you may have jumped directly to this chapter. In fact, it would have been my first choice, too. Your kids are likely avid Minecraft players who try to play the game every chance they get. "Mom, can I use your iPad?" is an often-heard call in our home. Or "Dad, can you log in to the PC for us?" You're probably trying to figure out why they're so enamored by the game and whether playing is good for them.

In this chapter, I hope to put your mind at ease by sharing what we've done in our family of seven kids, whose ages range from newborn to 14. (Five of the seven are old enough to play Minecraft, and they truly enjoy the game.) The truth is that Minecraft is an amazing teaching tool and a product that every parent can use to encourage exploratory learning, where children get to explore new concepts in a controlled environment.

Teaching Through Minecraft

When I asked a couple of parents on Facebook what their concerns are about Minecraft, the first questions they asked were, "What's the hook?" and "Why do kids spend so much time playing it?" For a parent like me, I look at the game and see an old-style graphical world in what looks like 8-bit graphics from the 1990s. And then I can't help but wonder why this game is interesting in any way to the current generation, which is intensely interested in 3D and high-resolution graphics.

However, I asked my son Thomas to write most of this book because I wanted him to be the one to show me what topics pique his interest and to explain why they're interesting to him. If you spend some time reading the chapters in this book, you'll quickly realize that Minecraft is much more than a silly-looking game. It lets you explore an entire world where you experience life by engaging in these types of activities:

- **Mining and geography/geology:** The sole premise of Minecraft is that you dig into your world's natural resources and gather different types of stone, precious metals, ore, and wood in order to build and create structures, as shown in Figure 17-1. The more you mine, the more you can build and create.

Figure 17-1: The first concept that your kids explore in Minecraft is likely to be geology and the process of mining to "create" structures.

Kids can quickly see that certain types of metal and stone cut faster than others. Wood can burn if placed near a flame or lava. Lava lurks deep within the earth. And dangerous creatures roam among the trees and plants!

- **Farming:** Our family announced our latest pregnancy by taking a screen shot of a pink sheep and a blue sheep that had just produced a random pink sheep. (Yes, it was a girl. See Figure 17-2 to see the announcement.) In Minecraft farming, you get to learn about "the birds and the bees" through animals in 8-bit format — a format that's safe for young kids to view (and fun, too).

Figure 17-2: We used two sheep mating in Minecraft to announce an upcoming birth.

On a Minecraft farm, you learn about growing plants and about needing to water plants to make them grow. You learn about preventing pests and other creatures that can harm your plants and animals. You also learn that the meat you eat comes from real-life animals that you have to kill before eating them. (Don't worry: It's all in 8-bit format, so kids don't see real violence.)

On a Minecraft farm, you can do things like shear sheep and collect wool. Thomas even created a farm that automatically breeds, hatches, collects, kills, and cooks chickens for eating later.

- **Nutrition:** In Minecraft, you have to keep your character healthy. (Every default user is named Steve.) Gathering nutritious foods best maintains your health. Try some beetroot soup. Or have an apple. Keeping your character's nutrition level stable helps the character last longer in the game.
- **Art and architecture:** From full-tilt architecture to simply building fun designs and contraptions, you can express the artist in you in Minecraft. You can create dye from objects such as beets and flowers that you collect throughout the game. You can then use the dye to create panels to decorate your house, for example, or to color wool for other types of items in your house or dwelling place.

  Players have created extravagant items such as ships and castles and even entire reproductions of various landmarks, such as the Eiffel Tower and the *Millenium Falcon* (from *Star Wars*). Entire cities have been reproduced in Minecraft. The sky is, quite literally, the limit.
- **Logic and math:** This is one of our favorites, because we're computer nerds. Minecraft uses binary logic to implement contraptions out of an electricity-like dust called *redstone dust.* You can use redstone to create logic-based devices that react in different ways based on power supplied to them. Even if your children don't realize it, creating redstone contraptions helps them learn binary logic, which is a primary element of programming and electronics that can be applied later in life. Check out Chapter 8 to see more about the topics your child can learn about with redstone.
- **Electronics:** When you're working with redstone, you're creating simple electronic and mechanical devices. Many of the devices work as transistors, capacitors, and even resistors to some extent, which are the basic building blocks of any electronic device or chip. If you can figure out how to compare the different redstone devices, you'll be able to help your child apply these contraptions to real life to build their own real-life robots and other fun, electronic devices.

  We're big fans of LEGO Mindstorms. Using the concepts he learns about in Minecraft, Thomas builds real-life circuitry using LEGO blocks, a little programming, and some simple logic.
- **Computer programming:** Computer programming and electronics truly go hand in hand. Like electronics, computer programming uses logic to decide what happens in the computer program. Because the redstone circuits in Minecraft are virtual, each circuit is in essence a computer program.

In addition, you can do some fun things with actual computer programming if you want to let your kids experiment outside of Minecraft. For example, many players create their own mods of Minecraft to do fun things that are not natural to the game. Or you might let your kids set up their own Minecraft server and learn a little about systems administration in the process.

Knowing Where to Buy Minecraft

If you have kids or work with kids (Minecraft is great for teachers as a learning platform!), there's a good chance they're approaching you and asking you to buy Minecraft for them. Likely, they'll direct you to `http://minecraft.net` and ask you to buy them an account. This account is required if they want to play the PC version. If your kids are playing only the Pocket Edition (PE) for mobile devices, they don't need an account, but you still need to purchase the app to allow full gameplay. In this section, we describe the different game types and specify how to help your child get started.

Differentiating between game types

In Minecraft, you should be familiar with the following game types, all of which we discuss throughout this book:

- **PC Edition:** Though not as popular as the PE Edition (described in the following bullet), the PC edition, depicted in Figure 17-3, is played on a desktop computer. It lets players do much, much more than they can in any other edition. If you want your child to truly explore and learn everything they can from Minecraft — and expand their minds beyond any level you've imagined — be sure to download the PC edition for them to play on a desktop computer. The cost of the PC Edition and a Mojang account is a one-time fee of $26.95 per account (at the time of this writing). For us, it's totally worth the investment.

  Minecraft PC Edition is free, but every player must have an account. This edition also lets you play on other servers. We've found that this strategy is generally safe, but be sure that you know which servers your kids are playing on and which players they play with.

- **PE Edition:** PE stands for Pocket Edition, the edition of Minecraft that works on all mobile devices. PE Edition works on any iOS device or Android device, including Kindle.

Figure 17-3: The PC Edition requires a little more effort to play, but allows more ability to explore, unlike Minecraft PE.

PE Edition is much more limited than the PC Edition. On the PE Edition, you can play only with other players on your own network who are also playing on PE Edition. PE Edition players can't play with PC Edition players, and vice versa. Also, the PE Edition tends to be a little easier to play because you don't have to know how to arrange the items you acquire in order to create new structures. As soon as you have the right items in the inventory (where all your items are stored), Minecraft PE Edition gives you all the options for structures you can create with those items, as depicted in Figure 17-4.

Lastly, PE Edition doesn't require you to have a Minecraft account. Instead, you have to purchase the game from the app store for your device, which is usually much cheaper than buying a Minecraft PC Edition account.

Get your kids started on PE Edition first, and then as they get better, introduce them to the PC Edition. As a parent, you'll appreciate that the PC Edition is where the greatest level of learning occurs.

- **Minecraft for Xbox 360 and Xbox One:** Microsoft owns Mojang (the creator of Minecraft), so you can buy versions for your Xbox 360 or Xbox One console as well. They work similarly to the PE Edition, and you can play them only with other Xbox Live users. As a parent, this is my favorite edition to play because I can sit and play with a simple Xbox controller.

  However, gameplay on the Xbox and other consoles is limited, and most kids are likely to prefer the PC Edition (and maybe even the PE edition). The Xbox might be a good environment to play with your kids, though, because as many as four players can all play at the same time, and in the same place.

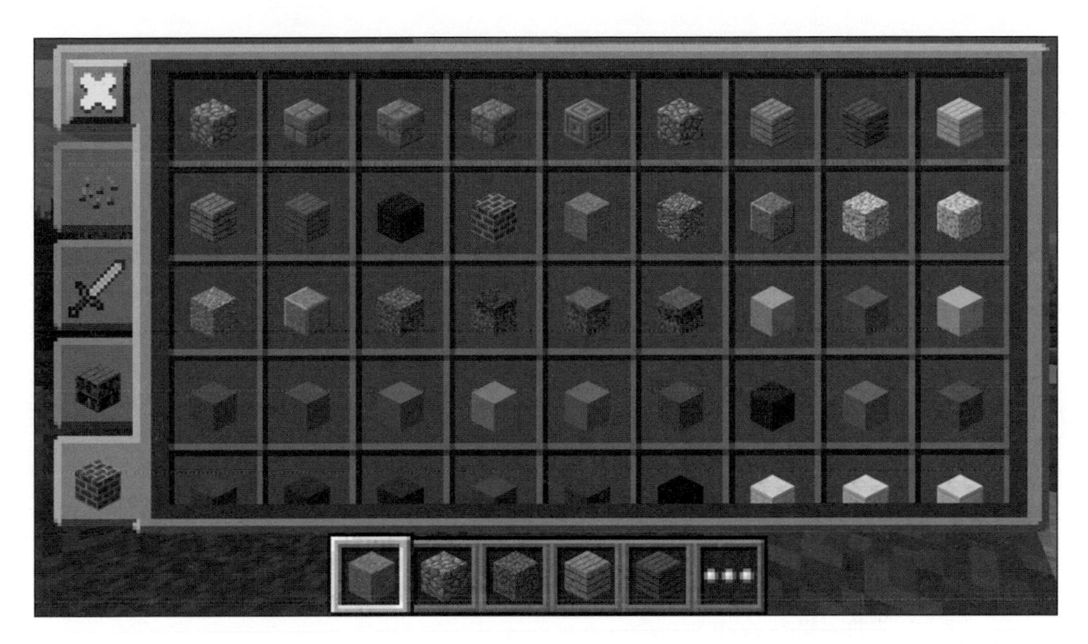

Figure 17-4: Minecraft PE doesn't require knowing how to arrange ingredients to create objects. The items simply show up when you acquire the required ingredients.

- **Minecraft on other consoles:** As of this writing, there's a PlayStation version of Minecraft and an anticipated release of a Wii version at some point. You can also set up a special version of Minecraft on Raspberry Pi devices, which are small computers that you can hook up to a TV. The Raspberry Pi is interesting because much of its code is accessible via the command line, and your kids can explore creating their own, custom versions of the game by playing with the underlying Minecraft code.

Ordering your child's first Minecraft account

After you know the different game types, and if your kids play the PC version, you can purchase your child's first Minecraft account. The following sections lay out the steps (reiterated from Chapter 1) for the sake of parents, to get you started:

Registering a Minecraft account

To jump into the action, you first have to register a Minecraft account. Then you can play in Demo mode or upgrade to the Premium account, which you need for the full version. Follow these steps to register an account:

1. **Go to** `http://minecraft.net`**.**

   The Minecraft home page opens.

2. **Click the Register link in the upper right corner of the page.**

   The Register New Mojang Account page appears.

3. **Fill out all the information requested in the text boxes, specify your date of birth, and answer the security questions.**

4. **Click the Register button to finish.**

5. **Check the e-mail account you entered for a verification message from Minecraft.**

6. **Click the link provided in the e-mail to complete your registration.**

   Check out the next section to find out how to purchase the game.

Purchasing and installing Minecraft

To buy and install the game, log in to your account at `http://minecraft.net`. (See the preceding section for details on registering.) Then follow these steps:

1. **Click the large Buy Now button on the home page.**

   The Minecraft Store page opens.

2. **Click the Buy Minecraft for This Account option in the upper left corner of the store, as shown in Figure 17-5.**

   At the time of this writing, the cost of the game is $26.95.

   If you can't click the button, you may not be logged in (or you may have already bought the game).

Figure 17-5: Buying the game.

3. **Fill out your payment information, and then click the Proceed to Checkout button.**

4. **Follow the necessary steps to complete your purchase.**
5. **Return to the Minecraft home page. On the right side of the screen, the large Buy Now button should now be labeled Download Now. Click this button to open the Download page.**
6. **If you're using Windows, click the download and save the file anywhere on your computer.**

   To view instructions for other operating systems, click the Show All Platforms button.
7. **Double-click the file to install the game.**

Congratulations! You've successfully registered your child and installed Minecraft. You may want a few tips on keeping them safe before you get started. Read on.

Keeping Your Kids Safe

As a parent of yes, seven children, I can relate to the constant, nagging feeling of wondering whether your kids are safe online. This feeling doesn't fade when your kids play Minecraft. Though I believe that Minecraft is a safer environment than lots of other games you can buy, I would at least follow a few principles to be sure that your children are staying out of trouble.

Knowing whom your kids are playing with

The biggest worry you should have as a parent of a child playing Minecraft, or perhaps any game or program, is not what they're playing but rather *whom* they are playing with. In the standalone game, players play alone, but if your children play on a server, they can be playing with *anyone,* anywhere around the world. And in a game played mostly by children, predators are *undoubtedly* trying to take advantage of this situation.

Another concern about children playing games online is whom they're playing with in person. Even on Minecraft PE, you can play on the same network with other players. Knowing who is physically present at their friends' houses when they play can be critical information.

Here are a few tips to keep your kids safe as they play Minecraft with other people:

- **Pay attention to whom they're chatting with.** Most interaction with players in Minecraft happens within the chat system. Your kids may even experience forms of cyberbullying (called *griefing*) that can trouble them, if you're not aware. You might want to look over your kids' shoulders every so often to understand what they're saying in chat and to ask them whom they're chatting with. You should know, and be comfortable with, every person your kids interact with in Minecraft.

- **Establish a list of safe servers.** The easiest way to avoid griefing on Minecraft is to establish a safe list of servers that your kids can join. Check out the list of family-friendly servers at `http://www.mediafire.com/download/a63m5vipfmcb6ni/mc-servers-list.txt`, where the administrators enforce family-friendly rules within the game to ensure that kids see no cursing or cyberbullying and that structures aren't mischievously destroyed by other players. Find a server or two that you're comfortable with, and work with your children to ensure that they connect only with those servers.
- **Set up your own server and establish rules on who can join.** This process may require a little more skill than you're willing to contribute, and the topic is well beyond the scope of this book. You can find many tutorials online, however, to show you how to set up your own Minecraft server. Doing so gives you the benefit of controlling what happens within the game and who is allowed to join. You can bar cursing and set gameplay rules, for example. My children play mostly on a server that our neighbors have set up, and the kids definitely know the rules that have been established.
- **Don't play with strangers.** The old adage "Don't talk to strangers" applies to Minecraft as well. Though players have opportunities to meet new people in the game, these opportunities can be dangerous for minors if they don't know whom they're chatting with.
- **Play with your kids.** The easiest way to keep your kids safe is to play the game with them. It's not only fun but also a great opportunity to interact with your kids at their level, to learn the same concepts they're learning, and to provide teaching experiences in the process. In addition, you get to know the other players that they interact with. Or, if the only person they interact with is you, that's okay too. We can't recommend this advice strongly enough. Who says that you have to interact with your kids only in real life? If they're still learning information that can improve their future, I say go for it!

Understanding Minecraft channels on YouTube

If your child is playing Minecraft, there's a pretty good chance that they not only play the game but also watch other people play it, *repeatedly,* on YouTube. We're extremely familiar with this phenomenon in our family: Minecraft is the new version of Saturday morning cartoons for our kids. They'd much rather watch Minecraft videos on YouTube than watch TV programs.

If the preceding paragraph describes your children, have no worries — your children are simply learning new ways to play the game. They're likely learning about new things they can create, and new ways to manipulate redstone and other blocks to build truly neat structures, which can likely apply to real-life knowledge.

Here are a few tips for protecting your children as they watch these videos:

- **Watch videos only from channels they've subscribed to.** My kids can watch videos only on YouTube channels that they subscribe to. My wife and I then have to approve each YouTube channel they're subscribed to. If we catch them watching a YouTube video on a channel they haven't subscribed to, or if they've subscribed to a channel we haven't approved, they're banned from watching YouTube videos.

  If a YouTube channel allows cursing or other objectionable material (you determine what's objectionable for your kids), it shows up in more than one video on their channel. So if I see it on one video, I generally disapprove of the channel as a whole. This way, my kids are more likely to be watching videos only on channels that have safe content for kids.

- **Watch a few of the videos your children watch.** Don't let your children randomly watch Minecraft videos. Objectionable, adult-oriented videos abound on YouTube, so be sure to establish a few guidelines to help your kids decide what to watch. Spend a little time watching a few of the videos your kids are watching. If you object, set some rules so that they don't watch the objectionable content again.

- **Limit the amount of time your kids spend on YouTube.** Set some time limits to control how much time your kids spend on YouTube. If you need help, parental control software such as Norton Internet Security can allow you to set limits on how long your kids are online, and monitor what sites they have access to. Use that if you need to completely enforce time limits for your children. Or tally it on your own — you should always know how often your kids use the Internet.

- **Place in a public area the computers your children use.** The best way to keep your kids safe is to put the computers they use in a public place in the home so that everyone can see what they're doing. This strategy also forces you to know more about what they're doing in the game (and other software). Our family also has a rule to prevent having mobile devices in our kids' rooms. Everything they do has to be in a public place so that we parents know what's going on.

- **Talk to your kids.** By all means, maintain a continual dialogue with your kids to keep tabs on what they do in Minecraft. This strategy becomes even more important as they get older and don't always play online at home. If they know they can talk to you about their experiences in the game, or on YouTube, or anywhere else on the Internet, they'll talk to you when they have problems or see things that make them uncomfortable.

You can subscribe to the official — and safe — YouTube channels for this book, as well as Jesse and Thomas's other book, *Minecraft Recipes For Dummies,* also published by Wiley Publishing. (Figure 17-6 shows the Minecraft For Dummies YouTube Channel.) You can subscribe to them at `http://youtube.com/minecraftdummiesbook` and `http://youtube.com/minecraftrecipesfd`. At these sites, I share examples from this book, and much more.

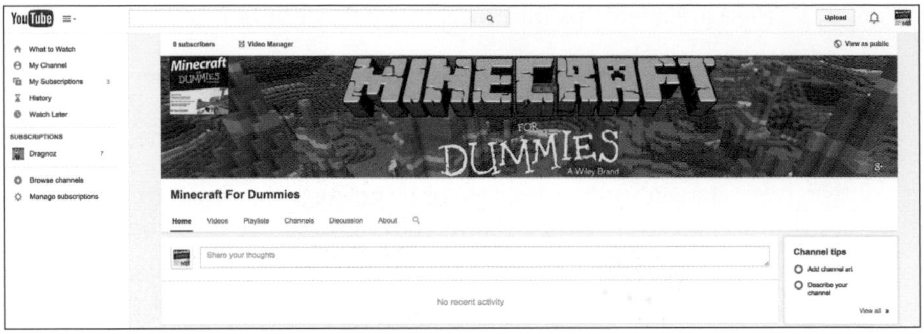

Figure 17-6: The Minecraft For Dummies YouTube Channel.

Installing safe software

Minecraft, the game, is safe to install. You'll have no worries downloading, installing, or running the game, as I discuss earlier in this chapter, in the section "Purchasing and installing Minecraft." However, as you soon discover, your kids will quickly find and download many skins, mods, and accompanying software. Many of these products come supplied with malware, spyware, and viruses that you'll want to be aware of. I immediately had to make sure antivirus software was installed to prevent this malware from taking over our family's computer.

The following list describes my favorite tools you can use to protect your computer — and your kids as they play Minecraft:

- **Norton Internet Security:** As shown in Figure 17-7, this tool helps keep my family's computers — and kids — safe from malware and other bad software like viruses, worms, or trojans. Not only does it protect us from viruses and malware, but we can also give each kid an account on the computer and establish their level of access to software. If they need more access, or if they want to install or download a particular program, they have to ask for permission first. We parents also receive email regularly from Norton, telling us which sites our kids have visited online.

  Norton Internet Security also lets you limit the length of time your kids spend on the Internet — it shuts off access at night and remains unavailable until the next morning. You can get a single license for this all-around solution for less than $100.

- **Net Nanny:** This product is solely an Internet filtering program for knowing what your children are doing on the Internet and for stopping them before they see objectionable content. Net Nanny usually doesn't protect against viruses or malware in the same way that antivirus software does, but it can stop them before they're downloaded.

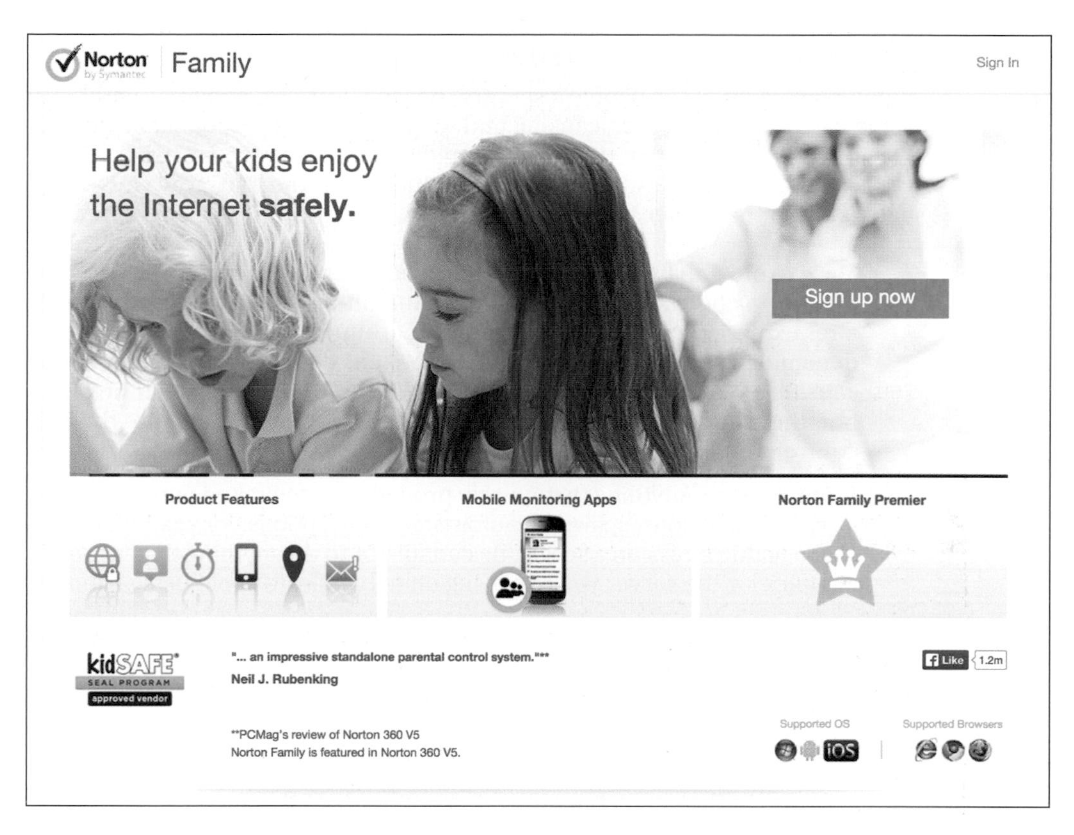

Figure 17-7: Norton Internet Security.

- **McAfee Family Protection:** This is the Internet filtering side of the protection that Norton Internet Security provides. If you want virus or malware protection, you have to purchase the McAfee antivirus product as well. The two combined can be comparatively close in price to Norton Internet Security, though, so compare the two at the time you read this section, in order to see which features you like best.

Teaching Proper Minecraft Etiquette

If you don't teach your kids good Minecraft etiquette, they may learn about it the hard way, by being banned from the server. Talk to them ahead of time, at their convenience, when they aren't playing the game. The following sections describe some "best practices" for interacting with other players.

Preventing server crashes

When playing on other people's servers, believe it or not, activities within the game can crash the server, causing undue stress for the person managing it. You should follow certain principles to avoid server overload. These are tips your kids ought to follow; otherwise, they may learn the hard way (by being banned from the server they're playing on).

- **Mass explosions:** My son Joseph crashed a server he participates on by creating a contraption that produced unlimited dynamite (which shortly after explodes and destroys everything around it) in the game. So much dynamite was generated that it caused a massive explosion of dynamite, causing an infinite loop that eventually crashed the server. Our neighbor, the administrator of that server, asked Joseph not to create that contraption again.
- **Infinite loops:** Anything that quickly produces an unlimited number of new items — explosions, spawn, or automated contraptions, for example — may cause undue stress on a server. Be careful not to do anything that is too complex for the server you're playing on to handle, to avoid being banned.

Stealing is wrong

In real life, everyone knows that stealing is wrong. You may not go to jail, especially if you don't get caught, but stealing in Minecraft can get you banned from the server you play on. Sometimes it's fun to play pranks on other players in the game, but always remember that the server administrator can tell who is doing what in the game. You *will* get caught, in the end.

In addition, vandalism and breaking items that others create are generally frowned on by most server managers. Treat other players' property with respect in Minecraft, and they'll treat yours with respect.

Asking permission

When in doubt, ask. If you're not sure whether a certain behavior is acceptable on a particular server, ask the server admin about it. Different servers have different rules and cultures, so what may be okay on one server may not be okay on another.

As a parent, see whether you can get to know some of the server admins on the servers your kids participate on. Get in the game and play with them. Chat with the admins or find out who they are. See whether you can find ways to get in contact with them and get to know them, or ask your kids about them. The more you know, the more you can help your children stay safe.

Playing with Your Children

The best thing you can do in Minecraft for your kids is to play with them. They'll bond with you in ways you never anticipated, and you'll get to know the game — and find new ways to teach them via the game. Minecraft is an excellent educational tool for kids, and gameplay is full of opportunities for parents and teachers to participate in the learning process.

Rather than refer you to Chapter 1 of this book to get started, I present a few highlights and cross-references in this section so that you can hit the ground running with your kids.

Mastering the basics

Peruse the official Minecraft wiki at `minecraft.gamepedia.com`. It has up-to-date information about Minecraft — more than you've ever wanted to know. Ads and downloads that are available on the wiki can introduce malware to your computer if you're not careful, so consider letting your kids focus on the information in this book and reserving the wiki for yourself.

Minecraft has two modes: Creative and Survival. In Survival mode, you can still play with other players, but dangerous mobs abound (usually, evil characters that can kill you), and you can die (see Figure 17-8). If you play in Survival mode, check out the section in Chapter 2 about setting up for your first night. Few people survive the first night on their first attempt.

Figure 17-8: A hostile mob in Minecraft.

If you truly want to play the game and dodge evil, Survival mode might be for you. But if you simply want to explore and learn by playing with your kids, try out Creative mode, as explained in the following section.

Playing in Creative mode

In Creative mode in Minecraft, you can truly do anything you want without having to risk dying — in this mode, nothing can kill you except yourself. And you have access to almost every resource in order to build anything you want. And you can even fly!

To get started in Creative mode, you can either select it as you start gameplay (see Figure 17-9) or, within Survival mode, if cheats are enabled, type `/gamemode creative` and it automatically switches to Creative mode. Refer to Chapter 16 to see what you can do within Creative mode.

After you're in Creative mode, you have just about every block available to you to start building. This might be an opportunity to start playing with redstone, as described in Chapter 8, or you can explore to see whether you can find the Nether. (It isn't difficult in Creative mode.)

Creative mode can be a helpful way to get the practice you need in order to truly survive the hostile mobs within Survival mode. I like to play in Survival mode and then switch to Creative mode to practice concepts from Survival mode so that I can try them out after I switch back.

Figure 17-9: Selecting Creative mode as you start Minecraft.

Winning the game

After you've had some practice in Creative mode, you can start playing in Survival mode to "win the game" — though the truth is that you never actually win the game. Minecraft is a *sandbox* game: It has no true beginning or end, so the focus of the game is entirely on exploring, and on surviving, as you explore the game.

You'll want to achieve some initial goals, however, as described in the following list, before you move on to plain ol' exploration (refer to Chapter 11 for details on each step):

- **Advance to the Nether.** You can find certain blocks and materials only in Survival mode, inside the Nether (which you can see in Figure 17-10). Take the necessary steps to reach the Nether and find this material needed to accomplish more things in the game, and expand your world. We detail how to find and reach the Nether in Chapter 11.

Figure 17-10: The Nether.

- **Find the Stronghold.** This huge, underground structure contains the end portal, which is what you need to find after you reach the Nether, achieve the materials you need, and return to the overworld. (Again, read Chapter 11 to see how to find the Stronghold.) After you find the Stronghold, you can advance to the final destination of the game: the End.
- **Reach the End.** The End is the final stage of the game. We explain how to find it in Chapter 11. In this stage, hostile mobs known as endermen attack you when you look at them, and you can build an army of snow golems to fight the endermen, as shown in Figure 17-11. The goal in this stage is to defeat the enderdragon. Defeat him, and you've accomplished everything you need in the game.

Figure 17-11: Snow golems fighting endermen.

Part VI
The Part of Tens

Visit www.dummies.com for more great *For Dummies* content online.

In this part . . .

- Get essential survival tips
- Build a successful house
- Make improvements with lighting
- Design with blocks
- Work with redstone

18

Ten Helpful Survival Tips

In This Chapter

- Getting the hang of digging safely
- Knowing how to cook efficiently
- Obtaining obsidian and portals quickly
- Finding the right location to mine
- Getting tips for avoiding overexertion
- Defeating basic mobs
- Obtaining experience points
- Figuring out how to craft quickly
- Taking inventory of basic equipment
- Finding natural comfort

Playing in survival mode in Minecraft can be tough! Just that first night can be hard to get through! With just a few simple techniques, you can easily stay alive and survive, building your empire along the way. We wrote this chapter to help you through that survival process.

Dig Safely

Digging underground in Minecraft presents quite a bit of danger, so mine carefully to avoid these common hazards:

- **Falling when digging straight down:** Breaking the block underneath you always increases the danger of falling into a pit or a pool of lava, as shown in Figure 18-1. Staircase mines (described in Chapter 6) are useful because they don't require you to dig straight down.
- **Falling sand and gravel or flowing lava when digging upward:** Quickly stop flowing lava with blocks such as cobblestone.

Figure 18-1: Watch out for lava when you dig straight down.

If you follow the safety tips covered throughout this book, you can navigate dark caves and huge lava lakes with no problem.

Cook Efficiently

Sometimes you want to cook or smelt a large amount of material such as beef to turn into steak or sand to burn into glass. Because you need a furnace and a plentiful source of fuel for this task, managing fuel efficiently is obviously an important skill.

You can cook with coal or any other hot or flammable material. Here are the best resources to use:

- **Wooden plank:** Cooks 3 items for every 2 planks
- **Coal:** Cooks 8 items per lump
- **Blaze rod:** Cooks 12 items per rod; see Figure 18-2
- **Lava bucket:** Cooks 100 items

The latter two resources are useful only if you've spent time in the Nether — a dimension that can also provide a good source of coal, from wither skeletons, as described in Chapter 11.

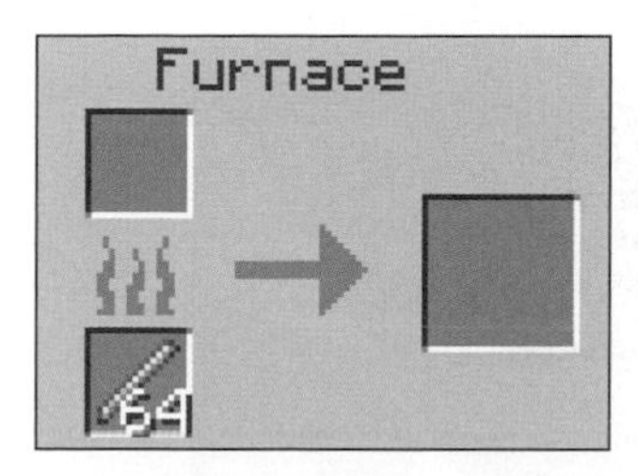

Figure 18-2: Cooking with a blaze rod.

In addition, you can cook 1 item using 2 saplings, so you can use saplings to your advantage if you don't need them for anything else. You can also cook an item with a wooden tool, providing a use for a neglected or near-broken wooden pickaxe.

You can also smelt logs into charcoal, which is slightly more efficient — but more time-consuming — than converting them into planks. This trick is probably more useful for crafting torches and similar items.

Obtain Obsidian and Portals Quickly

If you're playing in Survival mode and you're itching to go to the Nether (you can find more information about it in Chapter 11), gather obsidian as fast as possible. Even if you can't find the diamond you need for a pickaxe, you can still build a portal as long as you can find some lava.

Simply use a bucket to place some still lava in the location where you want to place the obsidian, and then dump water over the lava to harden it. Use cobblestone or another nonflammable block to form the "mold" for the portal and to form the container for the lava, as shown in Figure 18-3.

Figure 18-3: Building a portal mold.

Mine In the Right Location

Denser ores such as redstone and diamond appear deep underground, but they're statistically common about 10 blocks above the bedrock layer. However, this spot is also abundant in lava, which you can (mostly) evade by remaining 11 blocks above bedrock. To find a good spot to mine, you can dig down to this level: Either descend to bedrock and then move back up 11 blocks, or press F3 and dig until the *y*-coordinate is 11 (see Figure 18-4) — or find a sufficiently deep cave. Digging a tunnel stays more consistently at this depth, though a cave provides a larger surface area to search for minerals.

Avoid Overexertion

An action such as sprinting or jumping or suffering damage makes you hungry quite quickly. Hunger can become irritating when you need a lot of food in order to stay on your feet. Follow these guidelines to avoid exerting yourself:

- **Build roads with slabs and stairs.** These elements can help you move around without jumping.
- **Connect your destinations with a minecart track.** This strategy is helpful if you have to travel a long distance several times, as shown in Figure 18-5.
- **If you're using a staircase mine, use actual stair blocks.** Then you can leave the mine without having to jump.

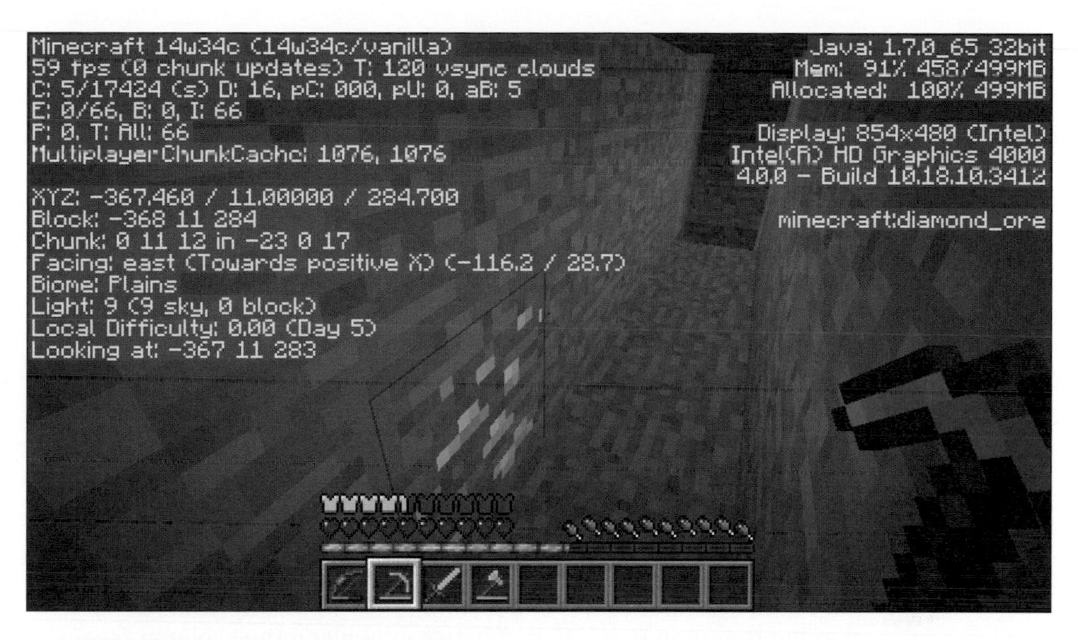

Figure 18-4: Digging until the y-coordinate is 11.

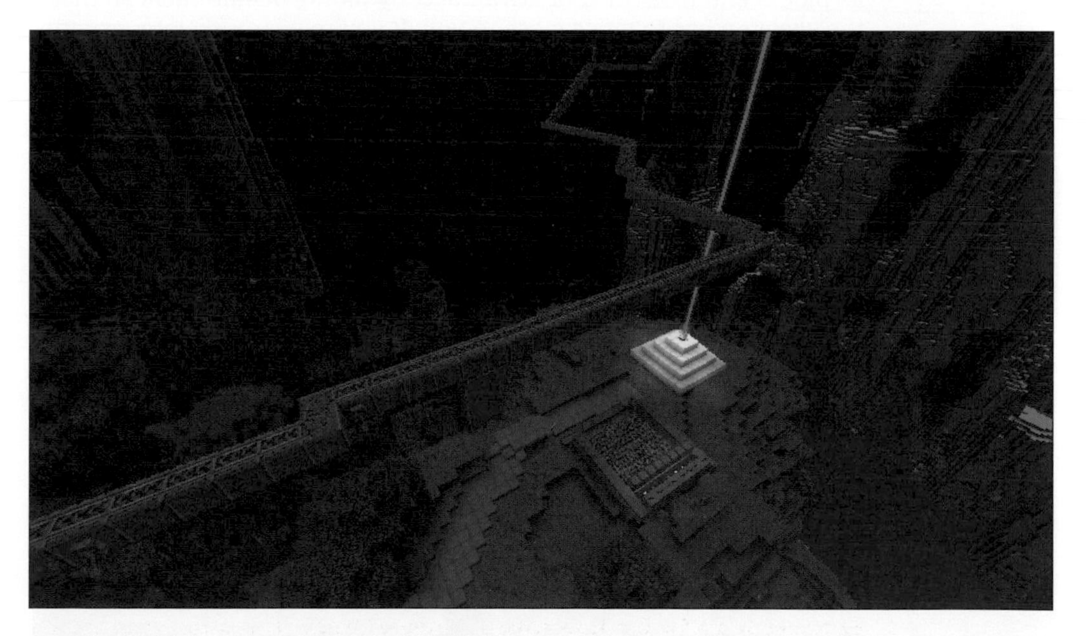

Figure 18-5: Building a road with slabs.

Defeat Basic Mobs

You have to face zombies, spiders, creepers, and skeletons many times during your Minecraft experience. (See Chapter 9 for more on mobs.) Each creature requires you to have a unique fighting style in order to defeat it. This list describes how to defeat each of these enemies (in order, from least to most threatening):

- **Zombie:** Sprint and attack this enemy to knock it backward, and jump and attack repeatedly to drain its health. Knock back the closest ones to keep the shape of the group manageable.
- **Spider:** Sprint-attack it! Try to predict a spider's jumps, and never let it gain the higher ground. Try to kill the spider quickly with a powerful sword because it has a low health level.
- **Creeper:** Sprint and attack the creeper to prevent it from exploding near you. (It's extremely harmful.) If you don't care how you kill it, try to lure it into exploding. If your timing is accurate, you can use creepers to destroy other pursuing mobs, especially spiders.
- **Skeleton:** This archer works best alone. Try to situate yourself so that another mob is positioned between you and the skeleton (see Figure 18-6) — it sometimes shoots its own teammates! Use items such as blocks and trees to your advantage, by hiding behind them so that the skeleton has to move close to you. If you're near a skeleton, simply kill it as fast as you can. Don't sprint-attack, or else the skeleton gains more shooting space.

Figure 18-6: Positioning another mob between yourself and a skeleton to protect yourself.

In addition, you can defeat a lot of these mobs easily by beating them into pits, cacti, or lava.

Obtain Experience Points

To advance into enchanting as you advance and explore through the game, you need experience. Mobs, breeding, and mining diamond, redstone, coal, emerald, and nether quartz ore give you experience. A helpful way to gain experience is to build an experience (also known as "XP" or "Mob") farm (we don't cover that in this book, but it can be found on the Minecraft wiki by searching for "mob farm"). Experience farms are farms you build to catch, and store mobs you can easily attack to build up experience without incurring damage as you do so. Building Experience farms may be a bit complicated, so we suggest mining for valuable minerals as an alternative.

We like to mine until we hit Level 11. On Levels 5–12, you can obtain diamonds in large numbers, and because your character is 2 blocks tall, you can get both Level 11 and Level 12. Levels 1–10 are where lava lakes form. Staying away from lava lakes and getting the most out of your diamonds through things like creating enchantment tables, or nether reactor cores, makes Levels 11 and 12 the best places to gain the greatest amount of experience. You should strip-mine these two levels (see Figure 18-7). Here's how:

Figure 18-7: Levels 11 and 12 are the best places to gain experience.

1. **When you're at Level 11, mine horizontally for about 50 blocks.**
2. **Return to where you started, and dig 3 blocks to the left of the tunnel you just mined.**
3. **On the third block, dig another 50, and then repeat this process.**

   Don't forget to mine the resources on the walls when you're done.

Light up tunnels to make sure that mobs don't spawn.

Craft Quickly

You can craft material in several ways:

- **Right-click a bunch of materials to split them in half.** Even if the materials are on the crafting grid, you can craft many items at a time, such as slabs or ladders.
- **Shift-click surplus materials when you finish crafting.** This action returns the materials to the inventory.
- **Craft several items at a time.** Figure 18-8 shows an efficient way to craft three tools at a time. When you take the axe, the remaining materials form a hoe, and the layer beneath it forms a shovel.

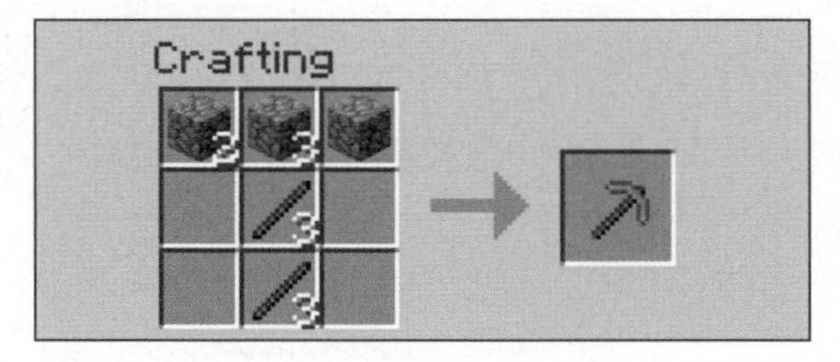

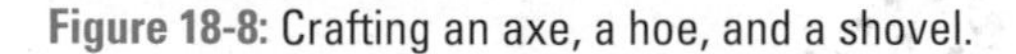

Figure 18-8: Crafting an axe, a hoe, and a shovel.

Check Basic Equipment

After playing Minecraft for a while and growing more confident in your ability to survive, you can keep more items in the inventory and worry less about losing them. Then you can work more efficiently and return home less often.

Always carry in the inventory certain equipment and supplies on a Minecraft exploration (see Figure 18-9) — as long as you know how to keep them safe:

- **Food:** Carry food that you have an abundance of and that doesn't take inventory space, such as bread or meat.
- **Weaponry:** Keep a sword ready, and possibly a bow or armor. Place a sword in the first slot of the inventory so that you can access it by pressing the 1 key.
- **Pickaxe, axe, and shovel:** Gathering materials while you're exploring is always useful, and if you ever need to break a block, you should have the proper tool ready, for efficiency's sake. A pickaxe is vital in underground areas.
- **Torch:** Never go mining without several torches to light the area.
- **Compass:** You can memorize the coordinates of your house (press F3 to view them) so that you can always return home. If this suggestion doesn't appeal to you, take along a compass instead, in case you get lost.

Figure 18-9: Carrying items in the inventory.

For recipes for these items, check out the appendix, available for download at `http://www.dummies.com/go/minecraftfd`.

Find Natural Comfort

If you need shelter before dark in the hills or the jungle for safety overnight, find an enclosed area (a shallow cave, natural copse, or large tree, for example) and fill in the cracks with blocks to turn it into a natural-looking house, as shown in Figure 18-10.

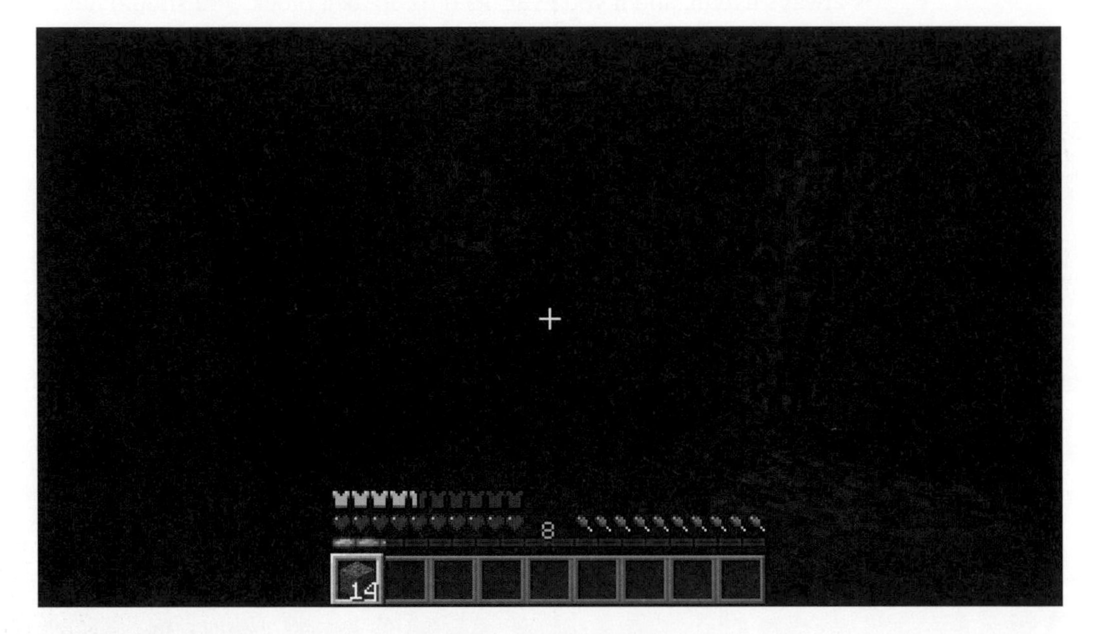

Figure 18-10: Building a treehouse for natural comfort before dark.

19

Ten Helpful Building Tips and Tricks

In This Chapter

- Building a successful house
- Managing lighting
- Designing with blocks

The basic premise of Minecraft is to literally dig in and build stuff — a house, the base, storage places, farms, and more! It's how you protect yourself from mobs, and how you progress in the game. In this chapter, we show you some simple tips for making it easier to build your next creation.

Making Your Starter Home Stylish

Building a stylish starter house, as shown in Figure 19-1, makes the game more fun and lets you show off to your friends. You can make your house a home by following a few simple steps.

Start with a square or rectangle. When building a rectangle, go to one of the longer sides of the house, and in the middle of the wall, knock out 1 block of the wall if there are an odd number of blocks on the row, or knock out 2 blocks if there are an even number of blocks. On a square house, choose any side and do the same thing.

Wherever you make the hold is where the door will be placed, so place the door (or double door) in the hole you just created. The door is 2 blocks tall. On the 1 block adjacent to both sides of the door, add 2 blocks upward, to make the wall 1 block taller than the door, creating pillars. Connect the two pillars you made at the top with a block.

Figure 19-1: Starter house.

Then go to each corner of the house, and build upward 3 more blocks. (The final block you place is on the roof level.) Then build 2 blocks upward on the blocks adjacent to each corner. The blocks don't respond to gravity, so you can simply place blocks all around at the third block height. The house should now have a base level and a top level.

Now add a flat roof to the top, fill in the holes on each wall with glass planes, and, finally, replace the floor with any material you want (such as wood or carpet). Place your chests, bed, crafting tables, bookshelves, and other items in your new, stylish house.

Improving the Exterior Design in Three Stylish Ways

After your starter home is set up, it's time to decorate! Here are three simple ideas for ways you can decorate the exterior of your new home (see Figure 19-2):

- **Shape:** After building a simple square or rectangle, make additional square wings that branch off the main building, creating U-shaped houses, L-shaped houses, second stories that are shifted a few blocks off center (gravity will not cause the second story to collapse), or outbuildings, such as storage sheds.

- **Depth:** Create a wall where the blocks alternate in depth, like the black square on the first two rows of a checkerboard (almost like a zig-zag).
- **Detail:** Add the small details, such as a chimney, a stained glass window, or even some stairs! Make the building look like it has been there for a long time, using moss stone or planting tall grass. Other finishing touches include flower beds, a hedge maze, a banner, and a mailbox.

Figure 19-2: Exterior house design.

Hiding Lighting

Many players like to hide the lighting that they use in the structures they build. Earlier in the game, when you have fewer ingredients available to you, try pot lights, which are recessed ceiling torches with glass under them. But that isn't the only option. The blocks that you can see through are

- Any type of glass
- Fancy graphical leaves (located in the video settings, discussed in Chapter 13)
- Glass panes
- Iron bars
- Ladders
- Fence gates

- Fences
- Nether brick fences
- Doors
- Trapdoors
- Cobblestone walls
- Any plant

Using any of the blocks in the preceding list can hide a lighting source (such as redstone, glowstone, or torches).

The blocks that you can't see through but that still let light through are

- Pistons
- Cake
- Beds
- Redstone repeaters
- Chests
- Ender chests
- Trapped chests
- Enchantment tables
- Anvils
- Brewing stands
- End portal frames
- Hoppers
- Lily pads
- Carpets
- Cauldrons
- Levers
- Pressure plates
- Buttons
- Redstone wire
- Signs

The blocks in the preceding list completely hide light sources without blocking the light. Carpet in particular is an easy and attractive solution, as shown in Figure 19-3. Ice and water are also blocks that let light through, but they subtract two from the light level, providing a dimly lit area.

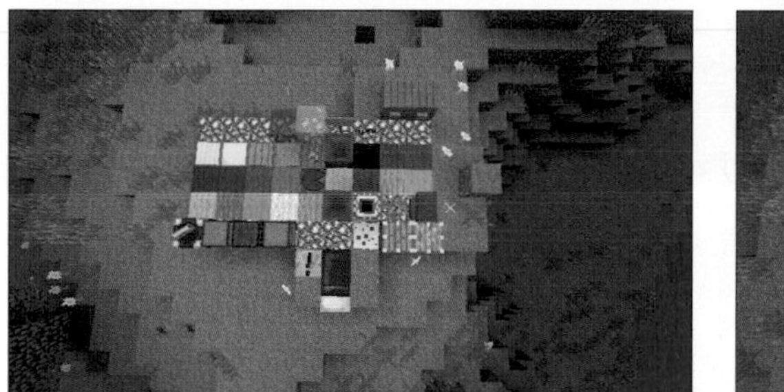

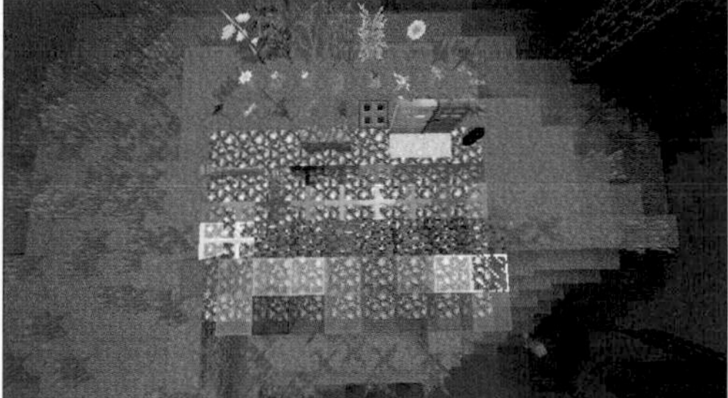

Figure 19-3: Hiding light with carpet.

Combining Blocks in Different Ways

Sometimes, finding the right blocks that look good together is difficult and confusing, so we list a few block combinations that can fit almost any condition. In Figure 19-4, we show you all possible block combinations, as described in this list:

- **Oak wood, oak wooden planks, and stone brick:** The stone brick contrasts well with the oak wood and wooden planks, making a great floor for a wooden house or a wall of stone brick with accents of oak wood.
- **Birch wooden planks, sandstone, and oak wooden planks:** The darkness of oak wood (not dark oak) contrasts with the bright birch wooden planks and sandstone, making it a great choice for an Arabian desert marketplace.
- **Spruce wooden planks, red stained clay, and hay bale:** The dark spruce with the red-stained clay complement each other, making a contrast against the bright yellow of the hay bale. These blocks form the recipe to make a well-designed barn.
- **Stone brick, cobblestone, and nether brick:** The gray tones of the stone brick and cobblestone make the dark purple of the nether brick stand out. This combination can look haunted or scary, if done well.
- **Cyan-stained clay, cyan wool, and block of quartz:** Both the cyan clay and cyan wool have a darker color that reflects off the whitish, yellowish quartz block. Make a border using cyan clay with indented cyan wool. Then add quartz to create an eye-catching building.
- **Stone brick, cobblestone, and brick:** The gray tones of the stone brick and cobblest — wait! Didn't we already do this? Oh, it has bricks in it now. This combination would make a great safe house or an old building.
- **Spruce wood, spruce wooden planks, and double stone slab:** The spruce is the real part of the house whereas the stone slab is more for decoration. Adding the double stone slab prevents this building from looking boring and ordinary.

- **Block of quartz, ice, and red-stained clay:** This combination has no focal point — nothing stands out. This combination simply blends well, creating a stunning look.
- **Glowstone, sandstone, and nether brick:** This is a nether base build. The sandstone with the glowstone can look good, but the glowstone surrounded by nether brick with a sandstone floor is outstanding. We believe that this is the ultimate nether base combination.

Figure 19-4: All block combinations!

Understanding Circles, Spheres, and Domes

Making any rounded item in Minecraft is extremely difficult. Circles in Minecraft? Unheard of.

Technically, Minecraft has no circles, but you can mimic the appearance of a circle. Follow these steps to build simple circles:

1. **Start out with a base row that's at least 2 blocks long (also called the first segment at the top of the circle). Then subtract 1 from the number of blocks you have in the base row and place that number of blocks in a row below the first segment, creating a stair step, as shown in Figure 19-5.**

   This is the second segment. Repeat this step until you have only 2 blocks in a segment.

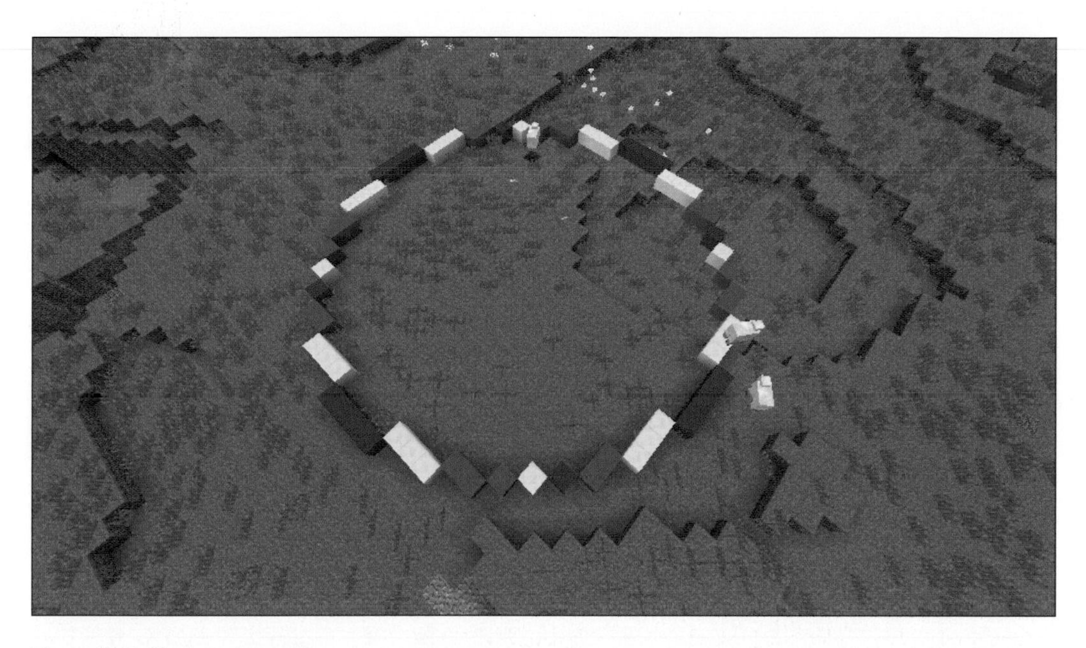

Figure 19-5: Circle construction.

2. **When you have only 2 blocks in a segment, look at how space you have to make your circle, and then place 1 block diagonally until you reach the edge of your available area.**
3. **Reverse what you did in Step 2 so that you add 1 block instead of subtract 1, creating sideways stair steps.**

   This step forms the sides of the circles. Repeat this step until you reach the original number of blocks of your base.
4. **Repeat this process to create the bottom of the circle.**

   Congratulations! For more tutorials on making other types of circles, visit these sites:

   ```
   http://www.plotz.co.uk
   https://donatstudios.com/PixelCircleGenerator
   http://oranj.io/sphere.html
   ```

Designing the Interior

What is a living room without a couch? Or a study without an impressive desk? Or, how would you feel about having a nice table on which to eat some cake? You can customize furniture in a million different ways, so you should experiment to see what works (see Figure 19-6). Several websites and YouTube channels also offer tutorials. One of our favorite websites to visit to learn how to build furniture is at http://forum.citycraft.co.uk/viewtopic.php?f=3&t=23684.

The following sections describe some of our favorite furniture builds.

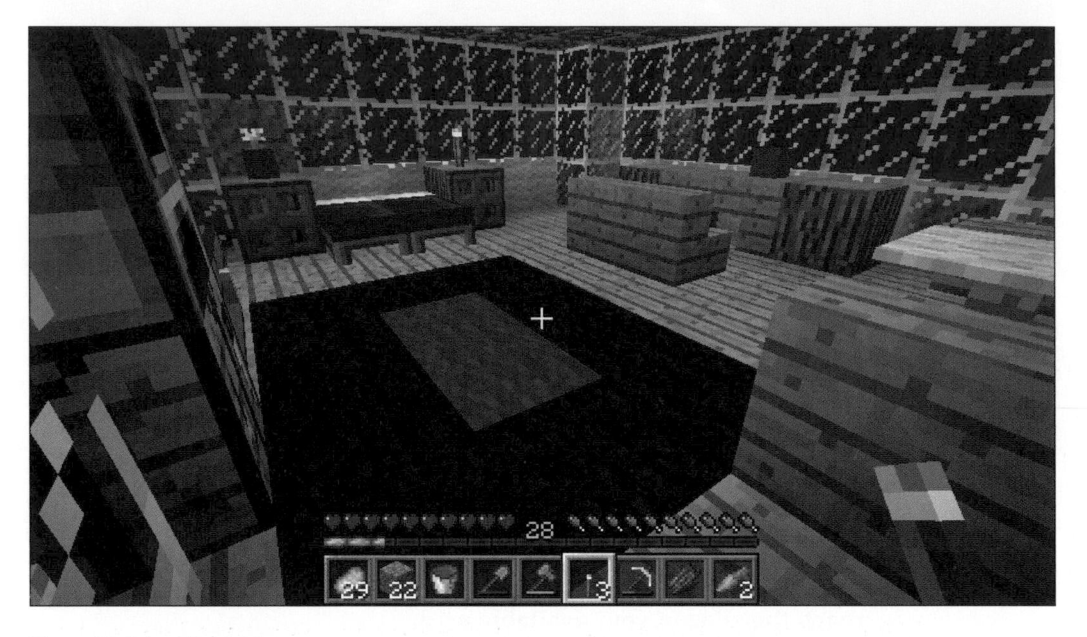

Figure 19-6: Interior design.

Building tables

To create the simplest type of table, place a pressure plate on top of a fence, or place a carpet on top of a fence. The problem with this design is that you can't place anything on the table. In another type of design, you can place 2 stair blocks upside down, next to each other and facing each other. Then you can display your wonderfully crafted cakes for your pets to admire (including your dog, cat, slime, or pet zombie named Fred).

Arranging chairs

What is a table without a chair? You can create a simple chair by placing a stair block. Then add a couple of signs to the sides for armrests. Add a half-slab to the end of the new chair to make an outdoor lounge chair.

You create a couch by placing 1 stair block, adding as many slabs as you want for seat cushions, and then adding another stair block on each end. Finally, add a block (of the same material that you used to make the slabs and stairs) to the back to finish the couch.

Creating bunk beds

Create a bunk bed by placing a bed on top of another bed and then adding 2 doors on both ends of the beds. Alternatively, place a couple of blocks on either end. Finally, add 2 ladders, allowing you to access the top bunk.

Lighting the fireplace

Why not add a fireplace to cozy up a room? You create a basic fireplace by placing nether rack on the floor and then lighting the nether rack on fire. (Lit nether rack doesn't burn out, making a permanent fire.) Then surround the nether rack with nonflammable blocks such as stone brick. Finally, put a couple of glass panes on top of the stone bricks to create a beautiful fireplace.

Playing with Sand and Gravel

Do you ever need to build scaffolding (often called *towering up,* in Minecraft)? No problem: Use sand or gravel! The special quality of these two blocks is that they are some of the few blocks that are affected by gravity. When sand or gravel fall on blocks that are not full size (such as torches), the sand and gravel simply drop without affecting the block they hit.

To build the scaffolding, first place a less-than-full-size block, such as a torch. Then jump while placing sand or gravel below you. Continue to jump and place blocks until you reach the height you want. This lets you reach high places without having to create a permanent ladder.

When you finish building at the top of the construction, you can simply jump straight down, using a water bucket at the last moment to prevent yourself from taking fall damage. Now break the bottom block of the sand/gravel scaffolding, and watch the tower crumble, as shown in Figure 19-7. An even better scaffold is using carpet, which is both efficient and easily obtained. Jumping down and using the bucket water trick "washes away" the carpet, causing all other carpets to break almost instantly.

Laying Roofs

A roof shields you from the elements of water and snow, and from those pesky spiders, which can climb walls. Stairs are often used as roofs. Ever looked at a villager's house? It has stairs for a roof. Just go around the top of the building to place the stair blocks. When you finish the first layer, go 1 block up and in, and go around in circles again. Each layer stair-steps, as shown in Figure 19-8. After you have made a simple roof, you can always stop after a few stair-step layers and simply place a flat roof as the final layer.

Figure 19-7: Sand tower.

Figure 19-8: Stair-stepped roof.

To make a simple roof for a shack or a smaller building, make the roof slanted on one side. A good construction rule to prevent a roof from being too sharply angled or too flat is to build each stair step 2 blocks wide for every 8 or so blocks that the house is long. In Figure 19-9, the house is roughly 16 blocks long, so each stair-step layer is 4 blocks deep. To build a house with this roof, you use half-slabs for a smoother ascent.

Figure 19-9: Angled roof.

In the final design, shown in Figure 19-10, we used a plain flat roof with wood and half-slabs. (Now, that is an easy roof to build.)

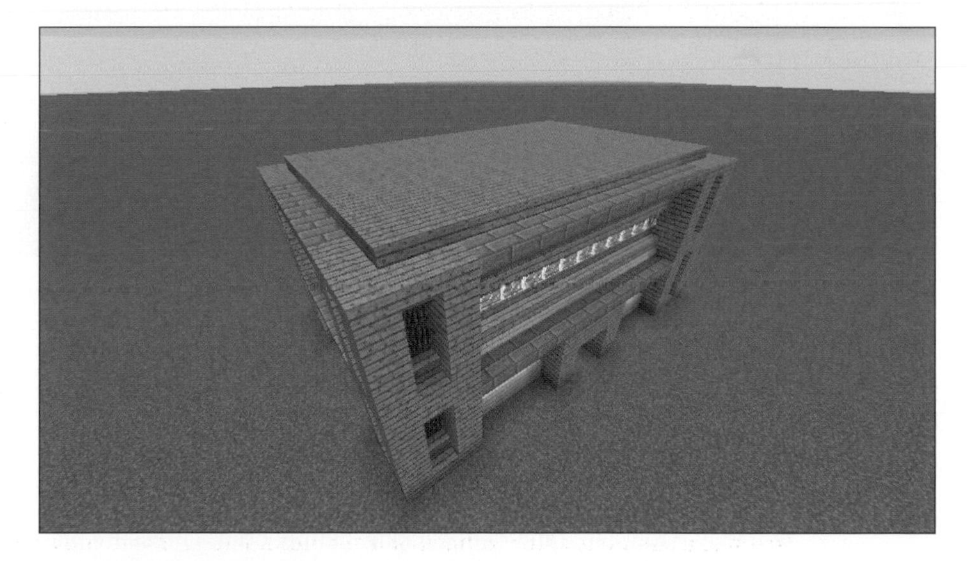

Figure 19-10: Plain, flat roof.

Terraforming the Terrain

Terraforming in real life involves earth-shaping. When you terraform in Minecraft, you make an item look like it was already there in the naturally generated world. Terraforming is used largely to hide bases, traps, or obstacle courses (often called *parkour courses*). When we want to hide the base, we often create a hill — though we need for the hill to look as natural as possible. We place uneven stair steps of dirt or sand moving upward and then place random blocks on the hill, such as dirt blocks enhanced with bone meal (see Figure 19-11). You may find other types of terraforming, depending on the biome.

Figure 19-11: Terraformed landscape.

Using Pressure Plates

The pressure plate, as you can see in Figure 19-12, is the way to go. Minecraft now has four different types of pressure plates: stone, wood, iron, and gold. Pressure plates work well to help you open and close the door so that you don't have to waste time right-clicking. Simply craft a pressure plate by placing 2 matching blocks (such as 2 wooden planks or 2 iron ingots) in a horizontal row. Then place the pressure plate in front of the door. Pressure plates can power lots of items, including trapdoors and fence gates (be careful — animals can also open the gate, by stepping on the pressure plate), and they can even light your TNT.

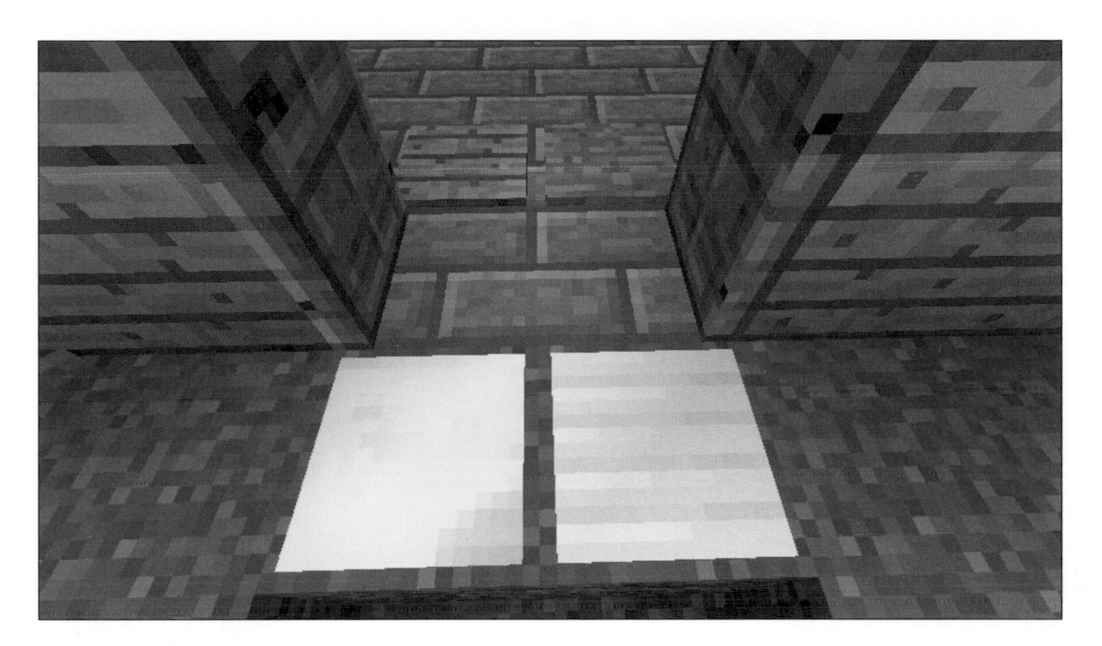

Figure 19-12: Pressure plates.

20

Ten Helpful Redstone Tips and Contraptions

In This Chapter

- Creating redstone circuit designs
- Building redstone contraptions
- Using TNT in redstone design

Redstone contraptions are some of the most complex, yet fun things you can build in the game. Just like society has advanced from the vacuum tube, to the transistor, to the chip, knowing the basic switches, circuits, and levers that can be created with redstone will allow you to build much more complex contraptions in the game. Then you can automate every element of your game along the way! Here are our favorite ten tips and contraptions you can build in Minecraft:

Keeping the Power On with a T Flip-Flop

The useful contraption known in Minecraft as a T flip-flop (T stands for "toggle") turns an *input* (where the power goes in) into a continuous *output* (where the power goes out). To turn a button (which turns on an item only as long as you push it) into a lever (which keeps the power on as long as the lever is flipped), you use a T flip-flop.

Building Design A

The first T flip-flop design, Design A, is a compact, simple design. To build it, you need 2 sticky pistons, 1 redstone torch, 1 comparator, 1 full caldron, and 1 input — in this case, a button. (You can see in Chapter 8 how to craft the sticky piston and the other items in that list.) The output is shown by the redstone lamp (again, described in Chapter 8), which lights when the T flip-flop is activated. Simply build it as shown in Figure 20-1.

Figure 20-1: Design A.

When the button is pushed, the sticky pistons pull the cauldron back and down, powering the comparator that then lights the redstone lamp. The lamp continues to stay lit, as though the button were a lever sending continuous power rather than sending the signal only briefly, as a button would normally do.

Building Design B

To build Design B, which is silent (doesn't make any noise) and resource friendly (uses much fewer items to complete), you need 3 droppers, 1 hopper, 1 comparator, 1 item that is not a tool (don't use items such as swords or hoes), and an input (a button will work for now). Again, you can read about all these items in Chapter 8.

To build the T flip-flop using Design B, follow these steps:

1. **Place a dropper in the middle section of the area you're building it in, facing the dropper toward you.**

   In the example shown in Figure 20-2, we have laid 3 blocks on the bottom — though you can build this contraption directly on the ground.

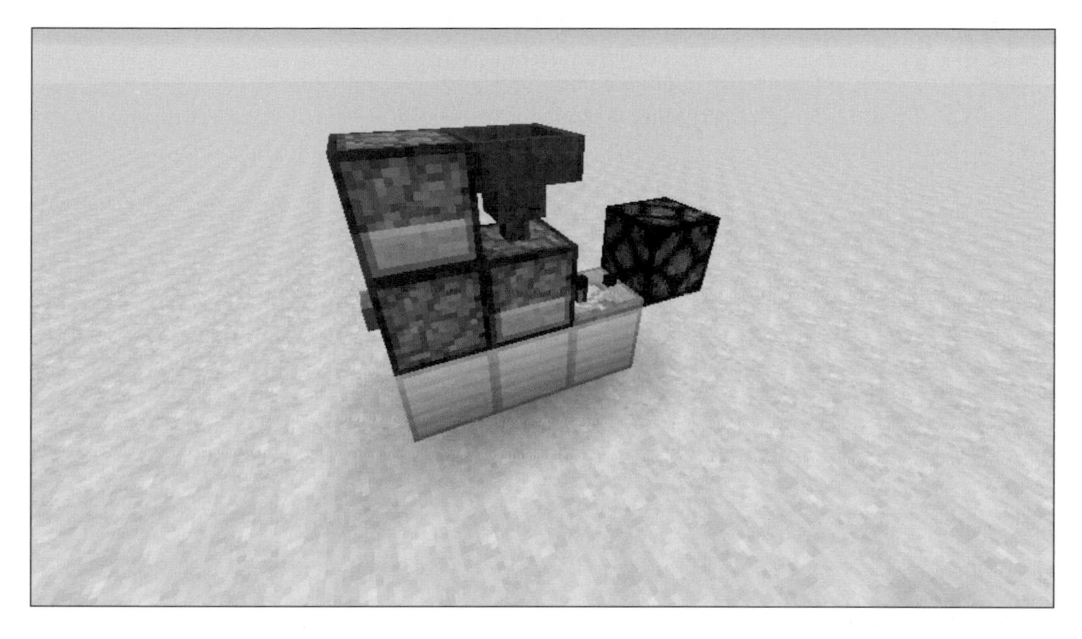

Figure 20-2: Design B.

2. **Look down, jump, and place a dropper next to the dropper that you placed in Step 1.**

   Place a new dropper facing into the dropper you placed in Step 1. On the top of the second dropper you placed, you should see a rectangular opening at the top. If you don't, repeat this step until the dropper's opening is at the top.

3. **Hold down the Shift key and then right-click to place one more dropper, which should be on top of the last dropper you placed.**

   This final dropper should be 1 block above and facing toward the dropper you placed in Step 1 (refer to Figure 20-2).

4. **Look down, press the Shift key, jump, and then right-click with the hopper on top of the dropper you placed in Step 1. Right-click the ground next to the dropper under the hopper to place the comparator. Right-click the dropper you placed in Step 2, and then place a block into its GUI. (We recommend wooden planks.)**

5. **Place the input (a button, in this case) on the side of the dropper from Step 2.**

   The comparator is the output.

Put a repeater after the comparator because the comparator on its own gives off only a single redstone signal. To fix this, put more than one item in the dropper.

Push the button, creating a pulse, and — voilà! — the contraption powers the redstone lamp.

Building Design C

Design C uses the least amount of resources. You don't even have to go to the Nether to get the ingredients to build it. To build it, you need 2 sticky pistons, 1 redstone torch, 2 repeaters, and 2 blocks. (See Chapter 8 to read more about sticky pistons, the redstone torch, and repeaters.) You need a 1 x 5 x 2 area. Then follow these steps:

1. **Start out by placing one repeater, as shown in Figure 20-3.**

Figure 20-3: Design C.

2. **Next to the repeater, mine 1 block down, get into the hole you've made, look down, jump, and then right-click to place the sticky piston.**

   You should see that the sticky piston is facing upward.

3. **Place a block on the sticky piston, get on top of that block, and right-click the ground next to the block. Get down from the block and move onto the repeater.**

4. **Continue walking forward until you're 2 blocks away from the repeater. Turn until you face the repeater, and place the second sticky piston next to the repeater. Place the next block on the side of the sticky piston that has green on it.**

5. **Next to the block, mine 1 block down and place the redstone torch in that hole.**

6. **Place an input, such as a button, on the first block (not visible in the figure).**

You have finished Design C. The output is directly after the hole with the redstone torch in it. (Refer to the redstone lamp shown in Figure 20-3.) Bravo! You have mastered the T flip-flop!

Getting Hopper Help

Hoppers are unique and can take some patience to get the hang of. We've used the hopper, which is one of only a few ways to transport items, to automate many redstone contraptions. An "available" hopper has open inventory slots, which can indicate either an empty inventory slot or not enough items within the occupied slots, which can be filled with as many as 64 of the same item per slot. When you place a Hopper on top of another Hopper, it checks to see if the Hopper underneath has empty inventory slots. If there's an available hopper, the item being stored within the hopper goes straight into the one beneath it.

Adding a comparator (see Chapter 8) next to a hopper sends a signal (which can be used to power redstone and other redstone contraptions) depending on how many items are in the hopper. One item sends out a signal strength of 1, 23 items sends out a signal strength of 2, 46 sends out three, and so on.

You can then use this combination of hoppers, available inventory, and comparators to construct a sorting system that sorts the items from a chest of random items (such as pumpkins and apples) into their own chests, as shown in Figure 20-4. You can see in the figure the chest of random items on the top, and the 6 chests that each individual item goes into on the bottom left. To make this work, inside each of the second row of hoppers, put exactly 19 of the same block (such as an apple) in one inventory slot (to see the inventory of the hopper, just right-click on the hopper) and 1 of the same block in all the other inventory slots inside the hopper.

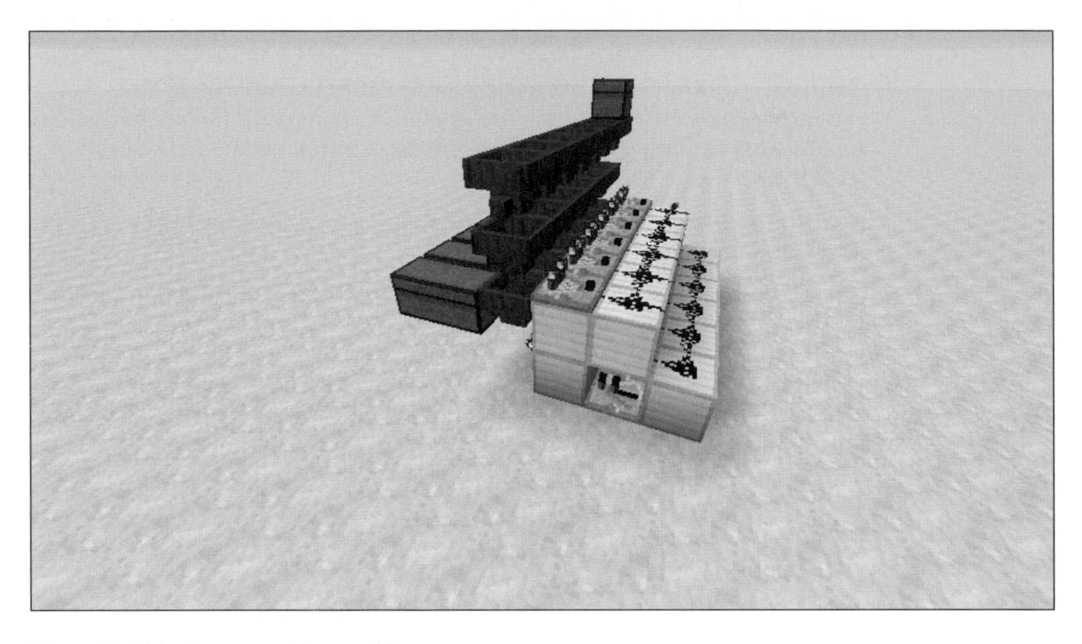

Figure 20-4: The hopper-sorting machine.

In addition to the hopper configuration (refer to Figure 20-4), we use a series of repeaters connected to redstone dust, followed by a row of comparators — this is what makes the items move from the chest to one hopper to another hopper, and so on, until all items are sorted. For this to work, the bottom row of hoppers remain closed from sending items from the hoppers to the chests next to them because of the redstone torches supplying power to the hoppers. (Refer to the blocks next to them in Figure 20-4.) When that power is turned off briefly, the hopper opens, allowing a single item through to the chest next to it, and the power then turns back on.

The comparators you see on the right detect that there are more than 22 items (sending a constant signal of 2 to the comparators until the number of items is fewer than 23, changing the signal of the comparator back to 1 — see Chapter 8 for more about how it works) inside the second row of hoppers, signal to repeaters and redstone torches next to the bottom row of hoppers to turn off briefly, allowing a single item through to the chest next to them. This process continues until the chest at the top is empty.

Building a Block Update Detector (BUD) Switch

In the BUD, or Block Update Detector, when a block placed next to it is *updated* (which can happen by changing the state of the block in any way, such as cooking in a furnace, breaking the block, or placing the block), it sets off a redstone signal. The BUD can be used for any number of purposes such as on a tree farm, to determine whether a sapling has grown into a tree. Or, perhaps you want to identify when your sheep are eating grass next to the BUD. Or, you may want to identify when other players are mining on your property.

The BUD works as the result of a minor glitch in the game: Its quasiconnectivity (partly connected) lets certain blocks be powered diagonally and even 1 block above the block, but activates only when a block update has happened next to the block. Two blocks that react to quasiconnectivity are pistons and dispensers. In Figure 20-5, you can see a sticky piston at the bottom, with a slime block on top of it, and a redstone block on top of that one, creating a BUD switch. Whenever a block is placed next to the sticky piston on the BUD switch, the sticky piston extends and then retracts quickly, triggering a redstone signal at the top that you can do other things with. (Chapter 8 describes all sorts of things you can do with redstone.)

Figure 20-5: BUD switch.

Creating a Constant Signal Switch with the RS-NOR Latch

The RS-NOR latch is sometimes called a *memory cell* because once a signal activates one input, it stays activated until a different signal is sent to the other input. However many times you press that button, it doesn't change the output until the other button is pressed.

The R stands for *r*eset, and the S stands for *s*et. NOR is a logic gate — the output is off when at least one input is on. If you've ever worked with electronics, this concept may be familiar to you.

The example we show you in the following step lists uses the common RS-NOR latch system, although you can keep a signal alive by way of a latch in other ways. To build the RS-NOR latch, follow these steps:

1. **Place 1 block with a redstone torch on the side of the block, as shown in Figure 20-6.**

   This step creates one input.

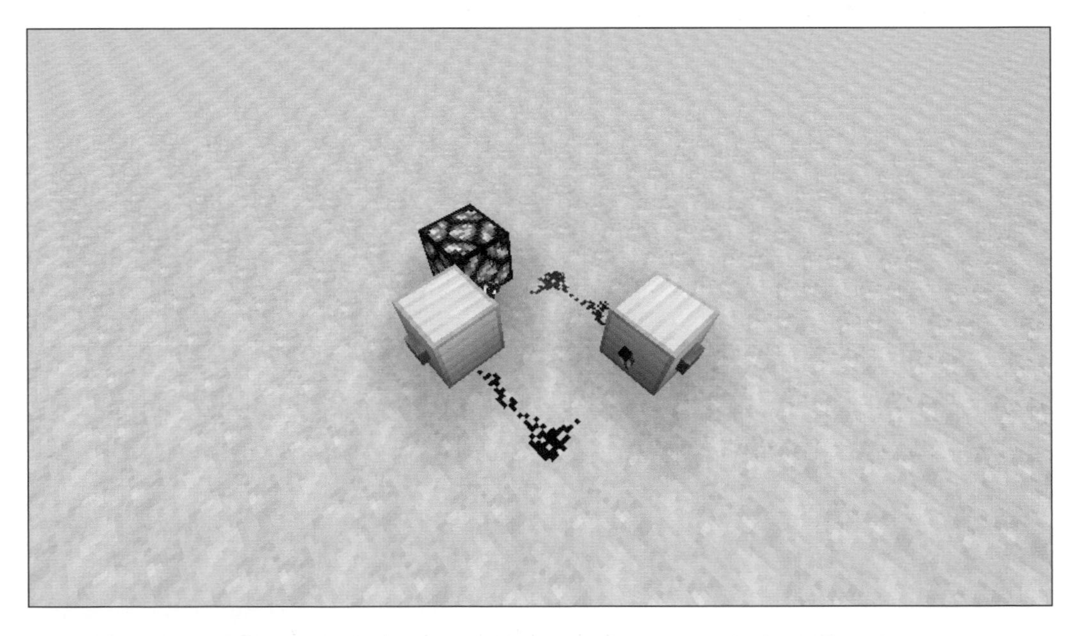

Figure 20-6: RS NOR-latch.

2. **Place 2 redstone dust parallel to the torch.**

   Refer to the darker red dust shown in Figure 20-6.

3. **Place another block at the end of the redstone dust trail with a redstone torch on the side of that block.**

   This step creates the second input.

4. **Place 2 redstone dust next to the original block that you placed.**

   Refer to the lighter red shown in Figure 20-6.

5. **Place buttons on the side of the blocks (though other input mechanisms would also work).**

To operate the RS-NOR latch, press the button on the block that has the lit redstone torch, thus turning off that torch and turning on the other one. In Figure 20-6, the glowstone lights up only when the redstone torch next to it is lit. If the button on the block of the unlit redstone torch is hit, nothing happens. That is the power of an RS-NOR latch.

Walking Through Walls with a Double Piston Extender

A *double piston extender* uses 2 pistons to push an item in and out (commonly used to create virtual doors out of walls by moving the blocks in the wall in and out). We show you how to do this in Figure 20-7. Below the pistons is a layer of redstone dust on 3 blocks. Then the rest of the platform is built with redstone on the outer blocks and 2 repeaters in the middle.

Here's how to build a double piston extender:

1. **Place the repeater on the left and set it to 2 ticks, to refer to the repeater delay.**

   You can read more about this process in Chapter 8. To set the repeater to 2 clicks, right-click it once after placing it, and it changes from 1 to 2 ticks.

2. **Place the repeater on the right and set it to 4 ticks. (Right-click three times on the repeater after placing it.)**

3. **Add the two pistons.**

4. **Add a lever to activate the block next to the redstone.**

5. **Add the block that you want to move (lapis, in this case) to the remaining piston closest to the wall. (Refer to Figure 20-7.)**

Figure 20-7: Double piston extender.

When the lever is turned on, the block is extended. When the lever is turned off, the block retracts. Now imagine this switch with multiple pistons on an entire wall!

Double pistons are much harder to use vertically than horizontally.

Creating Short Pulses with a Monostable Circuit

A monostable circuit has one stable state (Off) and one unstable state (On). When the monostable circuit is powered, it emits one short redstone pulse before turning off. A few monostable circuits are used in items such as RS-NOR latches and T flip-flops.

To build a simple monostable circuit, as shown in Figure 20-8, follow these steps:

1. **Start with a block with redstone dust on top. Put a sticky piston facing upward next to it.**
2. **Place a block on top of the sticky piston.**
3. **Place a block with a repeater on top of the set.**

   The repeater is set to 1 tick by default, which is perfect in this contraption.

4. **Add a button to activate the system and a redstone lamp at the end as the output.**

In this contraption, pushing the button briefly lights up the redstone lamp!

Figure 20-8: Monostable circuit.

Extending Pulses with Pulse Extenders

Unlike the monostable circuit, which shortens a pulse, the pulse extender extends a pulse. Because a button gives off only a brief redstone signal, adding a pulse extender causes the redstone signal to last longer. Here's how to create a pulse extender:

1. **Using the same redstone lamp shown in Figure 20-8, this contraption lights the redstone lamp longer but with the same button input. Place 6 blocks with redstone dust on the outer 4 blocks, as shown in Figure 20-9.**
2. **Place comparators facing each other on the middle blocks.**
3. **Add a button to the left side of the contraption, and add a redstone lamp to the right side.**

When you press the button, the redstone lamp lights up and stays on for a few seconds longer than would normally occur with only a button.

Figure 20-9: Pulse extenders.

Creating Hidden Doors with Sticky Piston Doors

Sticky piston doors are helpful because they hide within walls. Here's how to create a sticky piston door:

1. **The door starts with an archway of lapis lazuli. Add 4 sticky pistons to each side, as shown in Figure 20-10.** This sets the tone for Step 2.
2. **Add 4 sticky pistons in the back, as shown in Figure 20-11.** This completes what will move your doors.
3. **On top, place a layer of lapis with redstone dust and 2 repeaters facing each other and set to 2 ticks, as shown in Figure 20-12.** This will power your doors, moving the pistons.
4. **Add a lever to the front, as shown in Figure 20-13.** Now you have a switch that turns on the power, opening and closing your door.

   The figure shows how the contraption should look.

When you pull the lever to create a redstone signal, the door closes (refer to Figures 20-10 through 20-13).

Figure 20-10: Adding 4 sticky pistons to each side.

Figure 20-11: Adding 4 sticky pistons to the back.

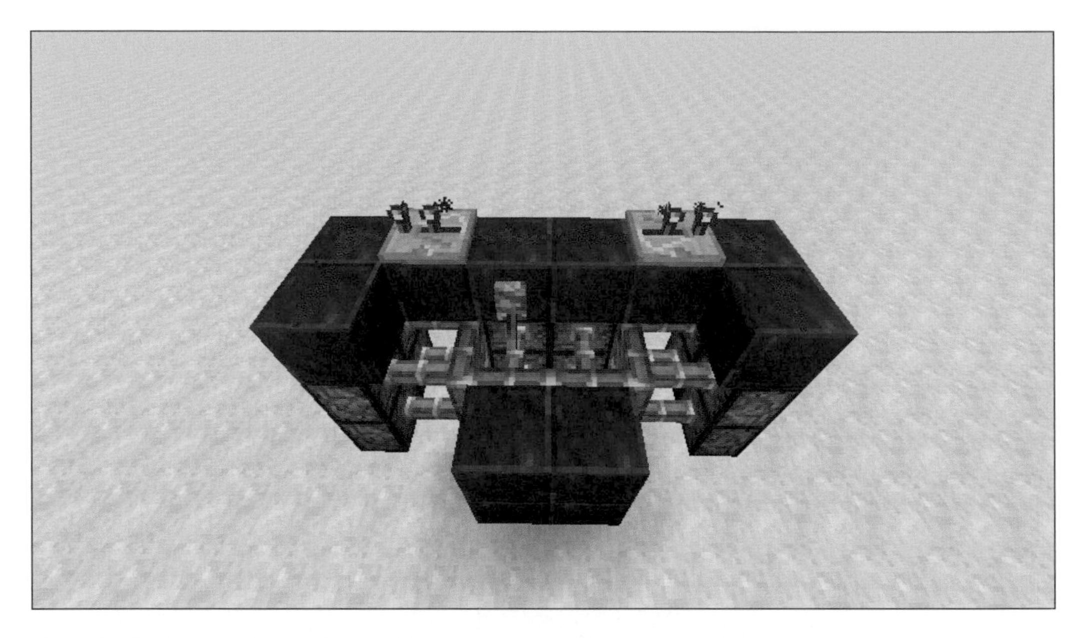

Figure 20-12: Placing a layer of lapis with redstone dust and 2 repeaters facing each other.

Figure 20-13: When the lever is off, the door is open.

To see how this door will function in a Minecraft game, add a wall around the lapis, using iron, in this case (as shown in Figure 20-13). Change the lever to the outside wall. When the lever is off, the door is open, as shown in Figure 20-13. When you activate the redstone signal by pulling on the lever, the doors close, as shown in Figure 20-14.

Figure 20-14: When the lever is pulled, the doors close.

This design completely hides the sticky pistons, giving the wall and door a sleek finish.

Creating Hidden Inputs

From a torch key to a BUD switch, a hidden input is a hidden way to trigger a contraption. Follow these steps for one way to create a hidden input:

1. **Build a hidden input is to start with 4 blocks in a row.**
2. **Place a sticky piston on top of the left block in the row, and next to that, place a redstone block.**
3. **Place another block on top of the sticky piston, and then place a sticky piston on top of the redstone block.**

   The redstone block powers the sticky piston, pushing the piston outward to the right if placed correctly (see Figure 20-15).

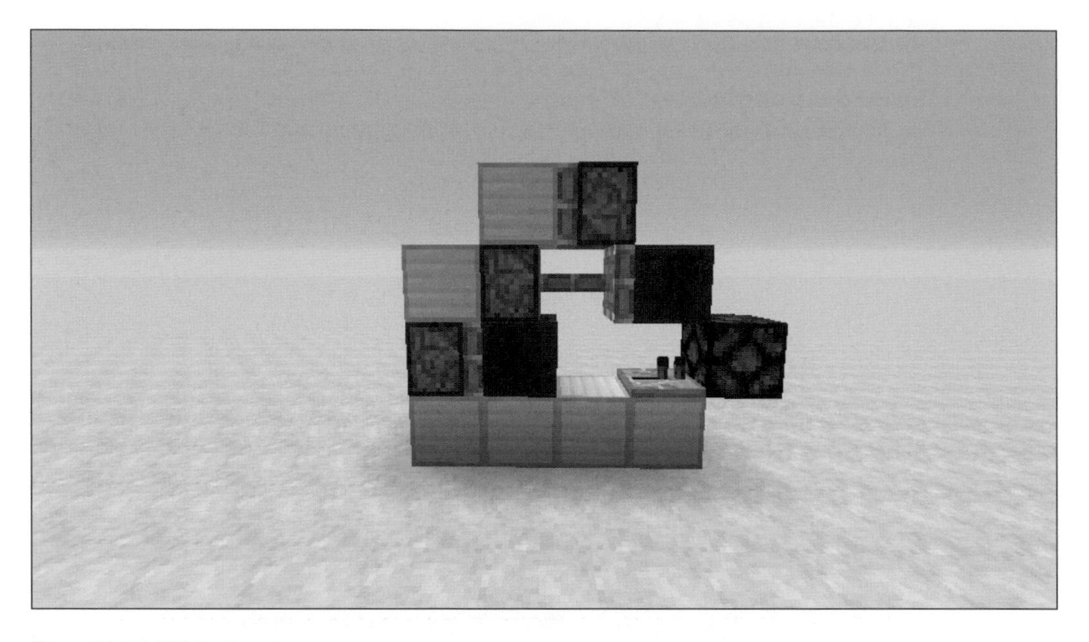

Figure 20-15: Hidden inputs.

4. **Place a redstone block on the extended sticky piston, and then place a block on top of the base part of the extended sticky piston (as shown in Figure 20-15).**
5. **Then place a sticky piston facing toward the block you just placed.**
6. **Place the items on which you want the contraption to operate on the right side of the contraption.**

For the example shown in Figure 20-15, place a repeater on the far right block, which is connected to a glowstone. To operate, put a redstone torch on the left corner of the contraption on the wall. In the example, that step powers the sticky piston on the bottom, extending the redstone block so that it touches the repeater, which then briefly lights up the glowstone block. Then the other sticky pistons are also activated, and the mechanism "resets" itself by waiting for a new torch to reactivate it.

Blowing Things Up with TNT Contraptions

Want to troll your friends? Or maybe you're on a faction server (a server where your friends get together and compete against each other) and you have to blow up someone's base. Well, this is the section for you, young trickster!

One of our favorite TNT contraptions is the time bomb. To build it, follow these steps:

1. **Place 2 hoppers in midair, facing each other (which connects them).**
2. **Place 2 torches under the hoppers.**
3. **Place a comparator next to one of the hoppers with the 2-torch side of the comparator touching the hopper.**
4. **Place a block with a torch in front of the comparator (see Figure 20-16).**
5. **Place the TNT block as shown in the figure.**
6. **Place any items into the hopper that's connected to the comparator. Then break the torch under that hopper.**

   The items begin filling the other hopper, working as a countdown clock. The more items, the longer the clock. When the last item empties from the hopper, the TNT explodes!

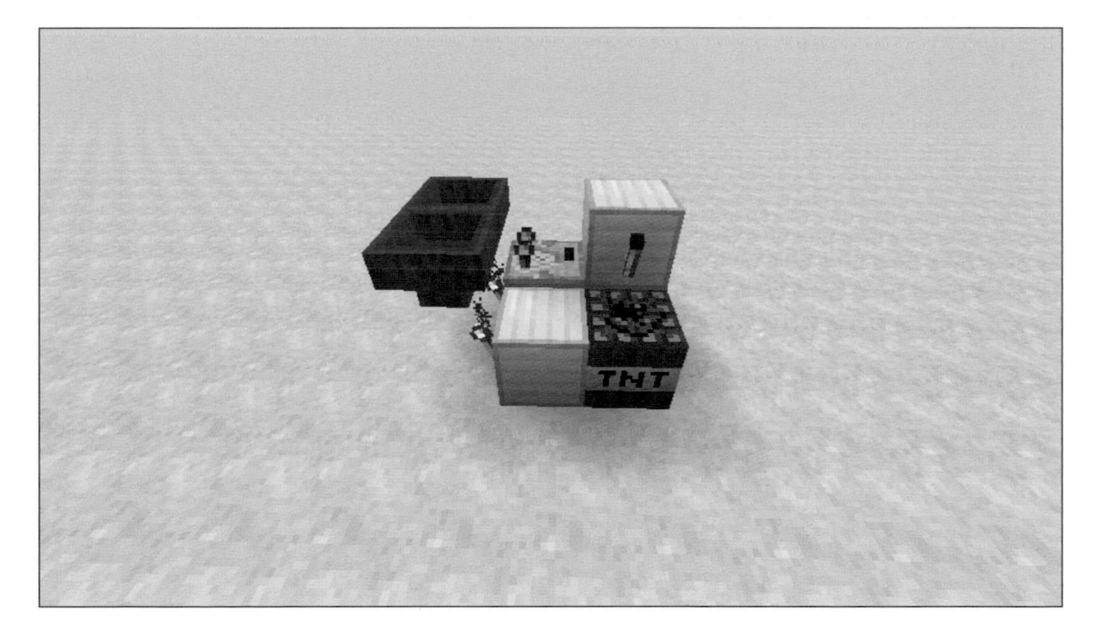

Figure 20-16: TNT time bomb contraption.

Index

Symbols

• A •

• D •

• E •

• F •

• G •

• H •

• I •

• J •

• K •

• L •

• M •

About the Author

Jesse Stay is an author of 8 previous books, an accomplished and world-renowned speaker, and all-around expert in technology, especially in the areas of social media and social media marketing. Jesse eats, breaths, and sleeps Facebook, Google+, Twitter, and other future-leaning and connecting technologies. A computer programmer since age 10 years old, Jesse understands what it's like to find an immersive piece of software that can teach you the further you explore. Not since he was a child has he seen an educational environment like Minecraft!

You can follow Jesse on his blog at `http://staynalive.com` or follow him on Facebook at http://facebook.com/stay!

Thomas Stay is Jesse's 12-year-old son, who eats, drinks, and breaths Minecraft. Thomas programs in Python, HTML, and CSS, and blogs at `http://tom.staynalive.com` where he writes about programming and software development. Thomas is a straight-A student enrolled a grade level ahead and starts high school soon. He likes to do LEGO Mindstorms robotics and plays the trumpet. He's often found late at night reading books. He loves to fix old Minecraft projects that don't work in the newer updates.

Jacob Cordeiro has been playing Minecraft since the Alpha pre-release. Jacob attends Stanford Online High School and won an award for his game entry in the 2011 Scholastic Art and Writing competition.

Dedication

To Rebecca (or Mom), who really put more effort into this book than any of us did. The person who truly deserves their name on the front of this book is her (Jesse keeps asking her to replace his name with hers and she is too humble to allow it!).

This was truly a family effort, and like the rest of our family, Mom was the one that powered it, kept it going, and even dug in and made it happen, all while pregnant! As you're reading this book, while they are Thomas and Jesse's words, you'll catch a hint of Mom throughout. Rebecca and Mom, we couldn't have done it without you!

And to grandma, Talma, who was in my dedication of my fake book that I wrote when I was 6.

Acknowledgments

Thanks to the entire family for pitching in on this. Even our friends who would all place their characters in one spot so we could get a screenshot, the Rikers who would let us use their Minecraft server until we could set up our own, and Hunter who helped get us into some of this world of Minecraft.

Thanks to Joseph and JJ for pitching in a few screenshots (and the Joseph's Corner!), and to Alex and Emily and even our big sister Elizabeth for letting us use the computer and devices while we played the game to be able to write this book. And to the little one on the way (should be born around when you read this!) who made a really interesting baby announcement using Minecraft sheep! Also, as always, thanks to the wonderful staff at Wiley and all those that worked with us in making this book – Douglas MacRostie our tech editor, our copy editor, (the outstanding) Becky Whitney, as well as those that were with us the entire way, Colleen Diamond and Amy Fandrei. We couldn't have done it without any of you.

Publisher's Acknowledgments

Executive Editor: Amy Fandrei

Project Editor: Colleen Diamond

Copy Editor: Becky Whitney

Technical Editor: Douglas MacRostie @Foosbag

Editorial Assistant: Claire Brock

Sr. Editorial Assistant: Cherie Case

Project Coordinator: Erin Zeltner

Cover Image: Courtesy of Jesse Stay